Second Edition

The Counterterrorism Handbook

Tactics, Procedures, and Techniques

CRC SERIES IN
PRACTICAL ASPECTS OF CRIMINAL
AND FORENSIC INVESTIGATIONS

VERNON J. GEBERTH, BBA, MPS, FBINA *Series Editor*

Second Edition

The Counterterrorism Handbook

Tactics, Procedures, and Techniques

Frank Bolz, Jr.
Kenneth J. Dudonis
David P. Schulz

CRC PRESS

Boca Raton   London   New York   Washington, D.C.

Library of Congress Cataloging-in-Publication Data

Bolz, Frank, 1930–
      The counterterrorism handbook : tactics, procedures, and techniques / Frank Bolz, Jr.,
Kenneth J. Dudonis, David P. Schulz.— 2nd ed.
            p.   cm. — (Practical aspects of criminal and forensic investigations (Series))
      Includes index.
      ISBN 0-8493-0964-6 (alk. paper)
            1. Terrorism—Prevention. I. Title: Counterterrorism handbook. II. Dudonis, Kenneth J.
III. Schulz, David P. IV. Title. V. Series. Practical aspects of criminal and
forensic investigations

      HV6431 .B65 2001
      363.3′2—dc21
                                                                                                2001035374
                                                                                                      CIP

© 2002 by CRC Press LLC

No claim to original U.S. Government works
International Standard Book Number 0-8493-0964-6
Library of Congress Card Number 2001035374
Printed in the United States of America   3   4   5   6   7   8   9   0
Printed on acid-free paper

Table of Contents

Section III: Post-Incident

10 Post-Blast Environment   183

11 Hostage/Kidnapping Aftermath   205

12   Interviewing Victims   221

By Dr. Frank Ochberg

13   Role of the Commander   233

Foreword

By
Dr. Robert Kupperman
Stephanie Lanz

Terrorism is a form of warfare that relies principally upon fear to deliver its message. The target of the violence often goes beyond the immediate victim. Its ultimate goal is theatrical, the Broadway of villainous acts. This holds especially true today with television news programs broadcasting images of the terrorist event even before senior officials have had time to assess the situation. This, together with the advent of cell phones, has led to just-in-time decision making, a new phenomenon in managing a crisis.

In recent years, we have witnessed a staccato of bombings, assassinations, and hostage-taking incidents, with every new threat spawning a new countermeasure and every new countermeasure resulting in new threats. While terrorists are unlikely to give up the truck bombs or spectacular suicide missions that afford them instant gratification and notoriety, a new cadre of terrorists exists that may look to nontraditional tactics and weapons. The young terrorist of today is often computer savvy and well educated, bringing a whole new level of sophistication to the table. Computers and the Internet are increasingly being used for planning terrorist activity, recruiting, and fundraising. And, while terrorists can afford the latest technological equipment, law enforcement and other officials more often than not find themselves lagging behind, making it difficult for them to keep up with the terrorists.

Further complicating terrorism warfare calibrations is the possibility that cyberattacks against critical infrastructures may be used as a force multiplier to extend the deadliness of an incident. Furthermore, the target of the attack, the critical infrastructure, currently is owned and operated primarily by the private sector, bringing a whole new group of players into the counterterrorism game.

In contrast with the period of the Cold War when terrorist groups were predominantly politically motivated, the most prominent groups today carry a religious banner. This makes them especially dangerous, for the only entity they need to justify their actions to is Gōd, in whose name they carry out the violence. Politically motivated groups traditionally looked for targets of symbolic value: a soldier, a government official, etc. Religious groups, on the other hand, feel that any mode of attacking the infidel is legitimate, even if it means killing innocent civilians. Anyone, anywhere, anytime can become a target.

What we end up with is an unholy marriage between advances in technology and indiscriminate targeting, an extremely lethal combination. Many experts in the emerging field of counterterrorism refuse to believe that terrorism will escalate to a level involving weapons of mass destruction even though the technology and expertise are readily available. This holds true despite the sarin gas attack in Tokyo subways in March 1995 by the religious cult Aum Shinrikyo that killed 12 people and injured thousands of others; it is often regarded as an anomaly — even by the Japanese.

The question is not so much whether or not there is a real probability of a terrorist incident involving weapons of mass destruction (WMD), but whether one can afford to not be prepared. The consequences of any incident involving WMD are so devastating that even if there is only an infinitesimal chance of one occurring, the framework has to be in place to swiftly and efficiently deal with the crisis.

So far, the United States' counterterrorism strategy, while impressive in appearance and number of acronyms, could in fact be a recipe for disaster should a grievous terrorist attack occur on American soil. The byzantine bureaucracy comprising the U.S. response, for example, could easily result in a delay in the deployment of the right tools to a local community dealing with an attack never before envisaged by its townspeople.

The Counterterrorism Handbook is among the first serious efforts to lay out a comprehensive strategy of how to deal with a whole gamut of possible terrorist incidents in a language that a first responder (policeman, fireman, medic, etc.) can understand. The book covers everything from bombings and hostage-taking, to nuclear terrorism and what needs to be done before, during, and after an event. The handbook combines what minimally needs to be understood about counterterrorism by the Washington-level policymaker while at the same time helping first responders who are planning to cope with what must at least initially seem like an overwhelming attack.

The book makes clear that the only way to effectively deal with terrorism is to have a thorough understanding of its present-day characteristics. Who is involved and what weapons and tactics are they likely to use. The players on the counterterrorism team need to take stock of what is in their tool kits; what works and what doesn't work; and what new capabilities need to be developed in order to face not only today's terrorist, but tomorrow's as well.

The authors of *The Counterterrorism Handbook*, Frank Bolz, Kenneth Dudonis, and David Schulz, each bring to the table unique insights and real-world experience based on years in the counterterrorism field. Their hands-on knowledge of the topic infuses the book with a down-to-earth practicality often missing from other counterterrorism studies. This book is a must read for anyone who may need to cope with a serious terrorist attack on U.S. soil.

Acknowledgments

We thank our families who sustained us — Ruth, Carol, and Dorothy — and the folks at P. J. Clarke's who put up with our meetings. Special thanks to Vernon Geberth and to the bomb technicians, investigators, tactical personnel, and hostage negotiators for professional assistance. And we gratefully acknowledge Neil Monaco, New York Police Department Bomb Squad (Retired); Detective John Breslin (Retired); Special Agent James Lyons; Frank Guerra, SIS Inc.; J. Christopher Ronay, president of the Institute of Makers of Explosives; Dr. Harvey Schlossberg; the late Lt. Justin McGarvey, NYPD for his unique contribution to the NYPD's hostage negotiating program; Bert Solivan, vice-president news information, Fox News Channel; Joseph Conley, FBI (Retired); Brian Jenkins, formerly of the Rand Institute and Kroll Associates; and Prof. Dorothy M. Schulz, John Jay College of Criminal Justice, for her invaluable assistance and contacts in a variety of fields.

SECTION I

Pre-Incident

Common Elements of Terrorism

1

The Meaning of Terrorism

The word terror derives from the Latin word *terrere*, meaning "to frighten." The word and its derivatives have been applied in a variety of contexts — from a sobriquet for a vicious despot (as in Ivan the Terrible), to eras of violent political turbulence (as in the Reign of Terror during the French Revolution), to the sporadic outbursts of violence the world knows today as international terrorism. Violence is not the key characteristic, however, since such violent confrontations as World Wars I and II are not considered terrorism. Rather than being an end in itself, violence is a means to instill fear into (i.e., to terrify) whole populations.

Instilling fear can be purposeful for criminal or political ends malevolent in nature. Yet populations can be frightened without terrorism being involved, for example, the cause may be disease, such as the west Nile-type avian virus that plagued the northeastern United States, the "mad cow" virus that struck England and continental Europe, and the deadly ebola epidemics in sub-Saharan Africa in the late 1990s and early 21st century. There are those who believe that the outbreaks of those diseases were not entirely natural but were intentionally spread by human intervention; in which case, they would be acts of bio-terrorism.

Since the intention of all terrorists is to instill fear into the population at large, there is a common motivation to the criminal acts they perpetrate. Because there is a common element to terrorism, counterterrorism has a foundation on which to base defensive strategies and tactics. Anything that can be done to reduce fear and anxiety among the general population is an effective defense against terrorism.

Nature of Terrorism

Brian Jenkins of the Rand Corporation has said terrorism is "the use or threatened use of force designed to bring about political change," while the Federal Bureau of Investigation (FBI) has defined terrorism as "the unlawful use of force or violence against persons or property to intimidate or coerce a government, the civilian population, or any segment thereof, in furtherance of political or social objectives."

Jenkins has identified the three most serious types of conflict short of nuclear war:

1. Conventional warfare
2. Guerrilla warfare
3. International terrorism

In the first two types of conflicts, noncombatants are usually able to distinguish themselves from combatants. This is not to say that noncombatants are never killed, because they are. It is just that these are isolated or unusual incidents, because in both guerilla and conventional warfare the major focus of killing is one armed force against another. Conflicts can be either high intensity, or low intensity in nature, such as the more than 90 confrontations currently taking place around the globe involving everything from former republics of the Soviet Union and former colonies of European countries to ages-old ethnic hatreds and narcotics trafficking.

However, the exploitation of noncombatants (i.e., their suffering and death) is the essence of international terrorism. Because of the covert nature of the activity, terrorist attacks are carried out by a small cohort of operatives who receive financial and logistical support from radical political and activist organizations, which can include governments of rogue nations. Political and other activist groups may be suspected of acting in support of terrorist goals, if not actually fostering and furthering those goals. Questions have been raised, and continue to be, concerning the integrity of some persons and groups or whether, in fact, they are being exploited or misused.

The U.S. Department of Defense has described terrorism as a phenomenon in transition and indicated that the nature of the terrorist threat has changed dramatically. The Defense Department attributed these changes to five factors:

1. Collapse of the Soviet Union
2. Changing motivations of terrorists
3. Proliferation in technologies of mass destruction
4. Increased access to information and information technologies
5. Accelerated centralization of vital components of the national infrastructure, which has increased vulnerability to terrorist attack

Much of the thrust of terrorism will continue to be directed toward U.S. targets, whether in North America or overseas. The attacks will be concentrated in urban locations, perpetrated by those acting on behalf of religious and ethnic causes and, as in the past, political points of view.

Table 1.1   Areas of Incidents

Regions	Incidents
Western Hemisphere	93
Europe	22
Sub-Saharan Africa	7
Neareast Asia	6
South Asia	3
East Asia and the Pacific	3

Table 1.2   Terrorists' Targets

Region	Incidents
Western Hemisphere	93
U.S. Government	4
U.S. Business	86
U.S. Private	3
Europe	22
U.S. Government	7
U.S. Business	15
Sub-Saharan Africa	7
U.S. Government	3
U.S. Business	2
U.S. Private	2
Neareast Asia	7
U.S. Government	3
U.S. Business	1
U.S. Private	1
Other U.S.	2
South Asia	3
U.S. Business	3
East Asia and the Pacific	18
U.S. Government	3
U.S. Business	15

Terrorism by the Numbers

According to the U.S. Department of State, in the last year of the 20th century, more than 135 terrorist attacks were directed at U.S. targets (Table 1.1 and 1.2).

Purpose of Terrorism

Terrorism for political purposes is usually a form of theater, and as such there are a number of elements which are almost universal in modern terrorist activities.

1. *The use of violence to persuade,* where bombings or other attacks are employed to "make a point" with target victims. The target victims are not necessarily those who are injured or killed. Rather, the attack may have been carried out to influence a government, or a group of

governments, to take a certain course of action or perhaps to terminate or cease a course of action.

2. *Selection of targets and victims for maximum propaganda value* means choosing targets and victims which will assure the heaviest possible media coverage. This consideration was particularly evident with terrorist attacks such as the World Trade Center bombing in New York City in 1993 and the hostage-taking of Israeli athletes during the 1972 Olympic Games in Munich. These were followed by terrorist activity including the bombing of the Murrah Federal Office Building in Oklahoma City and U.S. Embassies in Nairobi, Kenya, and Dar es Salaam, Tanzania.

3. *The use of unprovoked attacks*, which, truth be told, is just about any terrorist attack, because they were "provoked" is only the convoluted rationale offered by the terrorists themselves.

4. *Maximum publicity at minimum risk* is the principle behind many terrorist actions, particularly those involving explosive devices. Bombings typically generate a good deal of publicity, depending upon time and placement, so targets are usually selected for symbolic value, such as embassies, internationally known tourist attractions, and similar facilities. The use of sophisticated timing elements allows detonation to be programmed well in advance, reducing the risk to the bomber or bombers, who can be long gone by the time the devices are discovered or exploded. Moving up on the list of favored terrorist activities, kidnapping or assaults and assassinations may generate greater or prolonged publicity, but they also present a higher risk for the attackers. There is something of a cyclical pattern to terrorist activities. That is, if there has been a rash of kidnappings, the public may become somewhat inured, and subsequent abductions may not generate the same degree of front-page coverage, television news exposure, or Internet buzz. Bombings, just because they have been less frequent during the same period, may well generate more publicity than another kidnapping. A change in tactics, then, would produce more publicity than another kidnapping. Terrorists always want to remain in the forefront, so they will switch tactics in order to maximize publicity.

5. *Use of surprise to circumvent countermeasures* is one way terrorists try to attack hardened targets. Even though there are guards, detection devices, and increased perimeter security, the element of surprise can be employed to undermine the hardware and overwhelm the human factor in a fortified security system. Time is the terrorist's best friend. Even a well-protected and hardened target will experience slackened security measures during long periods of terrorist inactivity. Unless a suicide attack is planned, terrorists will wait to strike when security is relaxed.

6. *Threats, harassment, and violence* are tools terrorists use to create an atmosphere of fear. On occasion terrorists have planted small bombs or incendiary devices in public locations, such as department stores and movie theaters. In recent years, anti-government terrorists in Egypt have attacked groups of tourists visiting the Pyramids and other monuments. To the public, there is no rhyme or reason to the time or placement of the devices, and soon the mere threat of such activity is sufficient to send waves of fear through the populace.

7. *Disregarding women and children as victims*, often to the extent that locations with innocent victims are selected specifically to heighten the outrage, and fear, at the boldness of the terrorists' actions. This is yet another tactic to garner wider publicity and media coverage of the suffering and death of noncombatants. This characteristic differentiates the terrorist from a soldier or guerrilla. A soldier fights with the authority of a government for the protection of that government. A guerrilla fights the same kind of warfare as the soldier in technique and code of behavior, i.e., women and children are not specifically targeted. A terrorist, on the other hand, will focus on women and children, specifically, just to create a greater atmosphere of fear. Thus, the ethnic cleansing evidenced in Bosnia and Kosovo involving various population factions of the former Yugoslavia crossed the line from warfare to terrorism by militia.

8. *Propaganda is used to maximize the effect of violence*, particularly for economic or political goals. To carry out a particular operation without getting any publicity out of the action would be wasteful to a terrorist's cause. Thus, Black September, at the Olympic Games in Munich in 1972, and all those groups that mimicked that hostage-taking by claiming responsibility for attacks in other high-profile circumstances, wanted worldwide publicity for both political and economic goals. From a political standpoint, a group wants to show that it is a viable organization, a power to be reckoned with, and a force to be feared. On the economic level, the group shows sympathetic governments and others who support different terrorist groups that it, too, is worthy of funding. Even when terrorists do not publicly claim responsibility for an attack, many leave a signature or obvious clues during the action.

9. *Loyalty to themselves or kindred groups* is a common element of terrorist groups, existing among Armenians, Croatians, Kurds, Tamils, and Basques, to name a few. With these, and similar groups, the loyalty is so intense — distorted is not too strong a word — that the more radical elements of an otherwise peaceful movement will commit unspeakable criminal acts on behalf of that loyalty and associated

cause. For the most part, however, second- and third-generation terrorists have diminished loyalty to the original cause, the sense of pride associated with it, and a reduced vision of the original goal. Many of them engage in terrorism as a form of gratification and perpetuate criminal activity as an end in itself. They have thus become nihilistic and interested primarily in financial remuneration for themselves.

Terrorism of the 1960s and 1970s was carried out, for the most part, by college-age individuals and educated political activists. Now much of the low-intensity conflict and terrorist actions is being perpetrated by child soldiers, children, many of whom have not even reached puberty, who have become inured to violence and human emotion.

Characteristics of Terrorists

Terrorist groups are organized in many different ways, including the traditional pyramidal power chart with a leader or small clique at the top and ever-widening tiers of authority moving down the chain of command. Various other configurations for depicting the organization of terrorist groups include circles, squares, and bullseye target designs. One thing they all have in common is hardcore leadership surrounded by an active cadre; then, moving further from the center, a broader group of active supporters, and outside that, an even broader level of passive support.

In the shifting nature of terrorist groups — or at least the vocal justification they provide for their actions — religion and ethnicity seem to have replaced politics as the driving force toward their stated goals. Hiding behind the shield of accepted religious organizations, support groups are free to operate with virtual impunity, particularly in Western democracies. In addition to fundraising, religious and ethnic front groups provide cover for covert activities of more militant representatives of terrorist organizations.

Communication and cooperation exist between and among terrorist groups all around the world, regardless of political stripe or ethnicity. There is ample evidence of training camps organized for terrorist operatives conducted in Cuba, Lebanon, and countries in Eastern Europe when they were controlled by Communists. One of the most publicized gatherings of terrorists occurred in 1983 in Banghazi, Libya, when Muomar Khaddafy brought together more than 1000 representatives from such disparate organizations as the Palestine Liberation Army (PLO), Abu Nidal, Irish Republican Army, the Puerto Rican independence group FALN, the Black Liberation Army, the American Indian Movement, the Nation of Islam, and several unaffiliated freelance terrorists. (See Table 1.3.)

Table 1.3 Terrorist Leadership

Name	Organization
Abu-Abbas	Leader of the Palestine Liberation Front…Known as the Palestinian Rambo…Broke away from PFLP-GC over political differences…Responsible for the hijacking of the Achilles Lauro cruise ship
Omar Abdel-Rahman	Blinder Islamic cleric and spiritual leader of the deadly Egyptian group Jamaat al-Islamaya…Came to the U.S. in 1990, arrested in 1995…Sentenced to life in prison for "seditious conspiracy to wage urban war"
Sabrie-Banna, a.k.a. Abu Nidal	Although not a founder, a prominent member of Fatah's leadership…Linked to Black September, Hamas, and Osama bin-Laden
Osama bin-Laden	Arch-terrorist and the most sought after terrorist in the world…Suspected mastermind of a number of attacks against U.S. targets, including embassies in East Africa and the U.S.S. Cole in Yemen…Has issued a "fatwa" calling on Muslims around the world to slay Americans and their allies
George Habash, a.k.a. al-Hakim	Established the PFLP in 1967 as an alternative to Fatah…An uncompromising Marxist-Leninist implicated in a number of airplane hijackings…Led takeover of OPEC headquarters in Vienna in 1977
Ahmed-Jabril	Leader of PLFP-GC…Trained with Syrian Army…Considered an expert bombmaker…Suspected of helping bomb Pan Am Flight 103 over Lockerbie, Scotland
Hassan Nasrallah	Active with Hezbullah and believed to be the head of its military arm, Islamic Resistance…Keeps in close contact with Hamas leadership
Ahmed Yassin	Known as Sheikh or the Intifada…Founding member and spiritual leader of Hamas…Active in Damascus, Syria…Released by Israelis in 1985 in a prisoner exchange
Ramzi Ahmed Yousef	Active in Philippine terrorist group Abu Sayyaf…Came to U.S. in 1992, masterminded World Trade Center bombing in New York and fled to Philippines…Active in Project Bojinga aimed at blowing U.S. airliners out of Asian air space…Arrested in Pakistan, tried in the United States, serving a life sentence

Actions and characteristics of terrorist groups do change over time; for example, kneecapping was used as a signal or scar to demonstrate the wide reach of a terrorist organization. In Italy, they shot the victim in the knee; in Ireland, an electric drill was used to mutilate the knee. In both cases, victims walking the rest of their lives with a limp was a constant reminder to the populace of the terrorist group's power and omnipresence in the region.

In Africa, terrorists use a machete to chop off a hand or hands of victims, even children, accomplishing a similar effect on villagers and urban populations alike.

Counterterrorist Response

The United States has dramatically enhanced its counterterrorist response capability over the last decade in order to address the widening threat of global terrorism reaching domestic targets and U.S. interests abroad. The President sets the overall policy for counterterrorism, with the assistance of a special coordinating committee of the National Security Council. Presidential Directive 39, entitled United States Policy on Counterterrorism, recognizes that there must be rapid and decisive capability in defeating terrorism. The report spells out the need to protect U.S. citizens, arrest terrorists, respond to sponsors of terrorism, and provide assistance to the victims. As a result, the problems encountered in combating global terrorism are too complex to expect a single agency to deal with them successfully. As a result, in organizing the response to terrorism, the effort is divided into two broad phases: the crisis, or pre-incident, phase and the consequence, or post-incident, phase.

In response to the bombings of U.S. embassies in East Africa, Congress established a blue-ribbon panel to consider new approaches to combating the threat and actual acts of terrorism. The Advisory Panel to Access Domestic Response Capabilities for Terrorism Involving Weapons of Mass Destruction, familiarly referred to as the Gilmore Commission, was named for the chairperson, Virginia Governor James S. Gilmore. The commission addressed incidents involving weapons of mass destruction (WMD) against the U.S. home territory. In a departure from past policy, the commission suggested that the U.S. military assume the lead role in dealing with weapons of mass destruction.

Major points of U.S. counterterrorism policy include

- Make no concessions to terrorists and strike no deals.
- Bring terrorists to justice for their crimes.
- Isolate and apply pressure on states that sponsor terrorism to force them to change their behavior.
- Bolster the counterterrorism capabilities of those countries that work with the U.S. and that require assistance.

The Secret Service has the most defined role in protecting government officials from terrorist attacks, with responsibility for protecting the President and Vice President and their families, as well as selected other individuals including presidential candidates of major parties, President-elect and Vice President-elect and selected other senior government officials. The Secret Service and the U.S. Department of State share responsibility for protecting heads of foreign states and other international dignitaries visiting the United States. As a practical matter, these federal agencies coordinate their efforts with local law enforcement departments, particularly on such matters as crowd and traffic control, building security, and uniformed police presences.

The response to a terrorist action is addressed on three discrete levels:

1. Local: In a terrorist attack, such as a bombing or the taking of hostages, the first responders are typically local public safety and medical personnel. Unless the attack has occurred in a major municipality, local assets are usually not sufficient to meet the emergency, particularly when weapons of mass destruction are used.
2. State: If local authorities require help in responding to major terrorist activity, assistance can be requested through a state Office of Emergency Services, or similar agency. The state's substantially greater resources, including selected elements of the National Guard, can readily be dispatched to the affected area or location.
3. Federal: Contingency plans for most crisis and consequence intervention have been developed and refined in recent years. The Federal Bureau of Investigation (FBI) is the lead agency for crisis management involving domestic acts of terrorism. The FBI's role includes active measures for prevention, and immediate incident and post-incident response. In addition, in most cases, the FBI will utilize the assistance of local and state law enforcement officials.

The Federal Emergency Management Agency (FEMA) is the lead agency for consequence management for both preparedness and dealing with terrorist incidents. State and local governments are still the controlling agencies in rescue and medical functions during terrorist incidents. In an incident where weapons of mass destruction are used, the response capability of rescue and medical units may be impaired. In extraordinary cases, active military units garrisoned in the vicinity of the incident may be called upon for immediate deployment in order to save lives, prevent human suffering, and assist in protecting physical property.

Internationally, the U.S. State Department has increased its assistance to friendly nations in their efforts to combat terrorism. Such assistance includes financial support, as well as training and intelligence sharing. The Central Intelligence Agency (CIA) also plays a major role in combating international terrorism through it pro-active gathering and interaction with government and non-government agencies and organizations.

Counterterrorist Operations

Counterterrorist operations usually involve a blend of law enforcement agencies and the nation's military resources, particularly when terrorist activity occurs overseas. The National Security Council oversees the effort involving domestic terrorism. Among the agencies operating under the umbrella of the Counterterrorism Security Group are the departments of State, Justice (through the FBI), Treasury, Transportation (primarily the Federal Aviation Administration), and Energy, as well as the CIA and Joint Chiefs of Staff.

In all domestic terrorist actions and in many of those directed against U.S. government facilities abroad, the FBI is charged with being the lead agency in handling the crisis and post-incident investigation. As an example, in the aftermath of the 1998 bombings of the U.S. embassies in Kenya and Tanzania, the FBI sent investigators to the two countries along with evidence processing teams.

No single agency can be expected to successfully combat the multifaceted challenges of dealing with terrorist threats and activity. Joint operations involving federal, state, and local law enforcement agencies, coupled with military assistance when appropriate, are now the standard in combating terrorists. The threat of weapons of mass destruction has persuaded the federal government to adopt a more aggressive approach to the potential threat.

The Defense Authorization Act, also called the Nunn Luger Domenici Act, enhanced the nation's defense against attacks involving biological and chemical weapons. The legislation authorized the Department of Defense to provide initial training for "first responders" in major urban centers and other areas of likely attacks.

Counterterrorism is a challenge not just for the United States, but for most western European nations and industrialized states around the world. In most countries, the military plays a major role in combating terrorism through units such as the Delta Force in the United States, the United Kingdom's S.A.S., France's G.I.G.N. unit, and Germany's GSG-9 unit.

Weapons of Mass Destruction

Where once nuclear attack was considered the most destructive form a terrorist attack could take, there has been increased sophistication in the development of other types of weapons that can cause widespread death, suffering, and destruction. Since the Persian Gulf War of 1991, the threat of attack by rogue states such as Iraq using biological or chemical weapons has brought the specter of state-sponsored terrorism to new heights. There is the potential for rogue nations to arm their own operatives with these weapons, as well as to supply terrorist groups elsewhere. The most publicized use of a chemical weapon in a terrorist attack was by a Japanese religious cult which in the 1990s unleashed sarin gas in the Tokyo subway system.

In an effort to deal with such threats, the FBI operates the National Domestic Preparedness Office, which acts as a clearing house on weapons of mass destruction for federal, state, and local authorities. The NDPO facilitates and coordinates efforts of various government agencies in providing the emergency response community with detection, protection, analysis, and decontamination equipment, as needed, in dealing with weapons of mass destruction.

When an attack, or suspected attack, involves nuclear terrorism, the U.S. Energy Department becomes involved. Nuclear threats can involve more than surprise attacks. In the low-intensity conflict that for decades has involved India, Pakistan, and Bangladesh, the participant states have developed nuclear capabilities, raising the likelihood that nuclear weapons could be involved in a first-strike, or in a retaliatory response to terrorism.

Role of the Military

The Department of Defense has been assigned a much greater role than previously in dealing with terrorist attacks, both on U.S. and foreign soil or at sea. DOD supports local, state, and federal agencies in planning for, and responding to, emergencies, particularly those involving weapons of mass destruction. In the event a major incident occurs and the President, Secretary of Defense, or his executive agent declares an emergency condition exists, that individual may direct the military to assist.

For a number of traditional and pragmatic reasons, the military plays a greater role in combating terrorism overseas than it does on the domestic front; even after such attacks as the bombing of the World Trade Center in New York and the Murrah Federal Building in Oklahoma City. However, in the aftermath of the bombings of U.S. Embassies in East Africa in the late 1990s, Congress established the National Commission on Terrorism (Gilmore Commission) which proposed an increase in the role of the U.S. military in combating terrorism. Such units as the explosive ordinance teams, the Army's Technical Escort Unit, and the Marine Corps' Chemical Biological Incident Response Force have been involved in planning and establishing procedures for expanded counterterrorist operations.

The use of the military in counterterrorism efforts is still controversial, as witnessed in the events surrounding the siege of the Branch Davidian compound outside Waco, Texas, in 1993. It has been alleged that U.S. Army personnel were present as observers and perhaps as advisors, because military vehicles were used in the siege. If the Army personnel had taken a more active role, it would have been a violation of federal law.

Role of the Federal Aviation Administration

The Federal Aviation Administration (FAA) is the lead agency in dealing with the hijacking of airplanes and in airport security, even though the FBI, in all probability, coordinates the operation. There is a "memorandum of under-standing" between the FBI and FAA which indicates that should a skyjacking be attempted and the doors of the aircraft are open, the FBI has primary responsibility for the situation. If the doors of the aircraft are closed, however, the FAA assumes responsibility. In practice, though, the FAA does not have a full law-enforcement arm and, in most such situations, the agency will usually defer to the FBI.

In addition to airplane hijacking incidents, the FAA also monitors airport security involving both local police departments and private security companies under contract.

Financial Terrorism

Money laundering can lead to financial terrorism and many well-known financial institutions have had officers involved in moving money in and out of off-shore banks. Some manipulation and movement of money are done for the purpose of avoiding taxes or other regulations, but often it has been done to legitimize illgotten funds of illegal businesses or criminals. Major financial institutions and even governments of countries both large and small have been brought down as a result of money manipulations. More recently, there are reports of wholesale counterfeiting of U.S. currency by nations such as Iran and Iraq in an effort to destabilize U.S. and possibly European currencies.

Counterterrorist Capabilities

The original FBI Hostage Rescue Team (HRT) was a unit composed of highly trained agents working out of Quantico, Virginia, home of the National Academy. This team, which responds to anywhere in the country, and even outside the United States at the request of the President, is highly trained in weapons, tactics, and crisis management. Each individual agent has special skills which may be required in a hostage rescue attempt including rappeling down the side of a building; parachuting into a location, or shaping a directional explosive charge, to name just a few. This team was first deployed at the 1984 Olympic Games in Los Angeles where, as it turned out, their expertise was not required.

The tactical arm of the HRT has carried out a number of rescues, and the negotiating part of the unit also enjoyed success in several hostage incidents, notably in federal prisons in Georgia and Louisiana. The HRT was also involved in Waco, Texas, in 1993. ATF agents from the Bureau of Alcohol, Tobacco and Firearms were involved with the religious sect known as the Branch Davidians outside Waco. The FBI became involved after four ATF agents were killed and several others injured in a poorly executed attempt to serve search warrants covering illegal weapons and an arrest warrant for sect leader David Koresh. In a siege that lasted more than 50 days, the HRT, its policies, and procedures were the subject of much scrutiny and, afterward, severe criticism.

The HRT negotiators were able to secure the exit of a large number of Davidian members and their children from the Koresh-controlled compound. The negotiators were also successful in getting the cooperation of Koresh himself on several issues. During the drawnout siege, the lines of communication and coordination with the tactical portion of the HRT team deteriorated significantly. A series of miscommunications between tactical team members and negotiators resulted in improper or incorrect actions to positive responses Koresh and the Davidians had given negotiators. The tactical team engaged in psychological activity that was at odds with the efforts of negotiators. These conflicts would be brought to the attention of the whole country in the months and years afterward via Congressional testimony, investigative journalism, and statements from retiring FBI agents. The siege ended April 19, 1993 after the use of tear gas was followed by a fire which destroyed the Davidian compound and resulted in the death of 74 men, women, and children who were inside.

In the wake of the adverse publicity and subsequent inquiries, the FBI revamped and renamed the HRT. The newly launched Crisis Intervention Response Group (CIRG) is charged with placing a greater emphasis on negotiation and cooperation. Not withstanding the decision by a jury in a civil action brought by survivors and family members of individuals killed in the conflagration at the Branch Davidian compound, and the exoneration of FBI agents by a special investigative commission, public opinion is divided on the activities and responsibility of the government agents involved.

As a practical matter, in terrorist operations, the FBI's CIRG will have a long lead time before it can respond to a specific location. Notification and request must be made through FBI channels. The current lead time is approximately six hours, meaning that the team can be en route to a location about two hours after a formal request has been granted. Many local FBI field offices in major cities also have special weapons and tactics (SWAT)-trained agents and some trained negotiators who could respond more quickly to some incidents.

Counterterrorist Tactics

In combating terrorism, there are four major components that are utilized in addressing the threat: intelligence, antiterrorism, counterterrorism, and consequence management.

Intelligence-gathering is critical in combating any criminal activity, terrorist or otherwise. The gathering of information, on some occasions, may come up against privacy and other civil liberty concerns, particularly in protecting innocent parties. Major components of intelligence are collection, analysis, and dissemination to relevant parties. Intelligence can be collected in diverse ways, from old-fashioned legwork to sophisticated electronic voice and data capture. The use of human operatives is irreplaceable, and the ability of the CIA was severely restricted in 1995 when strict guidelines were adopted regarding the recruitment of terrorist informants. On the domestic front, FBI activity is subject to the Foreign Intelligence Surveillance Act, which allows agents to conduct electronic surveillance and physical searches of non-citizens, including individuals suspected of engaging in international terrorism.

Antiterrorism involves programs aimed at deterring potential activity by addressing security awareness, enhancing physical security, and actively pursuing individuals responsible for terrorism. Measures adopted to protect, or "harden," potential targets, is an effective step in deterring attack. Cooperation between private corporations and government agencies is another component of antiterrorism. In addition, virtually every law enforcement organization of any size has an antiterrorism program keyed to specific potential targets or individuals within its jurisdiction.

Counterterrorism efforts have been enhanced in recent years at all levels of government. This is particularly true where there are professionally trained units dealing with hostage, bombing, and kidnapping cases. In the case of the military, the United States maintains the vaunted and secretive Delta Force based at Fort Bragg, North Carolina. In almost all domestic terrorist incidents, local law enforcement personnel are first on the scene. Federal responder teams are at minimum a couple of hours away. For this reason, in recent years, there has been a heavy emphasis directed to the training of first responders. Virtually every major and mid-sized police department has specially trained hostage negotiators and special weapons and tactics (SWAT) teams, as well as explosives disposal personnel.

Intelligence research and analysis generally fall to large metropolitan, state, and federal agencies, up to and including the FBI, CIA, and various military units. The information is analyzed and compiled into reports that are disseminated to other agencies. This intelligence information is useful for investigators tracking terrorist operatives. It is also used by private security professionals in planning protection for overseas facilities and personnel.

There are a number of sources for private security professionals to access such intelligence, including relevant committees of the American Society for Industrial Security and Jane's Information Service.

Investigative Techniques

For a long time after its establishment in the 1920s, the FBI maintained an amicable but distant relationship with local law enforcement agencies, working together only when specific circumstances demanded it or legislation required it, as in the case of kidnappings or interstate commerce. In the late 1970s, however, the FBI began establishing a number of Joint Bank Robbery Task Forces in larger cities. This effort combined the technical capabilities and nationwide resources of the FBI with the street smarts of local police officers and detectives. Another positive factor in the success of these joint task forces was the Federal money available to pump into major investigations.

As cases were broken, those arrested were tried in federal courts under federal statutes, where violations are easier to prove than in state courts adjudicating state statutes. In addition, federal courts typically mete out greater penalties.

The success of the bank robbery task forces led to the creation of other joint efforts, including the innovative NYPD/FBI Joint Terrorist Task Force in New York City. This unit has been on the cutting edge in dealing with domestic terrorist activity. Since the FBI is the lead agency in dealing with domestic terrorist attacks on American territory, New York City police officers are sworn U.S. deputy marshals in addition to their NYPD ranks and titles. The federal rank allows them to have jurisdiction anywhere in the country and to cross state lines to travel to investigate activities of terrorist groups and suspected terrorists.

To illustrate just one advantage of combining federal and local law enforcement resources in counterterrorism, the FBI has trained specialists who respond to bomb scenes to organize and direct collection of physical evidence. Even when the State Department is the lead agency in dealing with attack, particularly overseas, the FBI is usually deferred to during the investigative stage of the incident.

Local Law Enforcement Capabilities

In hostage or barricaded situations, the local police department's guidelines are the basic operational procedures for the early stages of such terrorist activities. Information provided in this book should serve as an outline for forming those procedures, or in guiding actions in situations not directly covered by established procedures. In bombing incidents, unless intelligence provides foreknowledge, local police will be dealing with a suspected bomb or in a consequence investigation. In both instances, however, good liaison with the private sector on the part of local police and, conversely, good cooperation by private industry with local police will have the effect of hardening the target against terrorist activity.

Today, nearly all major police departments and many smaller agencies have hostage and barricaded situation procedures in place. Past events, even nonterrorist incidents such as the shootings at Columbine High School in Littleton, Colorado, illustrated the need for cooperative training between police agencies responding to a mutual aid call. The techniques that local law enforcement uses in responding to such a situation could just as easily be used during the opening stages of a terrorist attack or investigation or both. How the first responding officer or officers establish contact, seal off the affected area, conduct an evacuation, and/or protect the crime scene will greatly influence how the incident is played out.

Interagency Liaison

Interagency liaison involves cooperation from every type of law enforcement, ranging from local departments in contiguous jurisdictions to local or state-and-local relationships with the FBI, as well as cooperation between the FBI and such federal agencies as the Secret Service, Drug Enforcement Agency, Bureau of Alcohol, Tobacco and Firearms, Immigration and Naturalization, Customs et al.

By its nature, liaison implies contact prior to an incident or emergency conditions; for example, many smaller police agencies maintain a mutual response agreement with counterparts in adjacent jurisdictions. The importance of such contacts cannot be over-emphasized. Not only is it important for local authorities to maintain contact with each other, but with state and federal agencies as well. These contacts range from formal training sessions to conferences, workshops, joint practice emergency drills, and informal networking.

Local Significance

An important component of counterterrorism is intelligence-gathering. Much of the intelligence is not difficult to find, although assessing its importance and significance can be. One area in which this is especially true involves the names of people, location of places, and lists of dates which have particular significance locally.

For example, in Seattle, early December dates have special significance because that was when, in 1999, demonstrators disrupted a major conference on World Trade. April 19 is the date of the conflagration at the Branch Davidian compound outside Waco, Texas, and the bombing of the Murrah Federal Building in Oklahoma City two years later.

In coastal areas, dates of whale migrations could bring about activity by radical environmental groups. Dates of uprising and revolutions "in the old country" may have symbolic importance to ethnic or national groups living in a community.

There are many dates marked by terrorists that transcend local importance. May 19, for example, has double significance; it is the birthday of both Ho Chi Minh, who led North Vietnam during its war with South Vietnam, and Malcolm X, the Black Muslim. November 6 marks the date of the birth of Mohammed the Prophet, founder of Islam, while four days later, November 10, the U.S. Marine Corps celebrates its birthday. Any of these, and numerous other dates, could elicit some sort of terrorist action in an effort to garner publicity on a significant occasion.

Private Sector Cooperation

In order to harden a potential target against terrorist attack, a good deal of cooperation is required between private industry and law enforcement. The contacts by the private sector should also extend to emergency service agencies as well as state and federal agencies. As a matter of practical fact, in some areas, the security force of a private company may be significantly larger than the local police force. Many railroads are privately owned, but have sworn officers with multi-state commissions, giving them wider jurisdiction than municipal, county, and state police. Private industry has been a frequent supporter and sponsor of training programs that involve local and state agencies in a variety of emergency response scenarios. This cooperation may extend to allowing facilities to be used in practice drills for first responders.

The private sector has also contributed toward the purchase of specialized equipment for emergency services or law enforcement agencies for which no municipal funds had been budgeted. Such purchases have included tactical robots for remote entry in bomb and hostage situations as well as state-of-the-art bomb suits for explosive disposal personnel. Privately supported police foundations in a number of areas have provided funds for the purchase and training of horses for mounted units, dogs for bomb detection squads, and similar expenditures.

Another positive aspect of security cooperation between the public and private sectors involves local police specialists advising about private security guidelines and training for various emergency situations, so that the private security personnel can properly set the stage should such an incident occur.

Pre-Incident Planning

2

Introduction to Risk Assessment

In today's world of high stakes terrorism, there are few individuals or organizations in either the private sector or law enforcement who will question the need for planning to meet the threats terrorism presents. In fact, there is no other area in which there is greater need for cooperation between law enforcement and the private sector than in the area of terrorism defense. When questions do arise, they generally are about costs and potential benefits resulting from these expenditures. It must be remembered, however, that the moral obligation to protect people's lives cannot be evaluated in dollars. For law enforcement's consideration, there is a *legal* obligation to protect lives. It is the foundation of the police mandate. On the part of the private sector, the obligation can be derived from what the courts have called "foreseeability" in vicarious liability suits.

Thus, in the private sector, an incident such as a hostage-taking could be considered a foreseeable occurrence under vicarious liability statutes and case law, particularly if the company is doing business with a country or group that has been or is known to be a focal point of terrorist activity. In effect, such a company is a potential target of violent action and is under some obligation to protect its employees and property. Although terrorists are the most identifiable source of such violent action, disgruntled employees are also potential perpetrators of violence, as are common criminals, and courts have held companies liable for failure to react appropriately when such incidents occur. By way of illustration, there was an item in the *Wall Street Journal* that noted, "Business-executive kidnapping is on the rise as companies expand markets to unstable regions. The Hiscox Group, a London specialty insurer, says reported world-wide kidnappings for ransom last year hit a record 1789, up 6% from 1998."[1]

A defense plan is a guide to dealing with terrorist threats on a pragmatic level. Whether developed by a law enforcement agency or private security or, ideally, through a joint effort between the two, a defense plan is a living — rather than archival — document. It must be reviewed periodically and updated or altered as necessary. Terrorist defense planning can be divided into three component areas: pre-incident, incident, and post-incident.

Pre-incident involves all the planning, anticipation, and "what if" modeling and intelligence-gathering that can be done in advance. Cooperation between the police and private sector is especially crucial here, since information and intelligence can be shared and the most efficient use of resources can be made.

Incident planning involves the development of a course of action in the event a terrorist action, or suspected or potential terrorist action, should occur or even be threatened. Again, communication between the private sector target company or organization and law enforcement and public safety officials is essential.

Post-incident planning is concerned with handling events in the aftermath of a bomb threat, explosion, hostage-taking, or other attack, and deals with emergencies, physical damage, and the need to get operations back to normal as quickly and safely as possible. Continued cooperation between the private and public sectors is essential in this stage, too. Many companies maintain disaster recovery plans (DRPs) that will enable minimal operations to be relocated to a satellite location within a short period, before addressing long-term effects of an attack.

Structuring a Defense Plan

Pre-incident planning involves preparing for an occurrence that everyone hopes will never come to pass. The planning involves information-gathering, risk analysis, organization, training, determining logistical needs, and purchasing necessary supplies and equipment. What is the purpose of planning? First, it establishes the amount or level of potential risk to which a community, corporation, government entity, property, building, or other facilities, or an individual executive or group of individuals may be exposed vis-à-vis terrorist operatives. Once the risk is assessed, policy and procedures must be in place to implement the policy and adhere to procedures.

The incident segment of a defense plan is an operations manual for handling the initial phases of a terrorist attack of any nature. It should explain what actions are to be taken, when they should be taken, who should take them, and how these actions should be carried out.

Post-incident activity should include everything required to assist representatives of authorized agencies in investigating the incident as well in restoring the location to a point at which normal operations may resume. Post-incident planning also involves metrics for assessing the long-term effects of the incident and provides a vehicle for evaluating the strengths and weaknesses of the defense response so everyone can be better prepared should there be another incident.

Information-Gathering

Although this might seem contradictory, information-gathering is at once the easiest and yet the most difficult of tasks. It is easy because much information already exists — in files, letters, official documents, in the records of municipal and other governmental agencies, libraries, databases, and similar sources. The difficult part of information-gathering is that there is no certainty as to what kind of information will be most useful. Likewise, there are no guidelines for how much information is enough. One thing that is certain, new information will be flowing constantly, altering previous assumptions and conclusions, as well as opening whole new areas of concern.

There is a host of resources at the disposal of the security professional, including specialized repositories on everything from terrorist activity to security hardware. The Internet has made such information easily available to the security professional, although the same information is also accessible to terrorist operatives. A word of caution: information overload can easily occur, so the appropriate level of data gathering, both in amount and periodicity of updates, should be ascertained early in the process. For the most part, private security does not require the amount and depth of information that the law enforcement community requires. On the other hand, corporate security officials may require more geographically focused data, particularly when foreign operations are involved, than would a local police department. In either event, there is a tendency to gather so much information that it can be difficult to process and evaluate — almost to the point of rendering it worthless — not to mention organize and retrieve when needed in a timely fashion.

Whatever the sources, and however the data are collected, there are three general categories of information:

1. *Targets.* Information on targets can be subdivided into two categories. The first concerns the types of targets that are being attacked, not only involving American targets, but anywhere around the world. Another type of information covers the type or types of facilities and what it takes to get them up and running again after an emergency situation.Whether target identification information is being gathered on behalf of a municipality, quasipublic corporation, or a private company, the data are simply an enumeration of assets, including human resources, buildings and real estate, inventory, other physical assets, financial assets, and intangibles such as good will, name recognition, and publicity value. In other words, a target is anything or anybody that could be burned, bombed, stolen, damaged, contaminated, taken over, occupied, kidnapped, or held hostage. All of these potential

targets should be listed or inventoried, if you will, and major characteristics identified. Individuals have personnel files with home
addresses, medical histories, dependents' names, and name of next of
kin. Buildings have blueprints, floor plans, drawings of electrical, heating, ventilation and air-conditioning systems, as well as fire alarm and
other security systems. Vehicles have operating and repair manuals.
Real estate has site descriptions and dimensions in the deed and title
files. All this information must be gathered so it can be assessed, filed,
updated, copied, stored, or handled by whatever policy is decided
upon during the risk analysis phase. Target identification should
include rankings of vulnerability, and information on what it would
take to get them up and running again after an emergency situation.
Needless to say, all information on targets should be given the highest
security priority, and should be backed up with copies off premises,
but in a relatively easily accessible location.

2. *Target Profile.* This refers to subjective information dealing with people's perceptions of all the identified potential targets. If a municipality
is involved, likely targets include city hall and all schools, primarily
because of their high profile for media interest. The same goes for law
enforcement facilities, which have prime symbolic value. If a corporate
target is being examined, considerations encompass evaluating the
company's image in the local community, the country, and perhaps
even the world. Who are the company's suppliers, its customers, even
its investors? Individuals within the company should be evaluated as
to symbolic or strategic importance to terrorist operatives. An electric
utility may provide excellent security for corporate headquarters and
the main generating plants, but leave substations, service trucks, payment stations, and transmission lines with minimal protection. Even
if the decision is made not to protect the miles of transmission lines,
cost analysis must be done to justify the decision. In devising a target
profile, it is imperative to include the quality of responding emergency
services: the local police, fire, medical, and other emergency agencies.
Questions should cover whether the response teams are volunteer or
professional and if there are specialists such as bomb technicians or
hostage negotiators. What is the response time for emergency situations? What are the cooperative agreements with agencies that provide
support or supplemental backup? Are local hospital facilities adequate?
How long does it take local power and gas companies to respond to
emergencies? These subjective and qualitative questions will help in
evaluating the risk potential for possible terrorist targets.

3. *Terrorists.* The old adage about knowing your enemy comes into play
here. Much information must obviously come from police and other law

enforcement agencies, but a surprisingly large amount can also be gleaned from professional security publications and their archives and databases, newsletters, and even well-circulated publications available in any large library. The Internet allows access to a variety of governmental and private resources, including the FBI, Department of State, and Central Intelligence Agency, to name just a few. There are also helpful sites maintained by such organizations as the American Federation of Scientists and similar groups. Terrorist groups or their sympathizers may also maintain Web sites providing clues to current activities and specific references to enemies of their cause. The Earth Liberation Front and Animal Liberation Front are two of many such organizations.

Radicals and terrorist groups often disseminate tracts and manifestos during quiet periods when they may be engaged in proselytizing. For security professionals in the private sector, questions to be asked of local law enforcement officials are the same questions police should be asking themselves. What are the current trends in terrorism? Which, if any, terrorist or radical groups are active in the area? Terrorists come in a wide variety of political and activist stripes and ethnic backgrounds. Just because a group is not on the front page or the evening news does not mean that it is not capable of perpetrating a terrorist act. Local police should be aware of militant groups, political cadres, or ethnic populations from areas where there is conflict in the former homeland. A relatively easy tactic in information-gathering on groups that might cause problems is to monitor protest letters from the group or individuals associated with it. Almost every radical group, within and outside the U.S., started out as a concerned citizens organization that was subsequently radicalized or spawned radical splinter groups.

The information-gathering process of terrorist defense planning can be likened to collecting jigsaw puzzle pieces from an almost infinite variety of sources while not knowing how many pieces there are supposed to be or whether they fit one, two, or several different puzzles. And no one provides a picture of the finished puzzle, either.

Target Analysis

One of the more difficult challenges facing defense planners is accurately assessing the likelihood of any particular person, piece of property, or service becoming the target of a terrorist attack. Overestimating the threat potential means wasting dollars, personnel, time, and effort. On the other hand, underestimating the threat could result in physical injury or death, as well as millions of dollars in damages, ransoms, or potentially, liability judgments.

Target or threat analysis includes not only the likelihood of becoming a target, but also whether or not offered defenses are sufficient to discourage potential attacks or to protect individuals and organizations in liability suits.

Many terrorist attacks today, especially in the international arena, are directed at U.S. government facilities, but U.S. private sector organizations sustain the largest number of attacks, even if they are not of the same magnitude as those against official government facilities. According to the 1999 Report on Global Terrorism, U.S. interests sustained 196 terrorists attacks the previous year, which was a 52% increase from the year before. The largest number of attacks, 53, were directed at U.S.-owned or U.S.-based businesses.

In conducting an analysis, any business entity should consider these concepts and determine where it fits into the equation:

1. A company heavily involved in the military-industrial complex. This could include any company or subcontractor with a defense contract and anyone supplying goods or services or both to the defense sector of the economy.

2. Financial institutions, especially those involved in programs that finance programs (or are co-sponsored with the government) that are antithetical to various terrorist organizations and their causes; for example, a bank holding government-backed loans to countries where terrorist organizations are active.

3. Businesses that are working with advanced technologies, particularly if they are weapons or defense systems oriented or both.

4. Companies involved in the processing or use of petrochemicals or other environmentally sensitive products. This is especially applicable in South America, where oil pipelines and refinery operations are located in remote regions.

5. Utilities, particularly those whose service disruption would have a dramatic impact on the public.

6. Companies with manufacturing operations in the third world or developing countries, especially where low wage rates could leave the companies open to charges of exploitation.

7. Companies with operations in politically sensitive countries: traditionally, Israel, Sri Lanka, Spain (particularly in Basque areas), and current hot spots such as Colombia, Greece, Nigeria, and Yemen. Terrorist activity is fluid and subject to ebbs and flows, and thus can crop up almost anywhere, or recur after years of relative calm.

8. Companies, which by virtue of ever-changing political winds may find themselves on the wrong side of emotional political issues. These include, but are not limited to, forest product companies (particularly true of rain forest products), makers of abortion or birth control

products, researchers who use live animals in their testing process, consumer product manufacturers, food processors, real estate developers, and manufacturers or users of nuclear power products.
9. Corporations which because of their size, history, marketplace dominance, or status as cultural icons have become symbolic of America or capitalism or both, such as Coca-Cola, McDonalds, Microsoft, IBM, and virtually any international commercial bank.

Law enforcement officials with companies or organizations located in their jurisdictions that may be potential terrorist targets could ask such questions as:

1. Has the company or organization ever been the target of a terrorist attack?
2. Has the company or organization's name ever been mentioned in a derogatory manner in any radical oratory, literature, on Web sites or online chat rooms, or in any other communication medium? This includes whether the company has been the target of demonstrations locally, or at facilities outside the local jurisdiction.
3. Is the entity in any way affiliated with a company or organization that would have answered in the affirmative to either of the first two questions?
4. Does the company supply raw material, packaging, or any other goods or services to such a company or organization?
5. Does the company or organization receive materials from or ship goods to or through "sensitive" countries or territories?

The challenge in target analysis is to look at an operation through a microscope, noting suppliers, customers, distribution networks, end-users, financial supporters, even public statements and the personal politics of leading officials. If an organization is defensive enough, it will be able to surmise, even in "unlikeliest scenarios," who might want to mount an attack.

While many terrorist and radical groups are well-known, there are many others whose presence is virtually unknown and whose grievances are unaired. There are feuds which blow hot and cold over incidents which may seem inconsequential, or even resolved, to the mainstream population, but which burn in the memories of small cliques which use them to justify violent action. Witness the decades-, if not centuries-old animosity between Catholics and Protestants in Northern Ireland, Armenians and Turks, Turks and Greeks in Cyprus, virtually every group in the Balkans, the Tamils and the Sinhalese, Sikhs and Hindus in South Asia, to name just a few. Thus, the key component in determining who may pose a terrorist threat to a company, organization, or locality is identifying anyone who may be able to conjure grievances, however far-fetched or historically remote they may seem.

Organization

The organization of a defense plan requires the assignment of authority and responsibility for everybody, from the highest level of management down to the rank and file who must know whose orders to follow. The prime components of organizing are establishing levels of responsibility and structuring a chain of command. Individuals assigned to decision-making positions in a defense plan structure should be chosen for their ability to act under pressure. Bureaucrats, drones, slow-but-steady functionaries, or impulsive hunch players should be passed over in favor of those who possess the ability to keep their wits about them in difficult circumstances. This, of course, is a best-case scenario and reality may precipitate deviations from the ideal.

Any organization, whether a law enforcement agency, private company, or public institution such as a school or hospital, has established lines of authority and a chain of command for normal day-to-day operations. During emergency situations, such as might be precipitated by a terrorist attack, special operating rules go into effect. A terrorist defense plan could well call for a variation in the routine and a crisis team taking over control from the usual hierarchy. Such a change could include transferring the seat of power from the chief administrator's office to a command center that is better protected, has more space, or has better communications, at least until the arrival of public safety officials who will then assume command of the situation.

The structure of the chain of command — with lines of communications as short and direct as possible — can take many forms, depending upon the nature of the target and the type of emergency. More important than how the chain of command is structured is the fact that such a chain has been planned, exists, is in place, and everyone is aware of it. The changeover to crisis management can be effected rapidly and orderly as long as everyone knows who is in charge, who has what authority and what responsibility. Only then can the challenge of dealing with, and resolving, the emergency conditions proceed with any reasonable expectation of success.

Defining levels of responsibility is an important component in the chain of command. Each person in a decision-making or leadership role should be fully aware of, and well-schooled in, his or her responsibilities and extent of authority. The limits of that authority must also be well understood. Training for these individuals should include drills and quizzes as to who must make what decisions, as well as "what if" modeling in hypothetical situations.

In addition to individuals being fully aware of their roles, responsibilities should be spelled out in writing in the defense plan so that the operation can proceed accordingly even if key personnel have been replaced over time.

The organization of a well-defined, and thoroughly schooled, crisis team is required until public safety units arrive. Some elements of crisis teams may be in place, such as a first-aid squad or a fire brigade. Other teams which should be formed, if they are not already in place, are an evacuation team which, as we shall see later, is not the same group as the wardens who conduct fire drills; a bomb search team; and a consequence management unit to aid in such things as medical emergencies, evaluating the condition of the area where the incident occurred, and assisting authorities with their investigations. There should also be a risk assessment team that meets to plan defenses as well as to evaluate threats and situations as they arise.

In organizing a crisis team and its sub-units, every attempt should be made to eliminate overlap of duties among the members. In the event of an actual emergency, it is likely that each individual would be occupied with specified tasks and unable to handle multiple assignments. The amount of personnel available may be a limiting factor, but eliminating overlap as much as possible should be part of initial planning considerations.

In evaluating potential team members, there is an important distinction to be made between maintenance people and janitorial or clean-up crews. Janitorial staff is often composed of part-time or contract employees, and thus may not be available during an emergency.

The composition of an evacuation team should include supervisory and management personnel. People in positions of authority are more likely to be listened to in times of emergency. As a practical matter, more wardens will probably be needed for an evacuation team than, say, a search team, since every staircase and exit must be covered during an evacuation. Evacuation personnel will report to the same location each and every drill, or in the event of an actual emergency, so employees who are on the premises every day, all day, are preferred.

Training

Training in terrorist defense plan responsibilities must be addressed to all participants at all levels of involvement, since these people are members of a coordinated unit in which teamwork is required. The foundation for coordinated teamwork is a thorough understanding of individual assignments. Training of search teams can be accomplished without the necessity of outside assistance; however, local and state police agencies as well as specialized security consultants can provide assistance or supplemental training.

Training sessions should include a complete explanation of the defense plan, the theory involved, and the detailed application in order to provide operational flavor. The classroom sessions should be followed by tests and drills of each aspect or phase of the plan, which should then be critiqued so alterations can be made accordingly. Finally, a full-scale crisis simulation can be conducted.

Once the simulation has been conducted and evaluated, regular testing of plan components should be scheduled, at least as regularly as fire drills. A full-scale mock crisis drill should be conducted annually, at the minimum, unless local conditions dictate greater frequency.

Perhaps the biggest deficiency in terrorist defense planning and crisis management comes in the area of replacing and training personnel. When a plan is adopted initially, there usually are sufficient enthusiasm and commitment to assure well-trained teams. As individuals are promoted, transferred, or replaced within the organization, large gaps can develop in the defense plan's organization and/or personnel. Familiarizing newcomers with their responsibilities in the plan and regular simulations of crises and disasters — even just selected phases of the whole plan — is just good management. Such drills not only school newcomers, they also reacquaint experienced personnel with their roles and duties. The whole effort presents opportunities for reviewing the plan, and altering or updating where required.

Terrorist Tactics

To establish a meaningful defense plan requires knowledge of what is being defended. The four most important tactical operations involving terrorists are, in order of relative frequency:

1. Bombings
2. Assassinations and assaults
3. Kidnapping
4. Hostage-taking/skyjacking/barricade situations

Bombings are the most frequent, accounting for as much as 80% of terrorist-related violence. Currently popular are massive vehicle-borne explosive devices, frequently involving a suicide attack, which result in a large number of casualties. Although skyjackings and hostage-takings are relatively infrequent, they are the most spectacular in terms of garnering publicity for terrorist groups. Assassinations and assaults tend to be more selective in order to include symbolic targets, such as those in the 1980s involving the use of assault weapons by Arab terrorists in European airport passenger terminals during the Christmas season. In Spain, Euskadi ta Askatasuna, ETA or Freedom for the Basque Homeland, has favored assassination as a major instrument of terror.

Kidnappings by terrorists have included the taking of high government officials, such as occurred when Prime Minister Aldo Moro of Italy was abducted in the 1970s, or the capture of ambassadors and consular officials of foreign countries in an effort to embarrass local governments. Business executives and their families have also been targets of terrorist operatives.

Hostage-taking, skyjacking, and barricade situations include incidents by well-trained multinational hijack teams during the 1970s and 1980s. More recently, Shining Path terrorists in Peru attacked the Japanese ambassador's residence in Lima in late 1996 and held hostages for several days into 1997.

Whatever form the terrorist attacks take, a favorite tactic is to use multiple coincidental events in an effort to separate the defense's resources. The counter-tactic is to try to sever the terrorists' lines of communication, thus dividing and, eventually, conquering. Although the geography, location, type of tactic, and time involved may change, the terror remains the same.

Risk Analysis

Target analysis was discussed earlier, with guidelines for assessing whether or not a potential target is, in fact, a likely target. In risk analysis, an attempt is made to evaluate that likelihood and assign a degree of risk to it. The questions asked are more detailed, the modeling more complex, the analysis more sophisticated, and the conclusions more serious.

Risk, of course, is inherent in life. The danger could be presented by natural disasters such as hurricanes, earthquakes, or volcanic eruptions, or by industrial accidents such as occurred at Bhopal in India or at Chernobyl in the Soviet Union (finally shut down late in 2000). Danger can also come in the form of criminal acts such as bomb threats, espionage, sabotage, kidnapping, or murder.

Risk analysis is a survey to ascertain how high the probability is of one of these dangers occurring, how well the organization can respond should the threat become a reality, and how well the organization can carry on once that reality materializes. Inherent in the analysis is the identification of the vulnerabilities and threats that go along with the risk.

In the course of the analysis, one of the things to be determined is the extent of the organization's exposure, which could materially contribute to loss or damage in the event of a terrorist attack. Thus, a branch office or nonessential satellite facility is more susceptible to attack than the central office. Similarly, a police call box or temporary post is more vulnerable than headquarters or the communications center. In the private sector, a chain of retail stores exposes a company to more risks than does a manufacturing operation concentrated in a single location. Other factors in the risk analysis equation include considerations as to what could cause injury to employees and, in the event injuries are sustained, how well the organization could continue to function.

Risk exposure considerations which could affect the smooth operation of the organization include those involving persons — from the chief at the top down to the lowest-level employee. If the top administrator is kidnapped, killed, or otherwise harmed, the unique service the chief contributes would be gone. In the private sector, the price of a company's stock could be affected and its national or international standing or operational effectiveness jeopardized. This is exactly what happened in 1986 when George Besse of the Renault automobile works was assassinated by Action Directe terrorists. Not only were day-to-day workings of the company disrupted, but a proposed merger with American Motors Corporation was imperiled.

Even in situations in which an entry-level employee is threatened or harmed, the organization's perceived lack of sensitivity could bring about labor problems or a loss of public confidence in the organization.

Risk can be described in terms of its potential for occurrence and its capacity for loss. Risk measurement and quantification can be calculated by using any number of economic equations and mathematical models. Equations include weighted factors, such as loss of individual life, substantial interruption of the individual's activity, moderate interruption of the individual's activity, or little or no interruption. The amount of interruption may be indeterminable. One such risk analysis formula reads:

$$L = D + R + I - IC \ (2B)$$

Here, L equals loss; D is direct cost; R is replacement cost; I is indirect cost; and IC is insurance compensation.[2] This equation deals strictly with the dollars and cents of risk, although thorough analysis is required to put a figure on the indirect and replacement costs, as well as factoring in the cost of insurance premiums over time.

Risk Avoidance

When risk directly affects individuals, i.e., the likelihood that an individual would be killed, harmed, or taken captive, the subject of risk avoidance must be raised. In its simplest form, risk avoidance means identifying risks and neutralizing or eliminating the hazards creating the risk. For example, if there is a geographic area where kidnappings are very common, increased training for local law enforcement officers may cut down the risk by neutralizing the hazard. Perhaps the training could be underwritten by a local company whose executives would be likely targets of kidnappers.

Another common method of reducing risk is hardening the target; that is, making the target less vulnerable to attack, or reducing the likelihood of a successful attack. Although risk can rarely be eliminated totally, it can be reduced. Egress and ingress can be controlled in buildings and other locations;

protective barriers can be used and perimeters bolstered to segregate areas to which outsiders and the public have access; detection devices can be employed; and, for individuals considered high risk targets, defensive behavioral techniques can be implemented.

In the bluntest terms, an organization is trying to make sure that if a terrorist group is going to mount an attack, let it be some other organization that is the target. Preventing a terrorist attack may be impossible; shifting the focus of that attack is attainable.

Hostage/Kidnap Defense

Individuals likely to become targets of terrorist activities include those people of high wealth or status, travelers to politically unstable areas of the world, and particularly, corporate executives and overseas employees. Individuals in these latter two groups are at even higher risk if they are associated with companies that have a poor corporate image vis-à-vis terrorist groups or if they trade with the "wrong" countries or the "wrong" side in an internal political dispute. Other persons with above average chances of becoming hostages or kidnap victims are employees of non-corporate American organizations, such as schools, foundations, and the U.S. government, as well as U.S. citizens living abroad for whatever reasons.

Just being aware of these risk categories is the first step in an individual's defense plan to avoid being taken captive. Traveling is one of the highest risk activities for individuals who are potential terrorist targets. Defensive travel tactics include

1. Taking direct flights on U.S. carriers.
2. Checking in early and proceeding immediately to the secure area, being mindful to sit away from lockers, plate glass windows, or anything else that a bomb could turn into shrapnel.
3. If a foreign airline must be taken, use carriers from neutral countries or those with a reputation for high security, or both.
4. Avoid aisle seats and those facing bulkheads, since they have greater visibility and accessibility to terrorist skyjackers who roam the aisles.

These are just a few major actions which can assist a traveler in avoiding trouble.

Notes

1. *Wall Street Journal*, December 12, 2000, page 1, column 5.
2. *The Executive Protection Manual*, Paul Short and James Deiber, MTI Teleprograms, Sheila Park, IL, 1980.

Bomb Defense Planning

3

Types of Bomb Incidents

The bomb has been a favorite weapon of terrorists since the invention of explosives, and currently enjoys particular favor among such groups because of the 24/7 global media coverage of such events. In general, bomb incidents fall into three categories:

1. The bomb threat
2. A suspicious package or actual explosive device
3. An explosion

The most difficult of the three to deal with in terms of planning and developing procedures for a bomb defense plan is the bomb threat. The threat embraces so many variables that there is virtually no guaranteed defense against it. More often than not, the intended target will receive notification that a bomb or explosives have been planted, with the target then informing a law enforcement agency. It is difficult to assess the risk of a bomb threat. Overreacting can be expensive, disruptive, and play right into the hands of those responsible for the threat. Underreacting, however, can be even more costly in terms of time, money, and worst, human life.

Dealing with suspicious packages or actual explosive devices in a defense plan and the procedures involved should be much more concrete and specific. It makes no difference, in fact, whether a suspicious package turns out to be harmless or a live device, since once a package — be it a box, briefcase, backpack, pocketbook, or another other kind of container — is deemed suspicious, it should be treated as though it were an explosive device. Then the trained bomb technicians take over.

There are very few "always" prescribed in this book, and not many more "nevers;" however, one of the nevers is *never* touch a suspicious package unless you have been fully trained or are a certified bomb technician. The determination of a suspicious package as an explosive device and the removal and disposal of explosive devices are jobs for qualified bomb technicians, whether they are from the local law enforcement agency, or from county, state, or federal agencies, or even the military.

Planning and crisis response in the event of an explosion are the same whether the explosion is accidental or bomb related. Only after the determination has been made whether or not an explosion was accidental or intentional do the procedures vary (Figure 3.1). The use of weapons of mass destruction (WMD) other than explosives, such as gases or chemicals, requires different procedures, as discussed in Chapter 6.

The Bomb Threat

A bomb threat can be delivered in a number of ways and for a variety of reasons. In the past, it was often a means of claiming responsibility for a particular action by a terrorist or radical organization. The notification could be made by telephone, mailed notes, or hand-delivered messages to news media, proclamations secreted in public areas such as phone booths, or messages scrawled on restroom mirrors on the target premises. This latter tactic has been used for aircraft hijacking and/or bomb threats, as well as nuisance threats in large public offices and public facilities.

Although threats may be communicated in a number of ways, the most commonly employed medium by far is the telephone. The telephone affords the caller a great deal of anonymity, with public pay phones used to thwart caller identification systems. Even though the bomb threat is a tactic often employed by terrorists and radicals, the fact is that bomb threats are more often perpetrated by nonterrorists. These would be the threats received from individuals wanting to disrupt activities at the target or seeking the thrill of precipitating an emergency response to the threat. The number of terrorist bombings in the United States has decreased in recent years, but the threat of bombings is still a major concern of law enforcement agencies as well as facilities managers in both the private and public sectors.

Work locations, schools, theater, arenas, and stadiums, and centers of public transportation such as airports, train depots, and bus stations are favorite targets of bomb threats because of the considerable disruption and media attention they can create. Even in instances where no explosives have actually been placed, the threat alone becomes an instrument of harassment and disruption. A single telephone call can result in the evacuation of thousands of people from a named target location. In 1985, the Toronto, Canada, subway system was severely disrupted when a bomb threat was received. It was purported that an Armenian terrorist organization had placed a bomb in the system to protest the Canadian government's refusal to release several Armenians being held in connection with an earlier hostage situation at the Turkish Consulate. The threat, although real and believable, produced no explosive device. Several years later, however, a radical terrorist group in

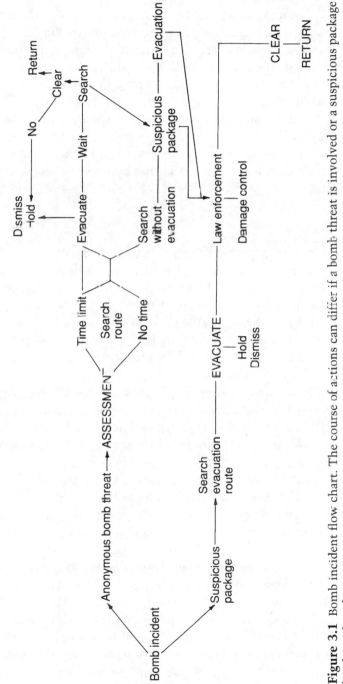

Figure 3.1 Bomb incident flow chart. The course of actions can differ if a bomb threat is involved or a suspicious package has been found.

Japan released sarin gas in the Tokyo subway system, in this case, not both-ering to issue a forewarning.

Statistically speaking, any given bomb threat is probably the work of a prankster, an emotionally disturbed person, someone looking for thrills or sexual fulfillment, or someone seeking revenge for some or imagined griev-ance. However, and this is an important consideration, any given bomb threat may also be the real thing. The caller may, in fact, have actual know-ledge that an explosive device or some other WMD has been placed, or will be placed, at the announced location, and for whatever reason wants to share that information.

No threats should be taken lightly. Threats should, however, be evaluated in the context in which they are made so that appropriate responses can be implemented.

Rationale of Bomb Threats

As already noted, most bomb threats are made when the caller knows that the threat is a hoax and no actual device has been placed. For whatever reason, the caller wishes to disrupt the intended target. Not only is this the most common type of bomb threat, it is the most successful, for by its very nature it achieves the desired result of disruption. In this type of threat, the offender usually is not apprehended or successfully prosecuted.

Types of threatmakers and their rationales for making bomb threats are limited only by imagination. Typical situations involve employees looking for a day off work, students seeking to avoid exams, dismissed employees getting even, jilted lovers striking back, family disputes spilling over into the work place, or pure pranksters and thrill-seekers with no definable motivation.

There are other instances of bomb threats in which the caller has a more serious purpose. The threatmaker may want to bring media attention to a particular cause or to assure that his or her organization gets proper credit for the threat. In utilizing the pre-incident call when a device has actually been planted, the organization or individual is assuring the media exposure that is so important to terrorist causes. In many instances, a follow-up communica-tion may be transmitted, expounding the aims, goals, and philosophy of the organization responsible.

There may be other reasons why warning calls are made in cases in which actual devices have been planted. It may be that the caller has had pangs of conscience or is having second thoughts about going through with the act. Perhaps he or she never thought a real bomb would be planted and now wants to distance himself or herself from the action.

Another rationale for the warning call may be to shift responsibility for any deaths or injuries away from the bombers and onto the police or the organization at which the attack is directed. This may be an attempt to build an affirmative defense in the event of apprehension. Those responsible for the incident may say something to the effect: "We gave fair warning to the police or intended target; the only reason people were killed or injured was because the police or the target or both failed to take proper action."

A Note of Warning

In the long tradition of modern terrorism, just such a communique was issued January 12, 1984 by a "revolutionary anti-imperialist organization" carrying out "armed attacks on military, police and governmental installations/personnel and on death merchants both military contractors and corporations engaged in oppression of the people and exploitation of our resources." This communique, delivered to several news organizations, said the group was going to use bombs and explosive devices in attacking intended targets. It continued, "It is not the intention of the United Freedom Front (UFF) to hurt any innocent civilians and workers and it has been our procedure, where applicable, to give *sufficient warning* [emphasis in the original] for evacuation of buildings and to use other methods to minimize the chances of personal injury." The message detailed how evacuation plans should be drawn up and employed whenever a bomb threat had been made. In addition, it also advised against touching suspicious packages once a threat had been received.

Though generally falling into the pattern of tactics and activities espoused by such terrorist theorists as Carlos Marighella, author of *The Minimanual of the Urban Terrorist*, this communication was unique because it so strongly appears to have been designed to establish a defense against the organization being held accountable for injury or death resulting from one of its attacks.

In practice, the UFF did employ a warning call prior to most of its attacks. It also used surveillance of the target to make sure that the warning message was acted upon. The group also called a third party with a warning call when members of the group felt that the target might not have received its warning call or was not acting upon it seriously. In one particular case, when a UFF caller indicated that a bomb would go off in 30 minutes and no apparent response was taking place, a second call was placed to reinforce the warning call and not that only 15 minutes were left before detonation.

There are variations of the pre-explosion call. On occasion, the warning calls have been made with a pre-recorded taped message intended to reduce the effectiveness of any voice identification techniques that might be employed.

Warning or Hoax?

When an individual calls with the knowledge that a bomb has been (or will be) placed, this should be considered a warning call. When a person makes a call knowing full well that no device is present, this should be considered a bomb threat or hoax. Unfortunately, it is not easy to distinguish between the two until after

- The bomb explodes.
- A search is conducted and a bomb is found.
- A suspicious package is located which may or may not be associated with the warning/hoax.
- A thorough search is conducted and nothing of an unusual nature is found.

To the law enforcement official, public safety officer or even private security practitioner, distinguishing a threat from a warning call is one of the most difficult determinations to make. There is no easy answer. To best be prepared to address the problem, a risk profile must be developed in pre-incident planning and a thorough risk assessment survey made of the affected area or facilities.

While a vast majority of bomb threats turn out to be hoaxes, the fact that a bomb was not planted does not automatically rule out the possibility of terrorist involvement. The group may be using the bomb threat as a tool, not only of disruption, but also for surveillance and intelligence-gathering concerning the target's preparedness for a bomb attack. The Irish Republican Army (IRA), for example, has developed a means of incorporating a code word in its warning calls to verify the validity of the call. But the IRA has also made a number, sometimes as many as a dozen, of validated calls that were hoaxes, before conducting an actual bomb attack.

In handling hoaxes — or to be more exact, bomb threats that may be hoaxes — experience has taught that there are some behavioral and psychological characteristics common to typical hoaxers. A risk profile based on these characteristics may be developed, as we will discuss later. Often, however, it is as much circumstances which create hoaxers as it is any particular pre-disposition to this type of behavior. An important factor, one which could play a role in the continuation of a hoax problem, is the reaction of the management of a targeted facility. Overreaction will almost invariably result in the escalation of these type of calls.

In retrospect, most nonterrorist bomb-threat hoaxers do not realize the seriousness of their actions, especially in terms of lost production time and injuries that could occur during an unnecessary evacuation. It is analogous to children being unaware of the possible consequences of transmitting a false fire alarm.

Responding to the Bomb Threat

Bomb threats can come from virtually any quarter. All bomb threats (even anonymous threats) must be treated as the real thing until determined otherwise. There are certain parameters or risk profiles that can assist in assessing the likelihood of a bomb threat being serious or frivolous. Much of the work in determining a credibility index, however, must be completed prior to the threat being received. This reinforces the need for pre-incident planning.

In developing a risk profile of a potential target, there are several points to be considered:

1. How tight is security at the target, particularly with respect to a potential bomb attack?
2. What is the target's previous experience with bomb threats or bomb attacks or both?
3. What is the current climate of terrorist or radical activity? Has there been an incident that could inspire copycat activity?
4. Does the warning call fit any of the known methods of terrorist activity currently or in the recent past? Is this intelligence up-to-date and reliable?
5. Is the target involved in labor contract negotiations, or has it been involved in labor/management confrontations in the past?
6. To whom was the threatening call made and what was the exact wording of the message? Did the caller indicate knowledge of the threatened area?
7. Evaluate distinctive traits in the caller's voice or speech mannerism: Was the speech slurred; did it contain accents, stutters, or other speech impediments? Was the caller rambling or excessive to the point of indicating alcohol or drug influences? Was there identifiable background noise such as street sounds, laughter, or music?
8. Has any employee of the target recently been discharged or disciplined to the extent that it might precipitate a bomb threat?
9. Could the target have caused the alienation of a consumer, member of the public, a special interest group, or a radical organization?

Consider how specific the wording of the threat is. The more specific the details, without being excessive, the greater the need to take the caller seriously. If a person is malicious enough to place an explosive device, or even threaten placement of such a device, there is no guarantee that he or she will be telling the truth about the time or place a bomb will explode. Yet the caller may be telling the truth. Both possibilities must be considered.

Bomb threats, even obvious hoaxes, cannot be totally ignored. If nothing else, a violation of law has been committed by the mere fact of a threat being made. In addition, if there is a series of calls or a pattern of harassment, serious criminal charges may be lodged when the callers are apprehended. In all cases, in addition to reporting the threat to the appropriate law enforcement agency, a search of the affected area should be conducted. The various search options are discussed in Chapter 8.

Evacuation Options

When a bomb incident results in evacuation of a building or other specific area, tight control must be exercised during the procedures. While a fire evacuation (drill or actual) calls for a speedy evacuation, a bomb evacuation must be more controlled to reduce risk of injury in the event of a premature detonation.

There are three options in handling a bomb threat:

1. Evacuation
2. Partial evacuation of the affected area
3. No evacuation

Which option is employed will depend upon the tactical demands of the situation, including the size of the suspected device. A letter bomb, for example, may require the evacuation of only the immediate area and not the entire building. In other cases, a suspected device may be placed in a location that does not allow a complete evacuation to proceed safely. Perhaps the warning call indicated only a certain area of the building has been targeted. In some situations, a full evacuation may not be possible, such as in a highrise building where people may have to be evacuated upward from the area rather than descending a stairway past the floor where the suspected device is located (Figure 3.2).

The size of the device dictates the distance required for safety. Construction, age of the building, and building materials must also be considered. And in truth, there are not answers to all possibilities. There were no warnings given prior to either the bombing of the World Trade Center in New York City nor the Murrah Federal Building in Oklahoma City. Even if there had been advance notice, in all likelihood there would not have been time for a full and complete evacuation and, given the power of the explosives used and the resulting damage, there could have been more death and injuries to hundreds of people exiting the buildings.

A bomb threat evacuation is entirely different from a fire evacuation. Primary evacuation routes must be searched prior to ordering an evacuation, and evacuees must be removed a distance sufficient to assure they will not be injured by blast effects or fragmentation in the event of detonation. Some of the most powerful bombs used in terrorist attacks have been delivered in vehicles parked outside the target, thus damaging not only the intended building or facility, but also much of the immediate vicinity.

The use of fire alarms is *not* recommended to give notice to evacuate for a bomb threat, since fire alarms elicit an automatic response and do not allow for a controlled evacuation. Additionally, when dealing with explosive devices, doors and windows should be left open in order to ventilate the area. An explosion follows the path of least resistance and open doors and windows will allow the explosive force to vent and, thus, somewhat reduce the amount of damage from the blast. In fire drills, doors and windows are usually closed to reduce drafts and the amount of oxygen available to feed the fire. Another reason for not using the fire alarm is that occupants of the building may assume there is an unannounced fire drill and, without the presence of smoke or fire, linger about or ignore the alarm altogether.

Evacuation Procedures

Anticipated or designated evacuation routes must be searched prior to giving an evacuation order. In many buildings and locations, there are many possible evacuation routes, making it time consuming to search each one individually, even with sufficient personnel. To reduce pre-evacuation search time, specific bomb evacuation routes should be predetermined and searched immediately upon receipt of a bomb threat, even before the decision has been whether or not to evacuate. Then, should the evacuation order be given, the escape routes will be clear for safe passage.

To reinforce the importance of searching the evacuation route, bear in mind that a number of terrorist organizations that were operating in the United States in the last third of the 20th century used fire stairwells as locations for their planted explosive devices. Fire stairs were used because of their accessibility and lack of traffic during normal business hours.

Damage control in a bomb incident differs from that used during a fire. As mentioned above, during a fire, the usual procedure is to shut windows and doors to reduce oxygen that could feed the fire. With bombs, it is desirable to ventilate the explosion. Also with bombs, lights, electrical devices, and office equipment should be turned off. If there is time, gas and fuel lines should be shut down.

Even when an evacuation has been initiated, it may be necessary to maintain a minimum workforce at a location in order to continue essential services. Contingency plans of high-risk companies and agencies should be reviewed and updated on a regular basis so that minimum operating requirements can be met with a maximum of automation. In some instances, remote or off-site backup systems may be employed on a short-term basis to maintain essential operations.

To facilitate safe and orderly evacuations, an Evacuation Warden should be appointed. The primary function of an evacuation warden is to assure that all people are removed from the affected area as quickly as possible. It is preferable to have supervisory or management personnel as wardens, because they command respect and possess enough authority to have their instructions carried out without argument. In additional, such personnel are more likely to have a better knowledge of who is assigned where, assuring that all employees are accounted for.

The number of evacuation wardens needed depends upon the size and layout of the areas that could be affected and the number of people occupying these spaces at any one time. In cases in which many wardens are required, an evacuation team coordinator should be designated. All those actually carrying out evacuation duties must be under the coordinator's direction. The coordinator need not be a member of the risk assessment team, because the evacuation is primarily a mechanical function.

Putting Out the Message

A major consideration in initiating an evacuation order is how to accomplish the evacuation without creating panic, yet at the same time communicating the need for immediate compliance. The best way to give an evacuation order is by utilizing an internal communication system. This could be an internal e-mail sent only to evacuation wardens, followed by messages over a public address system, universal intercom, or an emergency loud speaker network. The idea is to initiate immediate compliance, but without creating panic. In utilizing the internal communications system, it would be best to have recorded and previously scripted messages designed to create the least amount of alarm among the building occupants. As a backup to e-mail, a coding system, which should be confidential, could be used to alert key personnel needed to effect a successful search or evacuation. This prerecorded message should be prepared with the assistance of individuals trained in communications, so that confusion and potential misunderstandings are eliminated. The correct terminology must be used to reduce fear and anxiety. Keep the evacuation message simple, bilingual if necessary, and make sure it reaches everybody in the building.

Planning Issues

Even in terms of security plans, physical changes in the building are often overlooked. New interiors walls are constructed, staircases are remodeled or moved, doors and windows are blocked off, and similar alterations are made which can make a defense plan obsolete very quickly. More than once, bomb squads have been forced to conduct searches or postblast investigations using floor plans and other mechanical drawings that are several years out of date. Make sure the building engineer has floor plans; structural drawings; heating, ventilation, and air conditioning (HVAC) drawings; and design plans for remodeling or reconstructed sections of the building. Copies of all of these drawings should be maintained in a secure off-site location in the event it is not possible to retrieve working copies from the affected facility. Even with such drawings in hand, building engineers and maintenance personnel should be made available to investigators if an attack has occurred.

Continuity of effort, training, and current information are vital if a defense plan is to be worth the time, money, and effort spent on it. Since private security practitioners are more concerned with such day-to-day matters as employee screening, loss prevention, access control, and perimeter security than with potential terrorist attacks, it is up to the police professional to reinforce the message that preparation is also needed to defend against bomb attacks, hostage-takings, and kidnappings.

As previously discussed, the vast majority of bomb threats turn out to be hoaxes. However, if a company receives a series of threats which turn out to be hoaxes, police officers should work with the company's security professional to channel the energies of the internal security force into addressing the problem, whether it be a disgruntled employee, a prankster, or — just maybe — a terrorist. Threats cannot be ignored. Yet some need to be taken more seriously than others. It is the responsibility of the police, working with a company's risk assessment team, to develop guidelines and procedures on how seriously each threat should be taken.

The Role of Police in Handling a Bomb Threat

In the initial stages of a bomb threat, the role of the police, fire department personnel, or other public safety officials is primarily advisory. A bomb threat that turns out to be a hoax is at least a harassment situation or, depending upon circumstances and local statutes, something more serious. When an actual device is involved, or a suspicious package located or the situation otherwise requires police action, it has escalated into something definitely far more serious. On-site security and first-arriving law enforcement and emergency personnel should confer in an effort to determine the seriousness of the threat. This should also be the time when the existence, or absence, of a bomb or emergency plan is determined.

If there is a prepared plan, with search and evacuation teams in place, law enforcement officials may allow these individuals to conduct a search.

The police should be prepared to take over in the event a device or suspicious package is found, or if there is an explosion. Even if there is no defense plan formulated, the officer should leave the evacuation decision to management of the facility after strongly advising the senior decisionmaker of the gravity of the situation. An explanation of the reasons for a controlled evacuation should be made. The ramifications of other options should also be outlined. The officer must realize, as should management personnel, that it is better to err on the side of caution rather than to act hastily and precipitate unnecessary concern or injury.

Why Terrorists Bomb

Over the last several years, the total number of bombings has decreased, although the number of large or spectacular bomb attacks has increased. Terrorists commit bombings for a number of reasons:

1. To gain media attention, particularly if the target is highly visible or symbolic.
2. Bombing is a cost effective and efficient way to attack a facility.
3. Bombing can be accomplished with a small number of personnel.
4. There is minimal risk of bombers being detected or apprehended.
5. Bombing is inexpensive in comparison to alternatives such as kidnapping or hostage-taking.
6. Random bombings make a considerable impact on the population, because more people fear a bomb attack than being kidnapped or taken hostage.
7. Explosives are readily available through theft, sympathetic supporters, or purchase. In addition, explosives can be constructed through the use of legitimately purchased chemicals, fertilizers, and other material.

In mounting a bomb campaign, or even a single bombing incident, terrorists undertake a great deal of reconnaissance and typically select whichever target looks most vulnerable, but still holds some symbolic or publicity value. The target need not be a corporate headquarters or a major facility, but could be a satellite, subsidiary, or temporary operation. The impact will be the same. Terrorists who hijack planes will, if passenger screening is enhanced, move their attack to the terminal area where passengers, family, and friends can be assaulted. When access to the terminal is tightened, the logical target will be the outer perimeter, such as a passenger drop-off area or parking lot. Downtown airline ticket offices or airport transportation terminals have also been chosen. Rocket and grenade launchers have been used against some organizations, further removing terrorist operatives from the scene of the attack. Like water, terrorists follow the path of least resistance.

Types of Bombers

There are four types of bombers:

1. Amateur
2. Professional
3. Psychopathic
4. Suicidal

Amateur bomb-makers can best be described as experimenters. For the most part, the devices amateurs construct are crude and unsophisticated. They are usually delivered against targets of inconsequential value or targets of opportunity, meaning those with low levels of security awareness. Amateurs also begin in their youth to experiment with fireworks and explosive devices fashioned with material found in school chemistry labs, the laundry room, and the garden shed. Amateur devices may have sophisticated firing mechanisms, but usually employ only a small amount of main charge explosives, which is usually a propellant explosive, such as smokeless powder, black powder, or common fireworks powder. What these substances have in common is that they are relative easy to obtain. In many instances, the amateur bomber may be a copycat bomber, such as a teenager looking for excitement or an attention-seeking individual.

The professional bomber, whether a terrorist, a mercenary who builds or bombs or does both for profit, or an operative in an organized crime syndicate, is distinguished from an amateur by the higher quality of his or her operational techniques. The devices are more sophisticated and reconnaissance, including the use of strict timetables, is an integral part of the operation. The placement of the device is done to assure inflicting maximum damage on the intended target. With time and study, the professional bomber can attack almost any target, using devices that are sufficiently sophisticated to exact a considerable toll.

The psychopathic bomber acts without rhyme or reason. There is little or no predictability to his or her actions. Equally unpredictable is the construction of the explosive device or the rationale behind target selection. The types of devices constructed by these individuals may range from extremely crude to very sophisticated. The sobriquet "mad bomber" has been applied to several different individuals, including Theodore Kaczynski, known for years as the Unabomber, a name coined by the FBI after a device was planted and exploded aboard a United Airlines plane. Over a period of 17 years, he mailed or delivered 16 bombs to various targets, many of which had no apparent connection with one another. Three people were killed and 23 others were injured in these attacks. After Kaczynski insisted that his 35,000-word manifesto be published by the news media, his brother recognized the writing style and informed the FBI. Kaczynski was tracked down and arrested at his home, a mountain cabin without electricity or running water. As a bombmaker, Kaczynski ranked among the best. Many of the components were handmade, including some of the fasteners and the wood boxes in which the devices were placed. Among the subjects that Kaczynski railed against was technology, yet his devices were products of sophisticated technology and handiwork. He was highly educated, yet a reclusive loner. Dr. John M. Oldham, chief medical examiner of the New York State Office of Mental Health, speculated that Kaczynski's behavior might be a mix of two personality styles run amok and theorized that the Unabomber displayed a loner personality that became schizoid, while his vigilant side drove him to paranoia.

The suicide bomber has emerged as a major attack weapon in recent years, particularly among Islamic terrorist groups. Little in the way of scientific study has been done on the training and motivation of suicide bombers, though speculation leads to parallels with the kamikaze bombers employed by Japan during World War II. Most of the well-publicized suicide bomb attacks have been attributed to the Hamas organization, carried out against Israeli and Western targets. The attacks are perpetrated by a *shahid,* or martyr, apparently carrying out a religious mission after having been assured that eternal life in paradise and the chance to see Allah's face await them upon completion of the mission. The profile that has emerged of suicide bombers is one of a male between the ages of 18 and 27, high school educated, from a poor family, and a student of fundamentalist Islamic beliefs. Suicide attacks are usually vehicle-borne improvised explosive devices [IED] packed in or on trucks, vans, cars, and even bicycles. The largest IED to date was delivered by an Islamic suicide bomber against the U.S. Marine Corps barracks in Beirut, Lebanon. It is estimated that the exploded device was the equivalent of about 15,000 pounds of high explosives. In a more recent suicide bombing, that of the naval destroyer U.S.S. Cole in Aden Harbor in Yemen, in October 2000, the bombers employed a Zodiac motorized raft carrying a charge that was estimated at approximately 400 pounds of high explosives.

Motivations of Bombers

There are a variety of motivations for persons who construct and plant improvised explosive devices:

1. *Ideology.* Ideological bombings carried out on behalf of, or in defense of, a wide range of political and/or philosophical beliefs from the extreme left wing to the radical right wing, and all sorts of permutations between. Ideological bombers are generally professional bombers motivated by radical politics, racial or ethnic hatred, or religious, environmental, or ecological fanaticism, or even a distorted fondness for animals. The bombing itself may be a gesture of protest or a purely symbolic attack.

2. *Experimental.* Experimental motivation is common among youthful offenders and immature adults. The experimental bomber is drawn by the excitement and noise created by the explosion, curiosity as to whether the device will actually work, and what the results of an explosion will be, and the thrill of seeing an explosion as a reward for the efforts involved. Bombers motivated by experimentation are usually amateurs.

3. *Vandalism.* Destruction for the sake of destruction is particularly common at times of the year when fireworks are readily available and can be used in bombmaking. Alcohol and drug use may also be involved. Targets of these bombers tend to be small, such as mail boxes and store windows, but public so the handiwork can be observed. Vandals will tend to use larger fireworks devices joined together to fashion pipe bombs and similar devices. As with experimentation bombers, they are usually amateurs, often youthful or immature adults.

4. *Profit.* Profit bombings occur for either direct or indirect monetary gain. The largest number of profit bombings are associated with organized crime operatives extorting money by intimidating or destroying businesses associated with the wrong side in a power struggle. Profit bombers can also be employed by terrorist or radical organizations that lack the expertise to carry out a particular action. Profit motive bombings usually are associated with the professional bomber. A mercenary carrying out the wishes of a client in bombing a target, such as for insurance fraud purposes, is also included in this category. Insurance may also be a profit factor in bomb attacks on commercial airliners. In addition, there is arson by bombing and the use of bombs to cover up a robbery or burglary, all of which are profit motivated.

5. *Emotional* release bombings are usually associated with psychopathic bombers seeking to let go of real or imagined frustrations. The Unabomber falls into this category because of his pathological hatred of technology. There are cases of bombers who have had a love/hate relationship with someone associated with the target. Jealousy and revenge on the part of a dysfunctional family or a jilted lover would fall into this category. The bombs in these cases range from the extreme

of anti-personnel devices to small charges used to harass the target by causing minor property damage.

6. *Revenge* bombings are closely associated with emotional release. The revenge bomber is motivated by earlier transgressions, real or imagined, committed by the intended target. Many psychopathic bombers are motivated by revenge.

7. *Recognition* bombings often overlap with other motivation categories, particularly emotional release. The bomber seeking recognition will place a device in a location where he or she can discover it and thus be recognized for performing an heroic act. What is so dangerous about this type of motivation is that the target is being attacked from within, often by an employee who is bored or wishes to draw attention to himself or herself in the hope of achieving public honor or advancement. A classic case of this motivation occurred during the 1984 summer Olympic Games in Los Angeles when a municipal police officer who was in trouble with his superiors used the ploy in an attempt to work his way back into their good graces. He planted an explosive device on one of the buses carrying Olympic athletes from a politically sensitive nation. He then called in a bomb threat, located the bomb himself, and became the hero of the day. Twelve years later, during the Olympic Games in Atlanta, a warning call involved an improvised explosive device that was actually detonated. Perhaps because of the Los Angeles incident, authorities and new media were quick to accuse, falsely as it turned out, a temporary security guard named Richard Jewell of planting the device.

Hostage Situations

A Rare Occurrence

The cop on the street never knows, or at least almost never knows, if when he or she responds to a call it will result in a hostage situation. The call could be a robbery in progress, a domestic dispute, or a man with a gun. Each of these, or any one of a number of other so-called routine incidents, could wind up in a hostage situation.

With improved communications systems and deployment techniques, the very fact that officers are able to respond quickly may precipitate a hostage situation. There have been many occasions in which officers have responded to robbery calls only to find the robbers still inside the store. With escape blocked, it is not inconceivable that clerks or customers could be taken hostage. However, there are appropriate response tactics, which if employed properly, could preclude such hostage-taking or at least minimize the chances of it happening.

Who Takes Hostages?

Persons who take hostages, whether in the course of a well-planned, well-thought out action or a spur-of-the-moment reaction, can be divided into four categories:

1. Professional criminals
2. Inadequate personalities
3. Loose groups, such as prison inmates
4. Structured groups, such as terrorists

Professional criminals make their livings (full or part-time) by robbery, burglary, and similar illegal activity. When they take a hostage, it means that the job has gone wrong. Usually the crime in progress is a felony and the criminal takes a hostage or hostages in order to escape. For the police, the professional criminal is, in the first moments of confrontation, the most dangerous type of hostage-taker. There is an initial period of panic that generates a fight or flight reaction, so called because the instinct of cornered animals is to either flee or turn and attack. In humans, the fight or flight reaction is that brief time during which the trapped person most wants to strike out at or flee from whatever is causing the panic. In this case, it is the police.

The police tactic here is to carefully contain the professional criminal in the smallest practical area and give him time to think, rationalize, and generally consider all the options regarding the situation in which he finds himself. In containing the professional criminal, the officer(s) should find good cover that affords sufficient protection. Cover is not the same as concealment, since a curtain or cardboard box can conceal but not afford much protection. We discuss the differences of cover vs. concealment elsewhere. After the panic reaction period has subsided, usually in 10 to 30 minutes, the professional criminal becomes the easiest type of hostage-taker with whom the police deal. This is because as a professional, the criminal realizes he has nothing to gain from keeping the hostages, much less harming or killing one of them.

The inadequate personality is an individual who police officers in the street may refer to as a psycho. The more delicate designation is inadequate personality or emotionally disturbed person. This individual is a self-professed loner and loser for whom nothing goes right, and who the whole world is against. He wants to get attention, and taking someone hostage is just the way to do it. The last thing this type of hostage-taker wants is escape. He wants to keep the incident going because he is enjoying it. Newspaper and broadcast reporters have repeatedly established contact with such hostage-takers, provided a public forum for them, and, incidentally, almost invariably prolonged an agonizing incident for the hostages.

Loose groups, such as prison inmates, also have attracting attention as their primary intent. They may not even know what their actual wants are, but they will demand things such as better food, conjugal visits, and improved recreational facilities. The loose group (this term is used because inmates usually are not organized into a tightly knit unit) is unique among hostage-takers. Accordingly, the strategy in dealing with them is different. Rather than stretching out time as a tactic, it is appropriate early on in the incident, during that period called a "window of time," to use a show of force. This use of force can break down the least adequate of the hostage-takers involved in the loose group.

Since most prison takeovers are spontaneous, this early show of force can be effective. However, if there is information or other suspicions that it is a carefully planned takeover, the show of force tactic should be abandoned lest it result in immediate harm to the hostages. In addition, even if a prison takeover is spontaneous and hostages are involved, if the appropriate show of force is not effected almost immediately, that window of time is closed and the use of force no longer appropriate or effective. In this event, it is best to resort to using time and delaying tactics because in reality the hostage-takers become a group of inadequate personalities. When in doubt, use time.

Terrorists who engage in hostage-taking, and this includes hijacking, are employing a tactic used primarily as a propaganda tool to maximize the effect of violence for political or economic gains. The selection of targets and victims is made with the aim of eliciting the maximum propaganda value from the incident. These incidents may be immediate reactions to world events, or an eruption in a long-standing feud or continuing animosity. Often, it is impossible to discern the motivation behind a particular hostage-taking incident.

Terrorists, particularly in hostage situations, will often use multiple incidents in an effort to separate and disperse law enforcement resources. The primary defensive tactic is to cut the terrorists' lines of communication while the police maintain and improve their own.

Panic Reaction

One element that is common to almost all hostage-taking situations is the panic reaction, that period early in the incident in which the fight or flight quandary arises in the perpetrators. This panic is dangerous to the hostage-taker, the hostage, and especially to the police officers who respond to the incident. More police officers are killed during the panic reaction than at any other time during a hostage situation, or other confrontation, for that matter.

Those first few minutes, which may last up to a half hour, after the hostages have been taken and the perpetrator or perpetrators are consolidating power, are the most dangerous. It is during this time period when hostage-takers are most likely to kill someone. It could be a security guard, one of the hostages trying to flee or not responding quickly enough to an order, or one of the responding police officers. An effective example of a panic reaction, one that did not even include a hostage situation, involved a group of adherents of a Caribbean religious sect and a City Marshal in New York City. A marshal in New York performs a number of civil functions, including serving eviction notices. It is not uncommon for breaches of the peace to occur during this service, so police officers sometimes accompany marshals on their rounds. The marshal can serve the eviction notice in one of three ways: by handing it to the person, affixing it to the door of the premises, or slipping it under the door. If a police officer is present, this would be noted in a memo book as evidence that the notice had been served. In this particular instance, the officer with the city marshal, it may have been the end of a long day of serving many notices, grew somewhat lax in procedures. When he knocked on the door of the premises where the group was living, a voice demanded, "Who's there?"

The officer, standing directly in front of the door, responded, "Police."

It was the last word he would ever utter; for unbeknownst to him, the occupants had created a bomb factory inside the dwelling. When the person behind the door heard the word police, he panicked and sent a shotgun blast through the door, killing the police officer.

This was a classic panic reaction. All the person behind the door had to do was ask the officer what he wanted. The officer, in turn, would have said something about an eviction notice and the occupant could have told him to slip it under the door. The incident would have ended there. Instead, one officer was shot and killed. A gun battle ensued, with a number of the occupants being killed or wounded and the rest being taken into custody.

Panic reaction results in the deaths of more police officers than any other facet of a hostage situation. Officers finding themselves in such a situation should step back behind cover to protect themselves, so as not to return fire until they are absolutely certain of target identification. This reduces the risk of some innocent person being hit by gunshots.

There is good reason for police to avoid confrontation with hostage-takers during the period when there could be a panic reaction. If a person were killed during the initial takeover or during its earliest stages, it would be ascribed to panic reaction. Although inexcusable from a legal or moral standpoint, it would be understandable. In contrast is the killing of a hostage later in the incident after communication has been established. If a person were killed on a deadline or to otherwise show the hostage-taker's resolve, this would be neither excusable nor understandable.

Suicide by Cop

Though the phenomenon known as suicide by cop is not necessarily new, it has been occurring with greater frequency while at the same time being effected more dramatically. An incident that occurred a few years ago is illustrative. Two individuals, Keith FOU Haggler and Kate FOU Haggler were members of a very small and extreme religious group in which each person took the name "FOU" (Father Of Us) as a middle name. The pair hijacked a bus in Jasper, Arkansas, to create a confrontation with the responding law enforcement officers. After a period of give-and-take with a negotiator from the sheriff's department, they agreed to release about 20 hostages in exchange for an interview with a television news camera crew. During that interview they indicated that part of their religious belief, which was from the *Bible's* Book of Revelation, was that they should be killed (by the police) so they could lie in state on the father's land and on the third day rise from the dead, and walk upon the earth. In their interview with the TV crew, they indicated that after the interview they would release the remaining hostages and then would exit the bus and approach the police. They stated that they would point their guns at the police in a threatening manner and that the police would have to shoot them. Having been made aware of their plan to bait the police into this incident, the sheriff decided he would use a sharpshooter with good cover to only wound the male by shooting him in the shoulder to disarm him. When the two armed subjects came out of the bus, they approached the police. After moving up about 20 feet, they went down on their knees and started to creep toward the police pointing their guns in that direction. When a sharpshooter fired, the bullet struck the male in the right shoulder. He turned and the two perpetrators turned their guns on each other with the female shooting the male and then turning the pistol on herself. Their plan was to have the police do it for them. But this time, it didn't work.

On November 14, 1997, the most classic of suicide by cop rituals took place. A 19-year-old college student who had amassed a series of gambling debts on the World Series totaling about $6000 would carry this out. Apparently this debt, though his family was not without means, was too much for him to bear. He was greatly depressed. On that Friday, he told his best friend that he wanted to drive into something. He talked about suicide. That evening he purchased a toy gun and a sheriff's badge for $1.97 at a local drug store. At about 10:20 p.m. on a dark and rain-swept Long Island Expressway, the young man drove his 1998 Honda Accord in a very fast and erratic manner. He was weaving in and out of traffic, sideswiping and sometimes pushing other cars. He exited the expressway then turned and reentered. Various calls from cell phones were made to the 911 operator reporting this violent auto behavior. At about 10:35 p.m., the Honda sped past a police patrol car. The officer gave chase with lights and siren. The Honda pulled onto the shoulder, with the patrol car in a position behind it. The young man jumped out of his car and started waving his arms. The officer told the youth to get back into his car. The youth continued to approach and as he reached the grill of the patrol car he pulled the silver toy pistol from his waistband and pointed it at the cop. The officer retreated behind his vehicle and called for backup. He continued to yell at the youth, "Drop the weapon, drop the weapon." An officer responding to the backup call arrived on the service road, saw the youth pointing the gun at the first officer and he, too, yelled at the youth to drop the gun. The youth turned and pointed the gun at the second officer, who was out in the open. He leveled the gun with two hands. Upon seeing this and believing that the officer was in mortal danger, the first officer opened fire. The second officer hearing the shots, believing that they were coming from the youth, also opened fire. Approximately 10 rounds were fired at the subject who was hit by at least one of the bullets. As he fell, the silver, plastic toy gun fell from his hand to the ground. Upon further investigation, the officer found a handwritten envelope on the passenger seat addressed "To the officer who shot me." Inside the envelope, there was a letter also handwritten which read:

Officer,

It was a plan. I'm sorry to get you involved. I just needed to die. Please send
my letters and break the news slowly to my family and let them know I had
to do this. And that I love them very much. I'm sorry for getting you involved.
Please remember that this was all my doing. You had no way of knowing.

(Signed by the youth)

These two officers became victims of this troubled young man. Fortunately, his letter did give them some understanding of how they were used,
helping them alleviate some of the guilt that is usually heaped upon officers
involved in the shooting of a civilian. Many times officers are not so fortunate.
They are saddled with the "if only, if only" syndrome, becoming victims
(often without any support) because of their involvement in suicide by cop.

It is been estimated that as many as 30% of the persons killed by police
are, in fact, victim-precipitated homicides. A thesis was prepared in 1996 by
a Canadian police officer, John Parent at Simon Fraser University in Burnaby,
British Columbia, titled "The Phenomenon of Victim-Precipitated Homicide."
In it, Parent said that suicide by such traditional methods as leaping off a tall
building or off a bridge required commitment of the victim. In suicide by cop,
the hard part is done for them by the police.

Why Hostages Are Taken

One of the principles of hostage negotiating is the assumption that the
hostage has no value to the hostage-taker other than the audience the incident
can create. In the case of the professional criminal, hostages are seen as a
possible means of escape from a difficult situation. Inadequate personalities
use hostages as a means of getting attention. People will start talking to them,
asking what's wrong. A disgruntled or dismissed employee then has the
opportunity to air grievances in public. A jilted lover may want to prove his
love is greater and somehow feels that by taking his ex-girlfriend hostage he
is expressing that love for all to see. For prisoners, hostages are used to give
inmates the power to negotiate with prison officials. Terrorists use hostages
to get the widest possible media coverage.

In all cases, however, the hostage-takers want to extract something from
the authorities or the outside world. They cannot get what they want from
the hostages, so it is not the hostages themselves who are the important factor;
they merely allow the hostage-taker to make an announcement. This
announcement may take the form of a telephone call to the police or news
media by the perpetrator, or it could be a shouted warning to passersby or

even gunshots fired into the air. If a bad guy took a hostage and no one knew, what would the hostage-taker accomplish? Even if he had all of his windows booby-trapped or had a well-written note or a prepared statement to make to the media, these preparations would be meaningless if no one was aware of the situation.

Of course, police must respond in order to protect the life of that hostage. You can't take a chance on what might happen if the police did not respond, or upon arriving, saying to the hostage-taker, "Good luck," then leave for lunch or some other assignment.

The Magic Triangle

For an organization to function, it needs manpower and money. In order to obtain money, manpower is needed. And to obtain manpower, the public must be made aware of the organization. Media attention is required. Whether the organization is a group of terrorists, the Girl Scouts of America, a business corporation, or the Federal Bureau of Investigation, it utilizes the media–manpower–money triangle. In each case, the organization will create attention or generate media coverage or both. The private business may call it a publicity stunt; the Girl Scouts will promote a story about a kid who sold thousands of boxes of cookies; the FBI might engage in some high-profile action against organized crime; and terrorists will take some well-chosen hostages or maybe bomb a few specially selected targets.

In each case, the media exposure leads directly to either more money or more recruits, usually both. The organization then has enough manpower and money to continue its operations. The concept of the Magic Triangle (see Figure 4.1) was developed many years ago in response to the activities

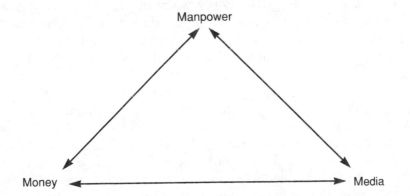

Figure 4.1 The magic triangle. A successful terrorist group — as with any business, organization, or government — relies on dynamic interaction between three essential elements: manpower, money, and communications media.

of the Popular Front for the Liberation of Palestine, sometimes referred to by its acronym in French which would be PLFP. In the late 1960s and early 1970s, many of these self-styled Palestinian freedom-fighter groups were receiving funds from the moderate Arab countries, such as Saudi Arabia, the United Arab Emirates, and similar nations. This was not so much out of any ideological agreement or particular desire to fund terrorists activities per se, but rather it was a form of protection payment for the Palestinians to keep their operations — and inevitable Israeli reprisals — out of those countries.

The PFLP was among the groups receiving such tribute. The situation took a dramatic turn on Hijack Sunday, September 6, 1970, when the organization hijacked four aircraft and successfully brought three of them to Dawson Field, an airstrip in what is now the country of Jordan. The runway had been built by the British during World War II and had been largely unused since then. The planes, an American, a French, and a Swiss airliner, were brought to this field and all the passengers released except those who were Israeli or who had Jewish-sounding names. On the sixth day following Hijack Sunday, all three airliners were blown up.

The big problem for the PFLP, however, was that Jordan's King Hussein was very much angered that these planes were brought into his sovereign territory without his knowledge or permission. He sent the Jordanian army against the Palestinians, with the result that during the month of September 1970, the PFLP sustained more casualties than it had while fighting Israel during the entire previous decade. There were more than 3400 PFLP troops killed and nearly 11,000 wounded. For the PFLP, that month became known as Black September, and an organization called Black September came into existence.

Following September 1970, the PFLP did not receive much money in the way of tribute. Not only had the organization lost manpower in its battle with the Jordanian army, it had also lost face. There was a downward spiral: the loss of face led to the loss of money, which in turn meant new members could not be recruited to replace those lost during Black September. The PFLP was forced to do something spectacular to get manpower, which would enable them to get more money, which would then allow them to get on with their avowed purpose of liberating Palestine from Israeli occupation.

The organization known as Black September, with its affiliation to the PFLP, staged a hostage-taking incident during the Olympic Games in Munich, West Germany, in September 1972. Its hostages were athletes and coaches of the Israeli national team. By carrying out the operation during the Olympic Games, Black September had some 3000 international newspaper, magazine, radio, and television reporters detail its actions and send its messages around the world. Almost immediately, other Arabs wanted to join the group, the kind of organization that could pull off something so daring and spectacular. As the ranks of Black September/PFLP swelled, those countries which had cut back or ceased paying tribute began to rethink their decisions. Black September was again in the position to extort money to finance its operations.

The media–manpower–money Magic Triangle helps explain why terrorists engage in activities such as hostage-takings, bombings, and kidnappings. Once it became known that these were the favored activities of terrorists, law enforcement and defense agencies in the free world were able to begin developing countermeasures and tactics to reduce their adversaries' effectiveness.

Munich, 1972

When the Olympic Games were held in Munich in 1972, one of the thoughts uppermost in the German planners' minds was that these games were going to be a showcase for peace. This would be in marked contrast to the militarism that permeated the Nazi-orchestrated Berlin Olympics of 1936, the last time the summer games were held on German soil. Whereas Adolf Hitler wanted to parade his master race philosophy for the world to see, the Munich Olympics were to demonstrate how much West Germany had distanced itself from Naziism since the end of World War II.

This was the atmosphere that confronted the terrorists of Black September as they plotted their strategy to secure worldwide recognition with the speed of satellite transmission. Just before dawn on September 5, 1972 — the eleventh day of Olympic competition and almost exactly two years to the day after the start of the Black September debacle in Jordan — six young Arab men scaled a chainlink fence to gain entry to the Olympic Village apartment complex that housed athletes, coaches, and trainers.

The six met up with two comrades who had been working in the village since before the Olympics had begun. They had managed to duplicate a key to the front door of the building in which 21 members of the Israeli men's team were staying on the lower floors. The terrorists were dressed like athletes, complete with small equipment bags; however, instead of holding shoes, towels, and athletic gear, the bags were filled with Soviet-made automatic weapons, including hand grenades and combat rifles. Apparently, the plan was to capture all 21 Israeli men without firing a shot, then demand that Israel release Arab terrorists being held prisoner in exchange for the Israeli hostages.

For all their careful planning, the Arabs found things going wrong almost from the start. The front door key failed to work immediately, with the resulting commotion awakening a sleeping Israeli who was able to shout warnings when the Arabs finally did make it inside. Another Israeli arriving back in his quarters in the wee hours of the morning was shot and killed, as was another who attacked the terrorists with a kitchen knife. The Arabs wound up with nine hostages, two dead bodies and — because shots had been fired and several Israelis had escaped — the local police were alerted to what was taking place.

Within a half hour or so, Manfred Schreiber, who held the dual role of Munich Police Commissioner and head of the Olympic security forces, had ordered all roads leading to the site closed to traffic. He arrived at the scene shortly afterward, but the terrorists had already begun to make their demands known in the form of a note passed through a window. The Arabs wanted Israel to release some 230 terrorists from prison, and also demanded that West Germany free five members of the left-wing terrorist group, the Baader-Meinhof gang. The note was signed "Black September."

The first thing that was apparent to Schreiber was that the local police were really just middlemen, because only the government of Israel could adequately respond to the terrorist demands. His own government officials in Bonn were involved not only with regard to the release of the Baader-Meinhof gang members but also in conducting diplomatic discussions with Israel, whose Prime Minister, Golda Meir, had stated previously that her government would never negotiate with terrorists. Schreiber's channel of communications with higher officials was Bruno Merk, the Interior Minister of Bavaria, the region in which Munich is located.

The Arabs holding the Israeli hostages announced the first of many deadlines: if the State of Israel did not respond positively to its demand by 9 a.m., a hostage would be killed. About 15 minutes prior to the deadline, a group approached the terrorist leader, Mohammed Mahmud Essafadi, with an offer: Interior Minister Merk; Walter Trager, head of the West German Olympic Committee; A. D. Touney, the Egyptian mayor of the Olympic Village; Hans-Dietrich Genscher, the West German federal Interior Minister; and former Munich Mayor Jochen Vogel would trade places with the Israeli hostages. It was an offer that would be repeated several times, and each time Essafadi would reject it.

Touney, the Egyptian, did ask Essafadi for a 6-hour extension of the deadline, maintaining that the Israelis had not had sufficient time to study the names on the list of prisoners whose releases were being demanded. Essafadi granted a 3-hour extension.

While West German Chancellor Willy Brandt consulted via telephone with Israel's Meir, at 9:10 a.m., 10 minutes after the original deadline, the Arabs passed another note with several demands and assertions. The first demand was that the police allow the terrorists to move the hostages to another location within the Olympic Village. Another demand was that three planes be readied for takeoffs at various times to different, unspecified locations. The note asserted that if any trickery was attempted, the hostages would be killed, that the noon deadline was absolute, and that other terrorists in unnamed locations were prepared to act if the more than 230 terrorists were not released from prison.

Shortly afterward, the Arabs verbally demanded that police officers who had taken up forward positions be pulled back because they were "spying from behind pillars." Schreiber ordered six officers to retreat. As the noon deadline approached, Touney, accompanied by Mohamed Khadif, the chief administrator of the Arab League in Germany, and two others approached Essadafi to ask for more time, claiming communications problems between Germany and Israel. Essadafi, with a grenade in each hand and a lieutenant identified only as Tony at his side, listened to the group. Khadif told the terrorists they could have safe passage out of Germany and a large sum of money as ransom, but that Israel was likely to release only some, perhaps as few as 10, prisoners. Essadafi responded that he was not interested in money, but in the release of all of his comrades. He also pushed the deadline back to 1 p.m., but noted that if Israel had not acted by then, two hostages would be killed.

Noting Israel's reluctance to negotiate or apparently make any concessions, Schreiber told the Israeli Ambassador to West Germany, who was at the scene, that there was little choice but to try to free the hostages by force. Schreiber also offered his opinion that this would likely lead to the death of most, if not all, of the hostages and most of the terrorists. As 1 p.m. neared, Schreiber and Merk were able to extract another 2-hour extension of the deadline. As 3 p.m. approached, Genscher led another group to speak with Essafadi and conceded that a final decision was not likely to be forthcoming from the Israelis who were still debating the issue. He also let it be known that Germany was not pleased with the way the Israelis were responding to the situation. Genscher asked whether there was a demand that perhaps the Germans themselves could satisfy. Essafadi then asked for two airplanes to transport the terrorists and hostages to Egypt. He added that the captives would be killed if the 230 prisoners whose releases had been demanded were not waiting for them in Cairo.

A seasoned politician adept at making deals, Genscher complained that two planes seemed extravagant and would present tremendous logistical problems. Soon Essafadi agreed that one plane would be enough and, not coincidentally, that the deadline would be pushed back another two hours to allow time to arrange for the plane.

It was the Germans' turn to make a demand, asking for proof that the hostages were still alive. First one, then another was trotted out. However, when the Arabs were asked to produce all the hostages, Essafadi was enraged. "You're trying to trick us," he shouted. "Your soldiers have surrounded the building and they're getting ready to attack us. Take a good look at that Jew! If you do not immediately order your men away, we will shoot him down where he is before your eyes and throw his corpse to you. And in another five minutes, two more hostages will be shot right on the spot where you are standing."

Schreiber, not certain that the riflemen had actually been spotted but also unwilling to call the terrorist's bluff, had no choice but to pull back his troops. Essadafi then agreed to allow Genscher to go inside the quarters to see the Israeli hostages. What he saw were nine hostages bound in groups of three, two sitting on separate beds and the third on chairs. In the middle was the bloody body of one of the Israelis slain hours before. A coach of the Israeli shooting team acted as spokesman, saying that morale was high and that no one would object to going to Cairo if the Israeli government gave assurances that the released prisoners would be waiting for them.

With a 7 p.m. deadline approaching, Genscher again asked for more time, claiming that it was difficult to find a volunteer crew to fly a plane to Egypt. Essadafi, whose men had been listening to newscasts reporting that Israel steadfastly refused to negotiate, demanded to know whether this was true. No, he was told, this was merely idle speculation on the part of the media. Another 2-hour extension was granted, but Essadafi let it be known that he was in the mood for no more delays.

Schreiber, for one, believed him and tried to formulate a plan of action. The Egyptians, meanwhile, let officials in Bonn know that they were unwilling participants in this drama and their cooperation could not be counted on for anything. It then became apparent that, given Israeli intransigence and Egyptian reluctance to help, the hostages could not be allowed to leave Germany. An assault would have to be mounted.

Schreiber had four options: he could attack the terrorists where they were; he could assault them in the underground passageway as they trans-ported the hostages to the waiting helicopters that would take them to the airport; he could attack as they boarded the helicopters; or he could mount the assault at the airstrip as they transferred from the helicopters to the aircraft. The airstrip was an abandoned military airfield located at Fursten-feldbruck outside of Munich. The second and fourth options seemed to hold the most promise of success, while exposing police and bystanders to the least risk; however, when the terrorists rejected the underground walk and demanded a bus be provided to take them to the helicopters, there was but a single course of action left.

In planning the ambush at the airport, Schreiber and his top aide, Georg Wolf, were (17 hours after the incident had begun) still uncertain how many terrorists were involved. Their best count was five individuals. Accordingly, five sharpshooters were ordered into position at Furstenfeldbruck. With Schreiber at the Olympic Village and Wolf at the airstrip, Schreiber was surprised to see 17 passengers board the helicopters. If there were nine hostages, that meant there were eight terrorists. Three more sharpshooters would be needed, but they never materialized since the information was never communicated to Wolf.

A dummy Lufthansa Boeing 727 had been set up at Furstenfeldbruck and as a defensive, last-ditch measure, Schreiber and Wolf had placed eight police officers aboard dressed as flight attendants and crew members. The cops were none too happy about the setup, feeling that the dummy plane would not fool anyone and that they would be overwhelmed by the superior firepower the terrorists possessed. The lieutenant in charge of the eight-person contingent was not in radio contact with his superiors, so there was little he could do to allay his officers' fears. Why there was no radio contact has never been fully explained — it could have been a malfunction, a communications line may have been severed, or no radios, in fact, may have been issued — but eventually, the whole group, including the lieutenant, abandoned the plan before the helicopters arrived.

Schreiber knew the assault would have to come when the terrorists and hostages alighted from the helicopters. Leaving six terrorists to guard the nine hostages and the two two-man helicopter crews, Essadafi and one other terrorist approached the plane to inspect it. As they walked back toward the helicopters, Schreiber noted for the first time that all the terrorists were not accompanied by hostages. Feeling this was the best opportunity he would get, and hoping that the action would shock the others into submission, he ordered his five sharpshooters to open fire on the two terrorists. The first round of fire missed.

Schreiber was later able to explain that by law and tradition, West German police were not trained to shoot to kill, but were taught to fire only at extremities. This, coupled with a long, tiring day, he surmised, contributed to the inaccuracy. It also led to a gun battle in which all nine hostages were killed, five terrorists died, and a German police officer in the tower next to Schreiber was fatally wounded.

The Munich Olympics hostage incident provides a touchstone for the handling of subsequent terrorist hostage-takings. A major question raised was why the Olympic Village, as controlled an environment as it was, was so susceptible to attack in the face of threats and forewarnings? Another question: Were all avenues of peaceful resolution explored before force was employed? Tactically, were the police adequately prepared when they finally did mount an attempt to rescue the hostages? Last, but not least, would the outcome have been different if the Israeli government had given Schreiber some latitude to negotiate?

In addition to these questions, there are three things that very obviously did go wrong and which serve as points to be expanded upon later. First, there was a lack of complete intelligence; the number of terrorists involved was not known until just before the shooting started. Second, there was a definite lack of communication, for whatever reason. Third, there was no discipline of firepower; the sharpshooters were given "shooter's prerogative" rather than specific targets.

Deadlines

In the years since Munich, very few hostages have been killed by their captors outside of the initial stages of the incident, when the fight or flight panic reaction occurs. In other words, there have been very few cases of hostages being killed on deadline. The best way to deal with a deadline is to seemingly ignore it. That is, do not be pressured by a deadline and do not call attention to it. The tactic is to talk the perpetrator or perpetrators through the deadline and not refer to it at all. If they bring it up, the negotiator can be reassuring and say that the demands, whatever they may be, are being worked on, but that these things take time. Then change the subject.

Calling attention to a deadline may precipitate an action that otherwise might not be taken. The hostage-taker will want to prove that he has power by firing a shot, or hurting someone, or both. In fact, one theory holds that if a perpetrator kills a hostage outside of the initial stages of a hostage incident, this evinces a depraved mind. The individual involved is a psychopath or sociopathic personality who, if he kills once, will kill again. Negotiations, in this case, would probably prove fruitless and a more parochial method of hostage recovery would best be attempted even though direct assault, for example, is extremely risky and dangerous.

Killing on Deadline

In all of the incidents around the world involving terrorist hijackings and hostage situations, there have been so few people killed on deadline that it is possible to track almost all of them. The ones that stand out most, in chronological order, are the hijacking of a British Overseas Air Corporation (BOAC, the forerunner of British Airways), the takeover of the Iranian embassy in London, the hijacking of a Dutch train by South Moluccans, and the killing of a U.S. sailor on a TWA flight hijacked to Iran in 1985.

The BOAC incident occurred in 1970 when an airliner was hijacked en route from Frankfurt in what was then called West Germany, to London. The jet was taken to Tunisia where it was allowed to land at an airstrip in the desert. It was so hot that even on television, one could see the heat rising over the desert floor. The Arab hijackers had made many demands and set various deadlines which had come and gone, and come and gone. Late in the afternoon of the first day that the hostages were held, the terrorists brought a man to the door of the plane, put a gun to his head, shot him, and dumped his body on the tarmac. A few minutes later, two men in white coats came out of the crowd with a stretcher, picked up the body and took it away. It was somewhat surprising that troops didn't go in, because the hypothesis was that if a hostage is killed after the panic fight or flight reaction subsides there could be more killing and the authorities might as well try to save as many hostages as possible by mounting an immediate assault. This is considered a preferable alternative to not acting at all and watching the hostages die one by one. The following day, however, all the hostages aboard the British airliner were set free and the terrorists accepted passage to another country.

Moluccans are people from islands popularly called the Spice Islands in what is now the country of Indonesia, but which at one time was a possession of The Netherlands and part of the Dutch East Indies. In the war for Indonesian independence fought after World War II, the Moluccans were on the side of the Dutch. When Indonesia gained independence, the Dutch government offered the Moluccans refuge in The Netherlands. Over the years, however, the Moluccans were not really assimilated into Dutch society and became ghettoized. There was chronic unemployment among them, and many existed solely by virtue of the government dole. As with many immigrant peoples, the elders spoke fondly and longingly of the old country while ignoring the political and economic realities of what was happening back home. The younger generation, hearing only good things about a homeland most of them had never seen, were more disgruntled and rebellious than their parents and grandparents. They resorted to terrorism, which included the hijacking of a train in Bellen. When these young Moluccans took over the train, a motorman was killed at the outset in the takeover (during the period of panic reaction) which is different, psychologically, from killing on a deadline once the hostage-taking has been accomplished. Unexpectedly, however, on the second day of the incident, the Moluccans killed a man and dumped his body out of the back of the train. Again, for whatever reason, the police failed to intervene. The incident continued another 12 days (December 2–14, 1975) before the Moluccans surrendered without another person being shot or killed.

The Iranian Embassy in London is located in an area known as Prince's Gate. It was here on April 30, 1980, at a time when several Americans were being held hostage in the U.S. Embassy in Teheran, the capital of Iran, that six dissident Iranians stormed the embassy and took a number of hostages. On May 5, the 6th day of the incident and after several deadlines had come and gone with scant attention paid to them, the terrorists brought a man to the front of the building, put a gun to his head, shot him, and rolled the body down the stairs. Within two hours, a team of commandos from the British Special Air Service went in on a direct assault, killing five of the terrorists and capturing one. One member of the assault team was wounded, but none of the hostages was hurt.

Other deadline killings include a case in which a Kuwaiti Airliner was hijacked to Teheran in late 1985, and while on the ground there, two Americans were beaten and killed on a deadline. In addition to this, there was also the hijacking of TWA Flight No. 847 in 1986 in which U.S. Navy diver Robert Dean Stethem was beaten and killed and his body mutilated.

Evaluation

If a person is killed during a panic reaction, the hypothesis says that fruitful negotiation can still be conducted. If a hostage is killed otherwise, it is presumed the terrorist is deranged and could kill again. Careful analysis of the deadline killings, however, adds a modification to the hypothesis. In the incident involving the British airliner taken to Tunisia, all of the hostages on the plane were British with the exception of one German man. At the time the hijackers effected their takeover, the German was, to put it bluntly, roaring drunk according to other passengers who were interviewed after the ordeal. Not only was the German drunk, they said that he was loud and arrogant. There was also some indication that he might have made what appeared to be homosexual advances toward one or more of the terrorists. It was the German who was killed and at least some of the surviving hostages said they felt he virtually committed suicide behaving in the manner he did.

On the train in Bellen, it was the second day of the hijacking and nothing was going right for the Moluccans. Almost anything that could go wrong did. One of the hostages was a man named Hans Prinz who was called "the Doctor" because he dispensed the medical supplies and prescriptions sent to the hostages. Afterward, Prinz described the man who was killed by the Moluccans as difficult and a troublemaker who was making things uncomfortable for everyone. When he was killed, Prinz added, nobody seemed to mind too much. He, too, apparently contributed to his own demise.

At Prince's Gate, when terrorists stormed the Iranian Embassy, they made statements about having purified themselves, how they were going to paradise, and how they were prepared to meet Allah. One of the employees of the embassy told the terrorists that he, too, was prepared to meet Allah and that in fact he was more deserving than they to go to paradise and see Allah. Six days later they accommodated him. The lack of hostage deaths during the police assault at Prince's Gate is attributable to the superior intelligence gathered during the long incident.

In the Kuwaiti airliner case, the only contribution the two victims made to their own demise was that they were Americans traveling on official passports.

In the case of TWA Flight No. 847, Robert Dean Stethem was military, traveling on military ID rather than a passport. When one of the hijackers asked about Stethem, a flight attendant replied that Stethem was from New Jersey and that he was a sailor or, in German, *bei der Marine dienen*, which means to serve in the Navy. The Lebanon-based hijackers may have thought Stethem was one of the U.S. Marines stationed in Beirut, or perhaps associated him with the battleship New Jersey which had bombarded the city, reportedly killing relatives of one of the hijackers.

In each of these cases, the victims contributed to their demise either actively, as in the first three examples, or passively, as in the cases of the American diplomats and the serviceman. These killings did not preclude negotiations, however. So the hypothesis about killing after the fight or flight stage has to be softened to include the fact that the victim could somehow contribute to his or her own demise. This places an even greater emphasis on the need for timely, accurate intelligence. The effort has to be raised to the *nth* degree. This is easy enough to recognize and acknowledge, but extremely difficult to accomplish because each hostage situation comes with its own unique set of circumstances. Still, every effort must be made because, for example, if a hostage tried to disarm a perpetrator and was killed in the ensuing ruckus, that would not evince a depraved mind. This would be no time to go in on an assault. Remember, an assault is a very dangerous act, bringing death — both potentially and statistically — to hostages, perpetrators, and the assault team alike.

Responsibilities of the First Responding Officers

In most cases, the cop on the street learns of a hostage situation when the perpetrator or perpetrators announce that hostages have been taken. This is often accomplished by the firing of shots. Then come the demands to be satisfied in return for the safety of the hostage. The first duty of the responding officers — whether advised by gunshots, announcement, or other communications that this is, indeed, a hostage situation — to take cover and protect themselves while assessing the situation. Only then can aid and assistance be offered to the innocent person or persons being held hostage. (See Figure 4.2.)

There have been times when an officer has responded to a man with a gun report that could have been a hostage incident but in reality was just a barricade situation. Occasionally, an officer might ask, "Have you got anybody in there with you?" The perpetrator might decide it is to his advantage to answer in the affirmative. All this does is make things unnecessarily complicated for the police. The appropriate procedure is not to make any suggestions about hostages. Don't put any ideas into anybody's head. Let the perpetrator do the talking.

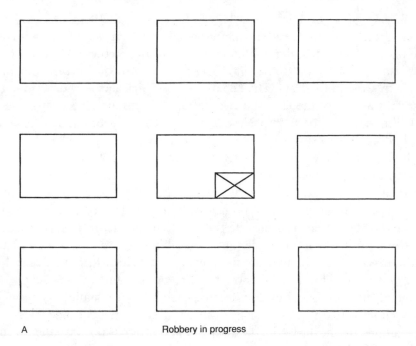

A   Robbery in progress

Figure 4.2 First response. (A) The report of a robbery in progress (B) triggers the response of patrol cars, which in turn advise the radio dispatcher of the nature of the danger area while requesting backup support (C). A mobilization point for next-responding cars and personnel is established within an inner perimeter around the area (D). Access to the inner perimeter is extremely limited, while an outer perimeter is established to allow some access by the media and others (E).

The hostage-taker should be confined to the smallest possible area, preferably without a face-to-face confrontation. If possible, the perpetrator should be locked in, i.e., by chocking the door or blocking it with a desk or other heavy, but movable, object. The physical blocking of an escape route precludes what is called a "push out" by the perpetrator in which he uses the hostage as a shield to effect a getaway while challenging the police to take a chance with the hostage's life.

The underlying assumption in hostage situations is that human life is the most important thing of all, much more so than apprehending the hostage-taker. In certain circumstances, then, it may be more prudent to let the perpetrator and hostage go in a push out. For example, if the perpetrator has a cocked weapon at the body of the hostage, even a well-placed shot may kill the perpetrator but still cause a reflex muscle reaction sufficient to fire the weapon and kill the hostage. A not-so-well-placed shot could kill the hostage rather than the hostage-taker. The only thing worse than the perpetrator killing the hostage would be the police killing the hostage, both from moral and liability standpoints.

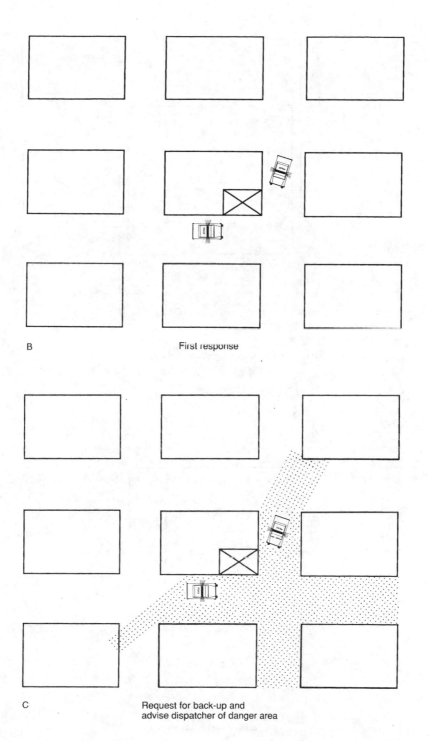

B   First response

C   Request for back-up and
advise dispatcher of danger area

Figure 4.2 (continued)

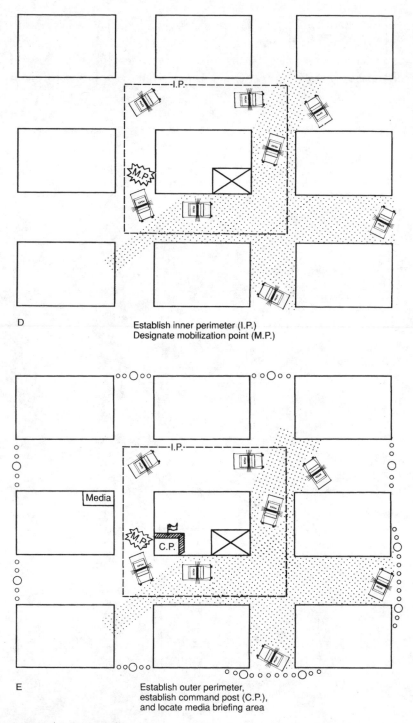

D   Establish inner perimeter (I.P.)
Designate mobilization point (M.P.)

E   Establish outer perimeter,
establish command post (C.P.),
and locate media briefing area

Figure 4.2 (continued)

The second duty is to call for backups. In many instances, if the initial report was a man with a gun or other serious felony, backups would be on the way. When radioing or calling in, the officer should mention the weapon or weapons involved and where the danger zone lies so that other responding officers do not blunder into the line of fire while responding to the scene. There was an incident in the late 1970s in Ottawa, Ontario, Canada, that illustrates the importance of identifying streets and directions within the danger zone, the location of the perpetrator within the building, weapons involved and, if possible, what precipitated the incident.

In this case, constables had attempted to serve a warrant on a man who responded by firing shots. He took refuge on the widow's walk of the house involved, which afforded him a 360° view of the neighborhood. Armed with a rifle and afforded this vantage point, he was able to observe the responding officers, who were unaware of his location. He managed to wound four different officers responding from four different directions. Although in this incident, every direction was fraught with danger, in most incidents there are safe routes to the scene. It is imperative, then, to provide such information as the size and shape of the danger zone, and the type of weapons, (i.e., rifles, handguns, knife, or bomb) to the radio dispatcher.

The Mobilization Point

If circumstances permit, the responding officer can indicate a mobilization point at the scene so backups can head there and be afforded some protection. The mobilization point should be close enough for the convenience of responding officers, but out of the perpetrator's view so he can't see the response. If the response is large, or the perpetrator perceives it to be, it might elicit a panic reaction and he might strike out at the police or one of the hostages.

Location of the Mobilization Point

There are some important reasons for selecting a concealed location for the mobilization point. For one thing, the hostage-taker should not be aware of who is, or is not, responding. Keeping this information from the perpetrator is a psychological tactic and becomes a psychological weapon. Imagination will be stimulated and he may think there are more police present than there really are. On the other hand, if he sees the force being assembled and all the cars coming and going, this might induce a panic reaction, fight or flight, which could result in violence, either internal or external. Internalized violence is suicide; externalized is homicide. In either case, it is not the outcome the police should want to precipitate.

One of the best illustrations of the value of concealment in hostage situations, although not a terrorist incident, occurred in DeKalb County, just outside Atlanta, Georgia. A man had kidnapped two babies of his common-law wife and told her that if she didn't come to his place by five o'clock he would kill her babies and himself. She called the police, who rushed to the scene. They used a shopping center parking lot as a mobilization point. The only problem was, unbeknownst to them, it was in full view from a window to which the man had access. The woman had also neglected to tell police about the five o'clock deadline. Tactical units began to arrive shortly before five; the SWAT team was on hand in full gear. They moved forward to take up assigned positions closer to the apartment complex. It was about 4:50 p.m. by this time and the perpetrator apparently misperceived the intentions of the police. He must have thought they were mounting an assault. He fired a couple of shots at the police, which had no effect, then put one into the heads of each of the babies and one shot into his own head. Newspaper photographs and television footage of police officers carrying out the dead babies were graphic portrayals of the tragic consequences of lack of concealment.

Decision-Makers

Once backups arrive and a decision-maker is on the scene, the command post can be established. The question always arises, "Can a chief negotiate?" Certainly, but *should* a chief negotiate? In almost all cases, probably not. It is impossible to be both a negotiator and in command of the situation. These are two hats that cannot be worn by one person. This may pose problems in smaller communities and in places where sheriffs and chiefs are elected or on tenuous appointment. It would probably be better if these individuals didn't show up at all; however, if they must be there, it is imperative that they turn over some of the reins to subordinates and rely on the advice of their experts. They may still be the top decision-makers, but there is no way they should handle the negotiations themselves. The actual mechanics and outlines of authority can vary. This is not as important as everyone knowing exactly who is in charge, and who has what responsibilities and what delegated authority. The decision-maker, commander if you will, at the scene must establish the lines of authority, and how the lines of communications are organized. Three foundation stones upon which to build the successful handling of a hostage situation are communications, intelligence, and discipline of firepower.

Evacuation

Once the backups arrive, evacuation of the area can begin. Evacuation should be conducted for two reasons. First, so innocent people don't get hurt; and, second, so no additional hostages can be taken. The evacuation process may have to be delicately handled because people may not want to leave their homes or offices. Local laws vary as to what police may or may not be able to do other than through the power of persuasion. Forcible evacuation could result in lawsuits, so more often than not, officers must cajole and coax people out of the area. Most people will cooperate, especially if they are faced with the possibility of a group of terrorists roaming through a building or marauding around a neighborhood accumulating hostages. Evacuation should be orderly, with all people accounted for and listed by office or street address or some other logical manner. The evacuees should be taken to a safe place so they don't mill around or be tempted to reenter, but also so they can be interrogated and perhaps provide some intelligence about the hostages and how the situation developed. Care should be taken during the evacuation because perpetrators or perhaps accomplices and lookouts may be exiting the scene. In more than one instance, criminals were shooed away by over-zealous officers clearing an area of civilians. It is important to discern whether the incident is a hostage situation or just an individual who has barricaded him- or herself.

A barricade situation does not have the same urgency. In fact, there is no urgency at all. Hypothetically, the perpetrator could be kept isolated for weeks if necessary. In a hostage situation, however, there is a greater urgency because of the concern for the safety of the hostages. When innocent people are taken hostage, the police are expected to take greater risks and chances in attempting to rescue them. If there is any doubt as to whether or not there are hostages, then police must assume there is a hostage until it is proven otherwise.

Keeping Track of People

An example that illustrates the importance of accounting for everyone involved in an evacuation is demonstrated by firefighters who routinely search a burning building. Although it is dangerous, the firefighters look for people who may be trapped by fire, were overcome by smoke, or who are otherwise still in the building. In this particular instance, police and firefighters were working together at the scene of a warehouse fire. At one point a lone fireman, burnt and injured, stumbled out of the building. Two police officers came to his assistance and sent him to the hospital in an ambulance. No fire department personnel were notified. A short time later, a fire lieutenant and three firefighters exited the building. When they counted noses, they realized one of their number was missing and assumed he was still inside the burning building. Intent on finding him, they reentered the building, only to be trapped inside when the structure collapsed. All four were killed.

As a result of this tragedy, police department rules require that no firemen be removed from the scene of a fire without permission of the fire chief at the scene. The same care and caution must be exercised when building searches and evacuations are conducted in hostage situations.

Start Intelligence-Gathering

As more backups arrive, some of the officers can be gathering intelligence. Remember the ICD building blocks:

1. Intelligence
2. Communication
3. Discipline of fire power

The intelligence-gathering begins with trying to find out exactly what is taking place. This information should be communicated as quickly, as concisely, and as accurately as possible to the communications or radio dispatcher who, in turn, can relay it to other responding officers and supervisors. There will be a constant demand on the officers to brief and update the others who are responding. More importantly, they are going to be asked repeatedly to brief responding higher-ranking officers who will then brief other responding officers. Later, we will explore methods of quick information transfer in the form of time bar charts.

Inner Perimeter

Once the evacuation is completed, or at least in its final stages, a perimeter must be established. This inner perimeter should be free of anybody who does not have a need to be there. Establishing this inner perimeter makes it easier to identify the principals involved, and to maintain control of the perpetrators and the situation. The area should be defined by police. It is not always feasible to rope off or tape off the area, but the reference should be transmitted to all at the scene. The area and its reference points should also be recorded at the command post so later arrivals can be briefed.

Police positions within the inner perimeter should be taken by officers wearing bullet-resistant garments, and carrying appropriate weaponry and sufficient communications equipment on the designated or tactical channel. If a mobilization point was not established earlier, or if the first mobilization point was not in the best of locations, this would be the time to designate a more suitable location to which manpower and equipment can respond. The mobilization point should be convenient, but it should also be concealed, situated in such a way that the perpetrator cannot observe the assembling officers and equipment.

Tactical Units

Tactical units are dispatched and deployed to replace the backup officers who responded initially and helped establish the inner perimeter. This is, of course, assuming the department is large enough to have the luxury of specialized units. When this change is made, the officers who initially responded and have been replaced should report to the command post where they can be debriefed as rapidly as is practical, so as much information as possible can be gleaned and disseminated quickly. This will supplement and confirm other intelligence reports and pinpoint areas of uncertainty such as the number of hostages, number of hostage-takers, types of weapons, etc. If, for example, there are reports of sighting seven people in garments of seven different colors, this could be any combination of perpetrators and hostages, but there can be reasonable certainty that seven people are involved, unless there is reason to believe that a deliberate attempt to mislead and confuse is being made.

Communications

In addition to intelligence, the other touchstones of a hostage incident procedure plan are communication and discipline of fire power. As early as possible, a communications frequency should be established on which all communications related to the particular incident will be carried. In jurisdictions that have a large number of frequencies, one may already be designated for emergency or tactical use. In those areas where a good deal of interaction exists between different agencies, a networking frequency may be employed. Often there is one frequency, usually statewide, that is used as a repeater system which permits police agencies throughout the state to be on one frequency should they have to interact and work on an incident together.

There have been disastrous situations, such as the one which occurred in New Orleans in 1973, in which a number of police agencies were involved in a hostage situation. In this case, there was no common communication frequency among the three different police agencies responding. Although they tried to cooperate, they started shooting at each other because one group was unaware of the location of another agency in the building. Several officers were wounded or killed, many by friendly fire, some by their own ricocheting bullets.

To insure that there is a thorough understanding of communications, one of the things to be considered is the nuance of language. This will be covered later.

First-Response Review

The duties and responsibilities of the first officer(s) on the scene are

1. Gather cursory information as quickly as possible on what is taking place.
2. Call for backup.
3. Evacuate the area in orderly fashion.
4. Communicate intelligence as rapidly and as accurately as possible, noting the safest approach routes.
5. Establish a mobilization point.
6. As backups arrive, establish an inner perimeter.
7. Upon being relieved, become an intelligence source.

For the initial responding officer, there is no urgent need to begin negotiations or even to converse with the perpetrator. Doing so, in fact, may lead to some problems. Deadlines may be set and the hostage-taker's clock may start ticking before reinforcements arrive on the scene, a negotiator is available, tactical people are in place, and commanders are on hand to make decisions. Certainly the best course of action for the first responding officers is to wait until a trained negotiator is on the scene. A second problem that could develop if negotiations are begun prematurely is that the perpetrator may not be confined to the smallest possible area. This can be done only when containment units are in place. If the hostage-taker has mobility, negotiations will not be fruitful.

Summary

There are four types of hostage-takers:

1. Professional criminals who are interrupted or trapped during the commission of another crime
2. Inadequate personalities, persons with psychological problems who want to air some grievance or otherwise attract attention to themselves
3. Loose-knit groups such as prison or jail inmates
4. Tightly knit and well-organized groups, such as terrorists

Hostages are taken because they provide the hostage-taker with a bargaining chip or a forum for making a statement. Terrorists use hijacking and hostage-taking as a means of gathering publicity and wide media exposure which, in turn, help them attract new recruits to their organizations and raise funds for their causes. The interconnected relationship of money, manpower, and media is called the Magic Triangle.

While there may be persons killed during the initial stages of a hostage-taking incident, it is rare that anyone is harmed once the hostage-takers have established control. In fact, if a hostage is killed after the initial takeover and period of power consolidation, it evinces depraved minds on the part of the perpetrators. If they killed once, they could kill again. However, if there are mitigating circumstances indicating that the killed hostages might have contributed to their own demise, this, in turn, lessens the probability that the perpetrators are depraved.

The first officers responding to a crime scene involving the taking of hostages have a number of duties and responsibilities. The one thing they should not do, however, is begin negotiations with hostage-takers unless this is unavoidable. The commanding officers at a hostage-taking incident should not participate directly in the negotiating. The negotiator's job is to establish a relationship with and communicate with the hostage-taker; the commander's job is to maintain control of the situation and make decisions involving all of the police personnel at the scene of the incident. The key elements to a successful resolution of a hostage incident are summarized in the acronym ICD: intelligence, communication, and discipline of fire power.

Defining Terrorism

5

What Is Terrorism?

The modern godfather of urban terrorism, Carlos Marighella, defined terrorism as action: "It is an action the urban guerilla must execute with the greatest cold-bloodedness, calmness and decision."[1] No police officer, legislator, or philosopher could better described the essence of terrorism: attacks are ruthless in nature and calculated in their impact on society at large.

On a more scholarly level, Brian Jenkins of the Rand Corporation described terrorism as "the calculated use of violence such as fear, intimidation or coercion, or the threat of such violence to attain goals that are political, religious, or ideological in nature. Terrorism involves a criminal act that is often symbolic in nature and intended to influence an audience beyond the immediate victims."[2]

On the political level, the U.S. Department of State acknowledges that there is a broad range of definitions for terrorism, influenced particularly by the definer's perspective on any given conflict or group. A middle-of-the-road definition used since the mid-1980s is, "Terrorism is a premeditated, politically motivated violence perpetuated against noncombatant targets by substantial groups of clandestine state agents, usually intended to influence an audience."[3]

Lack of a working definition of terrorism becomes a serious problem when terrorists are apprehended and brought to trial. Terrorism itself may not be prohibited by any statutes, but planting explosive devices, kidnapping, taking hostages, hijacking planes or other vehicles, use of firearms, killing, arson, robbery, conspiring to commit illegal acts, and similar activities are proscribed by federal, state, and local laws. In court, terrorists often argue they are being persecuted for supporting certain political or religious causes, and that the proceeding is a political trial rather than a criminal case. This raises concerns among law enforcement personnel and security executives who find it difficult to plan for contingencies that are not well defined and have not been inventoried.

However one describes terrorism, there are a few common elements: terrorists, supporters of terrorism, victims of terrorism, and once these elements are in place, counterterrorism operatives. Let us examine each of these categories more closely.

Figure 5.1 Organization charts. Whether the power chart is shaped like a pyramid or a bull's-eye target, terrorist organizations have a small elite leadership supported by a larger group of functionaries. This core group is bolstered by a larger group of active supporters who, in turn, are supported by an even larger group of passive supporters.

Terrorists can best be described as those individuals who plan, participate in, and execute acts of terrorism. These acts are usually perpetrated on behalf of a particular group or an avowed cause, although there are terrorist operatives who will barter their services, much like mercenary soldiers.

Supporters of terrorists include individuals, loose-knit groups, tightly knit groups, political factions, agencies of governments, and even governments themselves. The support can be passive, such as when supporters display ideological empathy, or active, which includes supplying money, weapons, or training or providing safe haven (Figure 5.1).

Victims of terrorism are the easiest group to identify because they are defined after a terrorist action has taken place. The victims can be individuals, family members, a community, or a whole race, ethnic group, or nation. The victims may be chosen as specific targets or they may be innocent victims of apparently random acts. Persons suffering as a result of counterterrorist retaliation must also be considered victims of terrorism.

Counterterrorist operatives are individuals actively engaged in the battle against terrorism. They may be agents of a federal or national government, including intelligence agents, investigators, and military personnel; or they may be law enforcement officers working at state or local levels. Private security and corporate security personnel may also be engaged in counterterrorism operations.

A Brief History of Terrorism

Political betrayal, treachery, deceit, and violence have been around as long as humans have formed themselves into political groups. Ancient texts such as the *Bible*, the *Iliad*, the *Odyssey*, Egyptian hieroglyphics, and letters inscribed in cuneiform on clay tablets have related some specific details about their occurrences in the eastern Mediterranean. The act of murder for political ends, a major component of terrorism, was raised to a fine art by a small group of Ismaili Shiite Muslims late in the 11th century under the direction of one Hasam-I Sabbah. His followers, who came to be known as Assassins, were a small, fundamentalist religious sect engaged in numerous confrontations with other Shiites and the more dominant Sunni Muslims. In the world of Islam, the demarcation between secular and religious authority is blurred so that a religion dispute may equally be viewed as political, and vice versa as well.

In addition to their name and legacy of terrorism, the Assassins are also credited with precipitating the invention of chain-mail body armor as protection against dagger attacks. Also, the loyal followers of Sabbah and his successors, the Assassins, were know as *fedai*, or faithful, and as *fedayeen*, men of sacrifice.

The Assassins, as religious and domestically political as their motives usually were, were not above engaging in terrorism on behalf of others, including, according to some accounts, Richard the Lion-Hearted (King Richard III of England) while he was engaged in one of the Crusades to the Holy Land. The Christian religious group, Order of the Knights Templar, was said to have adopted the Assassins' system of military organization.

The important thing to remember is that the Assassins were trained to participate in suicide missions. They were often paid in advance so they could give the money to their families. The only success was the death of the target, whether or not it cost the life of the individual Assassin. The Assassins themselves, falling prey to internal squabbles and internecine disputes, were effectively neutralized as a political power by the middle of the 13th century, but managed to remain cohesive enough to surface again in the 1830s and 1940s as foes of the Shah of Iran.

Although the Assassins were the most notorious group of historical terrorists, there have been others, including the celebrated Guy Fawkes, bomber of the English Parliament (who nonetheless is viewed by others as a fighter against oppression). The Barbary pirates of North Africa in the 18th and 19th centuries made their living kidnapping citizens of other countries and holding them for ransom. This activity led to the founding of another Christian religious group, the Redemptionist Order, whose members often acted as intermediaries between the states of the Barbary Coast and the foreign governments whose citizens were being held hostage.

In the United States, we can look at the early part of the 20th century when anarchists operating under the banner of the Black Hand preyed on newly arriving immigrants, especially on the lower east side of New York City. Their tactics of selective assassinations with guns and bombs proved extremely effective for a short period of time.

Many third-world leaders in Africa, the Middle East, the Caribbean, and the Pacific engaged in activities that could be described legitimately as terrorism against colonial governments prior to their countries gaining independence. In the post-World War II period, the Middle East became a particular focal point for wars of liberation, or terrorist insurrection, depending upon political perspective. In the area called Palestine, Zionists popularly called "the Stern Gang" and "Irgun" fought the British rulers for a state in the traditional Jewish homeland. When Israel was created and became an independent state in 1948, many Arab and Islamic residents of the immediate area settled outside the borders and began demanding a Palestinian state, a demand which continues to this day.

Terrorism as a Political Statement

One argument often advanced by radical apologists is that judgment of terrorists' actions is purely subjective, so that one man's terrorist is another man's patriot and revolutionary leader. In recent times, this view has been articulated by the Baader-Meinhof partisans in the Red Army Faction, the West German terrorist group, when one of its members declared that George Washington was a terrorist. More pointedly, early in 2001, German Foreign Minister Joschka Fischer, a member of the Green Party, admitted he had participated in terrorist activity in his youth, including incidents that resulted in the deaths of hostages. In a court trial, however, he swore he had never been a member of the Red Army Faction.

Many of today's terrorists believe that they will not see their goals achieved in their lifetimes, but view their activities as the base or building block of a greater movement yet to come. These individuals, especially those in the United States, see prison as an opportunity to further recruit, train, and indoctrinate new members, in addition to keeping old hands in line.

Examining, analyzing, and critiquing such philosophical arguments go beyond the scope of this book. It is important to note, however, that almost every terrorist group espouses a noble or, at least, rational and justifiable cause. The truth is, however, that the terrorists may be merely a group of common criminals using their stated cause as a smokescreen or front for nefarious activities; or the group may have legitimate origins as a political or activist organization but has degenerated into terrorist activity. On rare occasions, they may actually be a group of dedicated people acting on behalf of a legitimate statement against oppression or repression.

Regardless of which type of group it is, terrorist activities are all the same. The bombings, hostage-takings, kidnappings, or whatever, all present the same problems and challenges to law enforcement and private security personnel.

Modern Terrorist Groups

Terrorist groups come in virtually every size, shape, and political color, but the major ones operating today can be grouped under a few major headings.

Minority Nationalist Groups. Such groups, often styled as freedom fighters, depend for support on the sympathy of ethnic, religious, or linguistic minorities in conflict with the dominant culture, community, or political power. Groups in this category include what is now called the Real IRA (Irish Republican Army), the Basque National Movement (ETA) in Spain and southwestern France, the Kosovo Liberation Army (KLA) in Yugoslavia, Unikom in Macedonia as well as many areas of the former Soviet Union, and the Tamil Tigers in Sri Lanka. Nationalists in Chechnya have been accused of terrorist acts against Russia, which is dominating several former socialist republics of the U.S.S.R. In addition, there are many indigenous people's movements that have surfaced in different parts of the world, particularly in Latin America.

Marxist Revolutionary Groups. Since the collapse of the Soviet Union in the early 1990s, and the subsequent loss of financial and ideological support, Marxist organizations have withered in recent years. There are still some groups using rhetoric about fostering a socialist revolution, including the Shining Path in Peru and the Tamil Tigers in Sri Lanka. Historically, some of the more infamous Marxist terrorist groups were the Weather Underground in the United States, the Red Brigade in Italy, Action Directe in France, the Red Army Faction in West Germany, and the Communist Combatant Cells in Belgium.

Anarchist Groups. Anarchists have no particular political orientation or bias other than an anti-establishment sentiment. Largely a European phenomenon, with a history dating back to the 19th century, anarchism has had something of a revival among groups opposed to globalization. This was demonstrated by the "smash it up; bring it down" mentality witnessed during the World Trade Organization meeting in Seattle, Washington, in the spring of 2000. Individual anarchist organizations are usually short lived, because there is no central theme for their existence. The original members of West Germany's Baader-Meinhof Gang were anarchists, but with the emergence of the Red Army Faction, it was transformed into a Marxist organization.

Neo-Fascist/Right-Wing Extremists. Right-wing terrorists are only a minimal threat in Europe, but have persisted and even grown in number in the United States since the end of World War II. The recent rise has been fueled by Christian extremists, white supremacists, and anti-federal government activists. The traditional groups, including Aryan Nation, Posse Comitatus Committee, and the Ku Klux Klan, have been joined by various looser-knit groups using the word "militia" in their names. Their influence was demonstrated during the trial and conviction of Timothy McVeigh, the man responsible for the bomb attack on the Alfred P. Murrah Federal Building in Oklahoma City in April, 1994. The Jewish Defense Organization is also classified as a right-wing group.

Pathological Groups/Pathological Individuals. Pathological violence is perpetrated most often by individuals or small cult-like groups driven by a psychological need to make a particular statement or manipulate people. The multi-year bombing campaign of Unabomber Theodore Kaczynski was driven by his deep concern for the industrial society and its effect on the future of the world. The radical Japanese cult/terrorist group Aum Shinrikyo released sarin gas in an attack against the Tokyo subway system. This terrorist category encompasses single issues groups and includes anti-abortionist groups, animal rights terrorists such as People for the Ethical Treatment of Animals and the Animal Liberation Front, and anti-development groups such as the Earth Liberation Front. Early in 2001, President George W. Bush directed the Federal Emergency Management Administration, an agency that would normally deal with floods, tornados, and other natural disasters, to coordinate a comprehensive response to terrorist use of biological, chemical, and nuclear weapons. This is something that Dr. Robert Kupperman, who wrote the foreword for this book, called for more 20 years ago, when he was Chief Scientist for the U.S. Department of State.

Religious Groups. Religious fundamentalism, whether of the left or right, is the driving force behind many groups that commit terrorist acts. The Irish Republican Army, anti-abortion militants, and several groups based in the Middle East have used religion as a point of differentiation from the enemy or as a basis to justify their activities. Islamic fundamentalists have spread beyond the Middle East to foment terrorist activity as far away as the Philippines and the Americas. Organizations such as Hamas, the associates of Osama bin Laden, and the Egyptian Brotherhood have crossed international boundaries in pursuing their aims.

Ideological Mercenaries. Included here are individuals and groups who share a common faith and commitment to worldwide revolution (as opposed to several individual revolutions in many places). There are a number of organizations in the United States which follow the New World Order philosophy, while the Japanese Red Army was one group practicing mercenary terrorism in the recent past.

Terrorist Actions

By definition, terrorists espouse philosophical, religious, or political bases for their actions; thus they have strategic goals to achieve. The methods by which these goals are reached, or at least approached, are the tactics of terrorists. By and large these tactics are designed to gain as much media attention as possible through intimidation and fear, while at the same time enhancing the group's stature in its theater of political operation. Bomb attacks, hostage-taking, hijacking, and kidnapping have been the traditional tactics. New Age terrorists have, to some extent, taken a step back from the violent tendencies of their predecessors and engage in such activities as ecoterrorism, bioterrorism, and cyberterrorism, the last being favored by anti-globalization groups who attack communications facilities as well as business and financial computer networks.

The bomb, however, remains the weapon of choice among terrorists, both for the anonymity it affords operatives and the amount of media attention an explosion garners. This latter point is still valid, even in light of the relatively quick apprehension and trials held in the Oklahoma City and New York World Trade Center bombings. These successes have been attributed to more sophisticated investigative techniques coupled with an increase in intelligence operations, particularly on the trans-border international level.

The four types of bomb attacks are

1. Anti-personnel attacks
2. Symbolic target attacks
3. Selected target attacks
4. Sustained bombing attacks

Anti-personnel attacks include targeted individuals as well as improvised explosive devices (IEDs) placed in areas with a high population density which can be expected to produce a high casualty rate. Single-issue terrorists have made particular use of bombs directed at individuals, with the Unabomber mailing bombs and extreme abortion foes using strategically aimed IEDs. The device can be as simple as a pipe bomb or a vehicle filled with explosives driven to the attack site, sometimes by a driver prepared to commit suicide to ensure the bomb is delivered. Total disregard for human life, including the perpetrator's, is a common element of this type of terrorist action. Bombs directed at specific individuals are typically referred to as assassinations and assassination attempts.

Symbolic bomb attacks are generally carried out against government buildings, military installations, facilities of selected corporate enterprises, or historic landmarks. The devices used in these attacks are usually placed at a time or location in which casualties could be expected to be at a minimum, although this is not a condition that can be guaranteed to terrorists or would-be terrorists. Symbolic bomb attacks are often preceded by a warning call, which may be construed as an effort to reduce casualties, although it serves as a claim for credit by the perpetrating group. In recent years, symbolic bomb attacks have waned as a result of diligent securities measures. The heavy presence of law enforcement includes the use of bomb detection equipment, walkthrough metal detectors, and explosive-sniffing canines.

Selected target attackers aim at a specific facility or group of individuals in order to accommodate a belief or political ideology. The attack may be part of a series of actions against a government, a governmental agency, or private enterprise, its buildings, property, or personnel, or all of them. The Palestinian Liberation Organization letter bombs mailed to Israeli diplomats and prominent citizens are classic examples of selected target attacks (Figures 5.2, 5.3, 5.4).

Prolonged bomb campaigns are designed to draw attention to a particular cause or target such as the release of imprisoned comrades of the perpetrating group or operatives of the terrorist group. Some classic examples of this type of activity include the Unabomber's series of bombs, the Real I.R.A. attacks against British targets, and Osama bin Laden's campaign against U.S. targets.

Other Terrorist Actions

Hostage-taking, warehousing of hostages, and other incidents involving hostages may be used by terrorists to coerce governments or private enterprises to act in a certain fashion, desist from certain actions, or to modify a specific point or subject. Criminals may use hostages to abet their escape during a criminal act interrupted by the police; emotionally disturbed individuals may use hostages in times of rage and domestic disputes. Although there is a distinction between hostage-takings and kidnappings, both are used by terrorists in political contexts to elicit behavior modifications or change of heart on the part of governments or private companies. The distinction between hostage-taking and kidnapping is, in the simplest terms, knowledge of where the victim(s) is/are being held. Both are used to raise a group's profile and to garner media exposure. Kidnappings, in particular, are also used to raise funds via ransom payments. A dramatic example of this occurred in the spring of 2000 when terrorists from the Abu Sayyal Group (ASG) kidnapped a group of tourists from a resort in Indonesia and removed them to the ASG camp located in the Philippines. Police freed the abducted tourists, including two Americans, several months later.

Aircraft hijackings have been few in number in recent years, but they still occur often enough to remain a weapon in the terrorist arsenal.

Figure 5.2a Letter bomb. A letter bomb mailed from an overseas location. Notice the discoloration at the lower right-hand corner of the envelope. (Courtesy of F. Guerra.)

Figure 5.2b Letter bomb. A similar letter bomb that functioned as designed. (Courtesy of F. Guerra.)

Figure 5.3a An X-ray photo of a suspected letter bomb. (Courtesy of F. Guerra.)

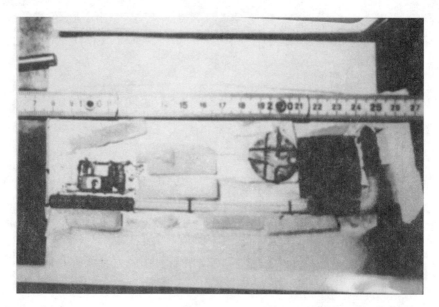

Figure 5.3b A photo of the actual device after being rendered safe. (Courtesy of F. Guerra.)

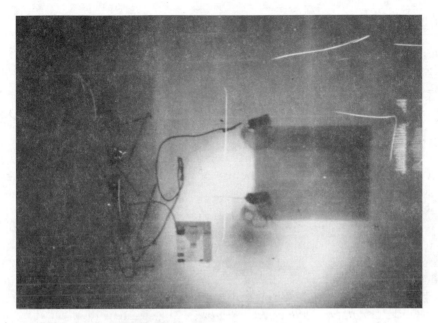

Figure 5.4a An X-ray photo of a suspected letter bomb. An electric blasting cap is clearly discernable on the upper right-hand portion of the photo. (Courtesy of F. Guerra.)

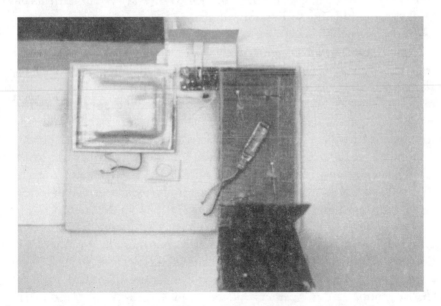

Figure 5.4b Photo of the actual device when rendered safe. Note the flat power pack in the upper left-hand corner. (Courtesy of F. Guerra.)

Intimidation and Use of Threats

Destructive or violent action is not the only option available to terrorists. The mere threat of action is itself a potent weapon. There are a number of different forms which these threats may take.

The bomb threat is still the most useful tool to harass or intimidate, particularly privately owned facilities and industrial installations, as well as such specialized targets as schools and abortion clinics. A bomb threat, especially one not handled properly, can cause as much disruption as an explosive device that is actually planted. The use of bomb threats is particularly successful in the aftermath of a successful terrorist bombing, at a time when public awareness and apprehension are intensified.

Scare or hoax bombs are simulated, improvised explosive devices that can cause an even longer disruption of operations than the use of an anonymous threat, because a search must be conducted and then an evacuation ordered once the simulated device is discovered. These devices must be treated as the real thing until they can be verified by trained bomb technicians as otherwise.

Environmental and public service threats can generate widespread disruption and unrest, particularly on a short-term basis. In recent years, the threat of biological and chemical agents in this type of attack has increased greatly in the wake of the sarin gas attack on the Tokyo subway system. Threats have included contaminating sources of public drinking water and disruption of mass transit systems.

Expropriation and extortion encompass everything from armed robbery to coerced protection money used to fund an organization and its terrorist activity, including, but not limited to purchasing arms, renting and maintaining safe houses, obtaining transportation, receiving advanced terrorist training, and paying day-to-day living expenses. In his tract, "Minimanual of the Urban Guerilla," Carlos Marighella recommends such illegal activities because they are the "expropriation of wealth of the principal enemies of the people."[4] Such activity is more common outside the United States, especially in Central and South America. However, one of the most spectacular terrorist acts of expropriation took place October 21, 1981 in Nanuet, NY, when members of several different terrorist groups acting under the umbrella of the Armed Revolutionary Task Force bungled an armored car robbery. They killed one guard and two police officers at a road block in the subsequent escape attempt. Members of the robbery gang were identified with such terrorist groups as the Weather Underground, the Black Liberation Army, the May 19th Communist Coalition, and the Republic of New Afrika.

Other criminal activities include almost anything that generates funds or furthers the aim of the terrorist organization or both. Drug trafficking is a major source of income, with virtually every major terrorist organization engaged in some sort of drug business either directly or by providing security and performing other services for smugglers and traffickers. Among the most prominent groups involved in drug trafficking are the FARC in Colombia, the Tamil Tigers in Sri Lanka, and Osama bin Laden's operatives in the Middle East, western Asia, and part of Africa.

Sabotage and subversive acts may not be immediately recognized as terrorist acts when they first occur. These actions involve blockading military installations and damaging property, looting during street demonstrations, civil disobedience disrupting transportation systems or government operations, and other actions carried out under the banner of "protest." These acts of selective indignation and spontaneous expressions of protected speech are often initiated by support groups of terrorist organizations.

Acts of sabotage are intentional destruction of property or disruption of an industrial or governmental operation by means other than an explosive device. These could include break-ins or other illegal entries in selected locations designed to harass or intimidate the owners or occupants of the premises. Computer hacking and electronic attacks against a Web site are other examples of sabotage, as is simple arson and various attacks staged by animal rights terrorists. More traditional incidents include damaging power transmission lines and oil pipelines.

Subversion is a systematic attempt to undermine a society. The ultimate objective is the total collapse of the state as a result of bringing its regime into disrepute, causing a loss of confidence in the ruling establishment's institutions and government, and provoking a breakdown of law and order.

Disinformation and Propaganda

Disinformation, propaganda, and media manipulation are not always clearly defined as terrorist activities, although these actions certainly must be included as tactics employed by terrorist organizations and their supporters. In his guerrilla warfare treatise, Carlos Marighella recommends these tactics as part of a "war of nerves." Such actions include "using the telephone and mail to announce false clues to the government and police," "letting false plans fall into the hands of the police to divert their attention," "planting rumors," and "exploiting by every means possible the corruption, the errors and failures of the government."[4]

Assassinations

Assassination is a specialized form of assault that has proven to be a very effective terrorist tool. It is the ultimate weapon of intimidation against target communities. These attacks are designed to gain maximum media attention as well as to have a major psychological impact on the organization the victim represented. Frequently, political leaders and their military or police officials will react to an assassination with a wave of repression aimed at the general population, which usually works to further the terrorists' aims.

Success of Terrorists

Terrorists have experienced a number of tactical successes for a variety of reasons, some of which are controllable and some of which are not, particularly in open and democratic societies. Factors aiding terrorists fall into six areas:

1. Mobility
2. Communications
3. Security
4. Democratic legal systems
5. Easy access to arms
6. Vulnerability of targets

Mobility

Terrorists enjoy the same freedom of movement within a country as do law-abiding citizens of those countries. When traveling internationally, terrorists have the protection of passports and other documents, often forged or obtained illegally, and even diplomatic passports provided by a sympathetic state. In developed countries, the national highspeed highway systems and internal rail and air networks allow terrorists to operate over long distances, commuting to the scene of an attack and back in a single day. Today, Russia, because of the relaxation of the totalitarian controls over civilians, has been experiencing acts of terrorism, including bombings of civilian targets as well as serious criminal activity. This criminal activity has created great disruption of the Russian economy. Organized crime has also engaged in the attempted sales of nuclear weapons. Apprehensions and recoveries have been made in Germany, as well as other countries. The borderless Europe created at the end of the 20th century only enhances such mobility. Above all, mobility aids terrorists in avoiding detection.

Communications

Communications technology has evolved so rapidly that its potential, for good or evil, is not yet fully appreciated. One definite attribute of today's communications, however, is that it enables a terrorist organization to plan more easily attacks on multiple targets and spread its own organization over a larger geographic area. In virtually all cases, electronic communication technology, from cellular telephones on up, is legitimately acquired, although stolen cell phones have been effectively applied to terrorist activities. Internet communication allows terrorist groups to be decentralized, and thus harder to identify, observe, and infiltrate.

Security

Security is a prime concern of terrorists. Having learned from past mistakes and the mistakes of others, they know that loose operating procedures make apprehension and prosecution much easier. A large, loosely run operation can be infiltrated by undercover law enforcement agents relatively simply. It was once said, only half in jest, that in the days of the Weather Underground movement there were more law enforcement agents in the organization than there were Weathermen. In an effort to maintain the highest level of security, successful terrorist organizations have long directives detailing policies and procedures regarding security. Whether the organization is being run from a single safe house or a mountain base camp, the terrorist organization can be very difficult to infiltrate by law enforcement operatives. From documents retrieved from a variety of locations, the following security measures were stressed:

- The need for total secrecy, keeping all knowledge of tasks, members, and organizational methods from even closest friends and relatives.
- The importance of punctuality, not missing meetings, and not being more than five minutes late because tardiness increases the time and amount of exposure of the group's other members.
- Prudence and discretion in conversations, even at organization meetings, because "the walls have ears." Use of euphemisms and generalities rather than specific events or names is urged.
- The need for telephone security, with phones employed only with great discretion. Only public telephones should be used because of the concern for electronic surveillance devices and call-tracing operations, unless, of course, a stolen cell phone is available.
- Meetings should be held in locations which are neither dangerous nor suspect. Specific suggestions included making use of soundproof rooms if possible, keeping a radio turned on in the background to frustrate efforts of eavesdroppers, and speaking in monotones that do not rise above the level of the radio. Each participant in a meeting should have a cover story for his or her attendance. Meetings should

be held in locations where alarm systems are in operation and with sufficient lookouts, a viable communications system for sounding an alarm, and even using watch dogs.

- Paper documents should be circulated only to those for whom it is absolutely necessary. One participant in the meeting should be designated as the person responsible for destroying documents if the meeting is disrupted.
- General security needs include using pseudonyms (which are to be used at all times); mapping out a route to go to meetings, making sure never to take a direct route, and being constantly alert for signs of surveillance; never revealing meeting locations to nonparticipants, even members of the group not involved in the operation; not writing notes on impressionable surfaces, and use of soft-tip pens; not staying at meetings longer than necessary; not discussing organization activities or members in public; and not acknowledging other members when chance meetings occur in public places.
- Operations security includes admonitions to not leaving fingerprints in any activity, to avoid cameras and reporters during coverage of street demonstrations or protest rallies, and to use care in handling explosives and firearms because "they are not toys."
- Safe-house precautions include remaining in the safe house until otherwise advised; contacting family or friends only through prearranged means and methods; never using a safe house for any reason other than the designated one; and leaving the safe house neat and orderly, removing all traces of occupation such as cigarette butts, bottles, cans, food containers, etc. because these can be the source of DNA evidence. Many jurisdictions now take DNA samples as well as fingerprints.

If arrested, the documents exhorted, "you are now a POW (prisoner of war). Give no information. Demand POW status." These documents also detail the need for developing a clandestine communications system by using mail drops, telephone answering services, codes, and leaving messages in predetermined locations. Security of the terrorist organization is so important to its success that the "Minimanual of the Urban Guerrilla" goes so far as to say that the worst enemy of the terrorist organization is the person who infiltrates it to spy or inform.

Legal Systems of Democratic Countries

The laws of a country and its systems and procedures for safeguarding the rights of its citizens are perverted by terrorists in order to help them achieve success in undermining that country. The need for court approval to obtain certain types of evidence or employ certain types of investigative techniques leads to long, time-consuming investigations in which every policy and procedure must be meticulously followed lest the letter of the law not be followed even if the spirit has not been violated. Once apprehension has been effected, civil rights guarantees and procedures make for long, drawn out, and costly trials. There is almost no reason why terrorists, actual or suspected, would want a speedy trial, because time works only in their favor as memories get hazy, people get bored, and witnesses or other key figures become sick or die. During these delays, costs to the taxpayers mount. The trials themselves are often used as a stage from which the terrorists can spout propagandistic rhetoric. Since the breakup of the Soviet Union and the freedom citizens of Russian and the other former socialist republics are enjoying, so come the problems of crime and dissidence.

Easy Access to Arms

With the advances in weapons technology, the terrorists of today have a wide variety of sophisticated weaponry with which to work, particularly when explosives are concerned. The use of miniature time-delay and detonating systems, along with the use of plastic explosives, makes concealment of improvised explosive devices frighteningly easy. The collapse of the Soviet Union late in the 20th century made the illegal arms market rich with possibilities. The former Soviet republics were a source of weapons for terrorists, as were weapons made in Western nations that were diverted to terrorist groups. To cite only one example, the Taliban freedom fighters in Afghanistan were armed by the CIA for a while because the Taliban opposed the Soviet puppet regime installed in Khabul, the country's capital. State-of-the-art weapons are readily available on the open market for use not only by terrorist organizations but also by groups involved in low-intensity conflicts. For instance, the Austrian-made 9-mm Glock automatic handgun is virtually made of plastics, thus making it easier to go undetected when passing through security metal detectors. Another concern is the easy access to chemical agents that may be used to produce weapons of mass destruction. Of course, today's technology allows even the most basic tools to be used to develop unsophisticated weapons capable of killing hundreds of people, including nuclear material said to be available from areas in the former Soviet Union through underground channels.

Vulnerability of Targets

Not very long ago, there was an almost endless list of potential targets available to terrorist operatives. Since the bombings of the World Trade Center in New York, the Murrah Federal Building in Oklahoma City, and the U.S. Embassies in East Africa, however, there has been a target hardening program at vulnerable government facilities. Private companies, on the other hand, frequently have multiple locations and bottom-line issues with which to contend. Because security is not revenue generating, this is presumed to be justification for low priority. During periods of high terrorist activity, security is typically enhanced; when the threat subsides, so does security awareness relating to terrorist threats. This point is not missed during planning sessions by terrorist operatives. They would rather attack a location with a lower degree of preparedness than a tight or hardened target. Given that, the security practitioner and law enforcement planner should always remember that a determined foe, with time and study, can attack virtually any target with a reasonable chance of success.

Notes

1. *Minimanual of the Urban Guerilla*, Carlos Marighella, New World Liberation Front, 1970, p. 32.

2. As introduced to the U.S. Senate by Senator Abraham Ribicoff of Connecticut on October 25, 1977, and indicated in "On Domestic Terrorism," a publication of the National Governors Association, Emergency Preparedness Project, Center for Policy Research, Washington, D.C., May 1979.

3. *Patterns of Global Terrorism — 1984*, U.S. Department of State, cover statement, 1985.

4. *Minimanual of the Urban Guerilla*, Carlos Marighella, New World Liberation Front, 1970.

Threat of Weapons of Mass Destruction

6

Introduction

World War I settled into static trench warfare, where gains were measured in yards rather than miles. Military leaders scrambled for methods of gaining a breakthrough. Then on April 22, 1915, at the Belgian town of Ypres, a new horror was unleashed on the world. On a beautiful spring day, with a slight breeze blowing toward the allied trenches occupied by French Colonial troops, the soldiers were alerted to a hissing sound emanating from the German trenches. The French troops watched with curiosity as a greenish-yellow fog rolled toward them, coming in low, barely head high. By the time the cloud of gas completely enveloped the trench line, thousands of men were retching and some were dying. The Germans had unleashed a lethal cloud of chlorine gas that incapacitated thousands of the French Colonial troops.[1]

Following the war, as a direct result of the liberal use of gas, not to mention the horrific injuries and death that it caused, most nations of the world signed a treaty banning the use of gas or gases in future warfare. Although the United States did not sign the treaty, a "no first use policy" has been in place from the beginning.

Nearly 80 years after the first recorded incident of gas warfare, a Japanese sect/terrorist group unleashed a gas attack against an unsuspecting civilian population in time of peace. In the wake of this attack, 12 people were killed and more than 5500 injured. Terrorists had adopted a new weapon of mass destruction.

The Threat Today

In the last four decades of international terrorism, the tactics employed by terrorist operatives have been significantly refined. No longer is the placing of explosive devices outside a building in the dead of the night or a suicide bomber using a large vehicle-borne IED the only option for causing widespread death and destruction. Terrorists, regardless of conviction, have now adopted new and deadlier weapons for their inventory. The chemical and biological weapons of mass destruction now can be included in their arsenals.

In what was once an option limited to the military of world powers, chemical and biological agents can be manufactured by virtually any determined group or individual who can scale the size and impact of the weapon to chosen targets. A case close to home occurred in December of 1995, when an Arkansas farmer was arrested for the possession of 130 grams of a deadly CB agent Ricin.[2] If released into the atmosphere, this amount of Ricin in a weaponized form may have killed thousands of people. The individual who was arrested in this matter hanged himself in his jail cell before his intentions could be made known.

An attack of this nature can come from any quarter. The United States can no longer be considered exempt from a major terrorist attack of this sort, whether the source is domestic or foreign. In addition to chemical and biological threats, the threat of nuclear attack against any one of a number of particular targets has been a concern for some time. For the most part, chemical and biological agents, or at least the building blocks to create them, are fairly easy to obtain through a number of venues by almost any organization.

The acquisition of nuclear material, however, is somewhat more difficult, but not impossible. Since the break up of the Soviet Union in the early 1990s, many former socialist republics in the union have become independent countries. Many of these newly, or once-again, independent nations laid claim to former assets of the Soviet Union, from factories and farms to Aeroflot, the national airline, and segments of the armed forces and military infrastructure, including nuclear weapons and the materials used in their manufacture. In many instances, these countries were left pressed for hard currency, and the nuclear materials in their possession became valuable commodities in the international arms market so often utilized by terrorist groups and the nations that support them. Weapons-grade nuclear material could bring a handsome price from a rogue nation or highly organized international terrorist group. Nuclear material trading has virtually escaped detection since record keeping and monitoring were virtually abandoned with the collapse of the Soviet Union. The situation now is that the accessibility of nuclear materials and the technology to build weapons using them have never been more accessible to interested parties.

Aum Shinrikyo Incident

Human destruction and fanatical cults have a long association with each other, through mass suicides or episodes that result in the deaths of others. In 1978, a messianic Jim Jones convinced his followers in a jungle encampment called Jonestown in Guyana to commit suicide. More than 900 of them did, including adults who first fed poison-laced Kool-Aid to their children. At the end of the 20th century a group of nearly 40 individuals belonging to a cult called Heaven's Gate committed suicide in a misguided effort to rendezvous with an alien spacecraft they thought would appear in the wake of the Hale-Bopp comet passing close to Earth. These inner-directed killings were horrific on one level, but what happened in Tokyo in 1994 prompted new cause for concern by counterterrorist planners dealing with potential uses of weapons of mass destruction.

The Aum Shinrikyo cult was unknown to the general public, especially outside of Japan. The leader of the group was a half-blind former acupuncturist named Shoko Ashara who turned to religion and mysticism. He was born in 1955 at Chizue Matsumoto. At one point he owned a folk medicine shop before traveling to Tibet to study Buddhism and Hinduism. In 1984 he founded his Aum Shinsen Club, recruiting 15 original followers. Within a few years the organization swelled to more than 1300 members. There was international growth as well, particularly in the Soviet Union and, following its collapse, Russia and the other newly independent republics. The ranks swelled with tens of thousands of new members. The organization later changed its name to Aum Shrinrikyo or The Supreme Truth Sect, with Ashara now considered a god by the followers.

His aim soon became the overthrow of the Japanese government. To accomplish this he planned to attack key points of Japanese government operations with a gas in order to neutralize the leadership. The gas to be used in the attack was manufactured by sect members in Kamikuishiki, Japan. During the group's growth years, their extreme radical views came to the attention of law enforcement officials and the sect was known to be manufacturing sarin gas. Although the group was responsible for a number of accidental spills that affected nearby areas and caused the group's activities to come to the attention of officials, the sect had violated no existing laws and, as a result, the police took no action. The cult launched its first attack at Matsumoto when they attacked an apartment complex as the occupants were asleep. The attack occurred on the morning of July 27, 1994 when sarin gas was released using a truck-mounted dispersal outside the complex. The gas traveled into the open windows of the building and before long there were 7 dead and 600 others sickened. The attack was launched in the hope of killing several judges who they felt were threats to their organization.

Although the Japanese police launched a massive investigation, they had little success in tracing the chemical agent to Aum Shinrikyo. As the investigation continued, the group launched another attack on March 20, 1995. This attack was made against Tokyo subway system at the height of the rush-hour. Aum Shinrikyo members produced approximately seven liters of high-grade sarin for the attack. The attack was well planned, and targeted the five different train lines that ran closest to the Tokyo police headquarters. The group hoped releasing the gas on these trains would kill those who worked in police headquarters and other government buildings. The sarin was packaged in plastic bags and was activated by a cult member who punctured the bag with an umbrella. Although sarin is an extremely deadly gas and caused more than 6000 victims, only 13 people died. This was attributed to the fact that the chemical was only 35% pure, as well as to the efficiency of the air-filtering system in the subway. The hospitals treated the attack victims with drug antidotes, mostly atropine, although a shortage of antidote serum resulted in only the most serious cases being given the drugs. The typical sarin poisoning symptoms are convulsion, vomiting, loss of balance, double vision, and slurred speech. Shortly after the attack, the police raided a number of Aum Shinrikyo locations and seized a large amount of chemicals that can be used in the manufacture of sarin, mustard gas, VX, and other biological agents.

These attacks brought home the vulnerability of a modern society to groups of fanatics or terrorists making biological and chemical attacks.

Chemical and Biological Agents

When the phrase chemical weapon is mentioned, it usually brings to mind military deployment, such as the ones used in World War I. In the closing months of the first World War, phosgene, chlorine, cyanide, riot control agents, and mustard gases were all used against enemy formations. After World War I, the rules governing warfare all but outlawed the use of such weapons of mass destruction. In 1925, a Geneva Protocol governing the rules of war prohibited the further use of chemical and biological weapons. The United States signed the document, but it was never ratified by Congress. In 1997, a more modern chemical weapons ban was signed by 160 nations.

In the major wars of the 20th century, i.e., World War II, Korea, and Vietnam, deadly gas was not an option to be used on the battlefield. Although many nations stockpiled biological and chemical weapons, especially in the Cold War era, none were ever used until the war between Iran and Iraq.

There are virtually thousands upon thousands of biological viruses and chemical agents that can be deadly to human and humankind. Not all can be listed here, but the following is an overview of the most common agents that are available to the terrorist groups and rogue nations of the world.

Chemical Agents

These agents vary in composition and how they affect the body, with most chemical agents coming in liquid form. The exceptions are riot control agents that are solids, usually in the form of a fine powder. Chemical agents can produce a variety of effects, depending upon their volatility and persistence to evaporation. Some of these effects can occur within seconds, while others arise hours and even days later. The components that constitute the chemical agent are a major factor in how quickly it will evaporate. There are also other factors to consider, including temperature, wind velocity, and the surface upon which the agent comes to rest.

Chemical agents can be categorized in following manner:

1. Nerve agents
2. Blistering agents
3. Choking agents

Nerve Agents

Jane's Bio-Chem Handbook describes these as agents "…that disrupt the mechanism by which nerves communicate with the organs they stimulate."[3] In other words, the agent gets the nerves to send the wrong signals to the muscles they control and hence, disrupt the muscle function of the body. When received in large doses, death will occur in a short time, preceded by tightness in the chest, blurred vision, nausea, convulsions, loss of consciousness, and stopped breath. These agents are and will affect the victim within a very short period of time. They are usually clear and colorless when released, and, being heavier than water, will affect lower terrain features. The common agents are sarin and VX. sarin was developed in the 1930s and can kill quickly after only small amounts come in contact with the skin or are inhaled. This is a chemical in the "G" series which also includes tabun, soman, and GF. The VX gas was developed in the 1950s and will act on the nervous system.[4]

Blistering Agents

There are three common agents of this type; the most widely known are mustard gas, lewisite, and phosgene oxime. Mustard gas, first used in World War I, will cause blistering on the exposed portions of the body, as well as on internal organs. It will generally cause blindness and then death by respiratory failure.

Choking Agents

One of the deadliest choking agents is phosgene gas. This agent damages the respiratory system and causes the lungs to fill with water, and thus chokes the victim. Chlorine gas is also included in this category.[4]

Biological Agents

Biological agents can appear in either liquid or dry form. In the hands of a well-organized, trained, and determined terrorist organization, biological weapons can be perhaps the worst case scenario that one could imagine. It has been estimated by experts that as little as one gram of anthrax, dispersed properly, can be enough to kill one third of the population of the United States.[4] Today's advanced biochemical manufacturing techniques allow for an almost endless progression of lethal pathogens which may be produced, allowing rogue nations and terrorists a whole new selection of weapons. The most common types of biological agents that may be utilized in terrorist incidents are categorized as bacteria, toxins, viruses, and rickettsia.

Common Agents

Anthrax

This is a single-cell organism that is produced by a fermentation process, such as that by which beer is made. The bacteria that causes anthrax is *Bacillus anthracis* and the effects of exposure include a severe infection that attacks the skin, lungs, and gastrointestinal tract. The location in the body that is attacked by the bacteria depends upon how the victim is infected. Coming in direct contact will cause formation of dry scabs all over the victim's body and can develop into a systematic infection. This form of anthrax can be readily treated with antibiotics. When inhaled, the agent attacks the respiratory system, with symptoms appearing from one to seven days after exposure. Initial flu-like symptoms increase to fever, followed by difficulty in breathing and then acute respiratory distress. Death can occur within 24 hours of this phase. Untreated anthrax in this form is usually 90% fatal. The vaccine for anthrax is not widely available and it is not really known how well it will protect against the inhalation of anthrax spores. It is estimated that a gram of anthrax is capable of killing millions of people if released against an unprepared nation.

Botulinum Toxin

This agent is a protein made by the *Clostridium botulinum* bacteria. This is one of the most toxic compounds known. When the victim is exposed to the toxin, the nerve cell synapses are affected, causing palsy, spasms, and then paralysis. The amount of exposure to this biological agent will determine how quickly the victim will die. The military has a vaccine for this agent, but at this point it is not cleared for civilian use.

Brucellosis

Also known as undulant fever, brucellosis is usually caused by infection by one of any number of closely related species, but most likely by *Brucella suis*, *Brucella abortus*, or *Brucella melitensis*. Symptoms can include intermittent or prolonged fever, headaches, profuse sweating, chills, pains in the joints and muscles, and fatigue. In most cases, exposure is more incapacitating than fatal. This agent may be dispersed by aerosol or through contamination of a food supply. The normal incubation period for a brucella infection is 5 to 21 days.

Cholera

This is an acute gastrointestinal disease caused by the germ *Vibrio cholera*. The symptoms include a sudden onset of nausea and/or vomiting accompanied by severe diarrhea and a rapid loss of body fluids. After exposure, an individual may experience the onset of symptoms within hours, or up to several days later. If the illness is left untreated, the fatality rate can run as high as 80%, although if treated, the fatality rate is greatly reduced.

Plague

Because it is extremely effective as well as deadly, it is the disease of choice, especially the pneumonic strain. In its natural transmittal form, the plague may be the bubonic plague, or Black Death, that eradicated a great number of Europeans in the Middle Ages. It is usually transmitted from person to person by respiratory transmission, through rats, or from the bite of an infected flea. If this disease is untreated, death may even occur within 24 to 48 hours. The symptoms are a high fever accompanied by general aches, severe weakness, and pneumonia. In extreme cases, hemorrhages in skin and mucous membranes may occur. A second type of plague results from the inhalation of the germ. The disease spreads quickly until the hemorraghic pneumonia infects the entire lung and, if not treated, brings on death. Although this killer disease is attractive to the terrorist because of the potential for developing a huge body count, a major drawback is the difficulty employing it. Sustaining the virulence of the germ is hard, and as a result of this instability, it is difficult to turn the disease into a viable weapon of mass destruction.

Typhoid Fever

This malady is caused by an organism called *Salmonella typhosa* which causes fever and frontal headaches and is usually accompanied by rose-colored spots on the skin. The potential use of typhoid bacteria as a terrorist weapon of mass destruction is limited. It is not able to be spread via an aerosol application, but must employed through food or limited water contamination.

Rickettsia

Q-Fever, a result of the hardy strain of this biological agent, makes it attractive as a biological agent, especially to terrorist organizations. Rickettsia is a disease that appears in domesticated animals such as sheep, cattle, and goats. It is spread to humans through inhalation of particles that have been contaminated with the organism. Because the agent is very hardy and easy to produce, it stores well. This agent can be distributed by aerosol and is very stable in that form in a wide range of temperatures. The incubation period, ranging from 10 to 14 days, is much longer than most agents. Of course, like any other agents, the more severe the exposure the more quickly the disease will take hold. The diagnosis of this fever is often overlooked or treated as just a fever of unknown origin.

Response to a WMD Incident

To properly combat the threat of weapons of mass destruction it takes an integrated response concept that includes local, state, and federal agencies. It is extremely important that a working relationship among all agencies be established, prior to incidents occurring, and not making the actual incident a learning experience. Presidential Directive #39, spelling out the U.S. policy on counterterrorism, recognizes that a rapid and decisive capability in responding to terrorist incidents is necessary. Emphasis must be put on deterrence, detection, and apprehension of terrorists, as well as providing assistance to the victims of terrorist attacks.

Local

When dealing with a terrorist attack, the local public safety or health agency will be, in almost all cases, the first responding authority. An attack utilizing a biochemical agent may not be recognized at first, although at other times it may be obvious immediately. The former is especially true in dealing with biological agents, where symptoms may not surface until many hours or days following the initial attack. To assist the all-important first responders, the federal government has provided funds to train them in the handling of the first hours of a WMD incident. The training encompasses programs not only for police and fire agencies, but also public health and hospital personnel. Instruction includes classroom training, providing basic instructions to specialized groups, with a full drill and critique as a final phase. The Nunn-Luger-Domenici Act of 1996 mandated the training and development of a response capability to terrorist attacks using chemical/biological agents in the United States. An initial round of training may be an excellent start, but it is not the complete answer. Constant follow-up training for new personnel and refresher courses for those who received the initial round of training are essential.

State

In almost all cases, states maintain emergency or disaster management teams or agencies. Local law enforcement or emergency services can call upon state authorities to lend assistance. National Guard units in each of the states fall under the control of the governor and possess highly trained specialized units to assist in WMD incidents. For further details, see the section below on federal military assistance. The state may request assistance in accordance with the Federal Response Plan, through a designated Defense Coordinating Officer (DCO). The DCO will coordinate all required military assistance during the consequence or aftermath phase. The Response Task Force (RTF) will deploy to support the federal lead agency in the handling of the crisis, consequence, or both stages of the incident.

Federal Law Enforcement

To coordinate the federal response, the Federal Bureau of Investigation (FBI) and the Federal Emergency Management Agency (FEMA) have been assigned as lead agencies for crisis and consequence management. The FBI is the lead agency in dealing with the crisis portion of terrorist incidents, while FEMA is charged with coordinating the aftermath of an attack. The FBI has been charged as on-the-scene manager for incident coordination with other federal, state, and local agencies. In order to complete this mission, the FBI will operate under its Nuclear Incident Contingency Plan and the Chemical/Biological Incident Contingency Plan, both of which are classified. In addition to providing investigative supports, the FBI conducts a number of schools and training courses for local law enforcement for dealing with WMD. One of the more unusual and operationally beneficial training activities centers on the processing of large vehicle-borne improvised explosive devices crime scenes. The training is provided through the efforts of the Los Angeles FBI office with the cooperation of the U.S. military components in the area. This week-long training program is open to certified bomb technicians from police departments across the country and covers processing of crime scenes where a large vehicle explosive device has detonated. Training devices of approximately 500 pounds are detonated in remote desert areas in California.

Federal Military Assistance

The Domestic Preparedness initiative was launched following the 1997 Defense Authorization Bill funding the Nunn-Luger-Domenici Act, and provides money for the Department of Defense to upgrade the capabilities of federal, state, and local agencies in dealing with WMD. Any issues dealing with biochemical issues have always been within the venue of the regular military services. The U.S. Army Chemical and Biological Defense Command (CBDCOM) located at Aberdeen Proving Grounds in Maryland has been at the forefront in dealing with these issues for a number of years. In the past, the threats from weapons of mass destruction were from the regular standing armies of the Soviets and their Communist allies. Within the last few years, this threat posture has radically changed with the collapse of the Soviet Union and the proliferation of rogue states and terrorists groups which have put the United States at the top of their enemies list. This problem has been compounded by the standing-down of a large number of U.S. regular military forces. To make up the short fall, more reliance has been thrust on Reserve and National Guard units. One of the missions that these units were given is assisting in defending the homeland of the United States, especially against the consequences of the use of weapons of mass destruction. The Defense Reform Initiative #25 that was issued in January 1998 is the Department of Defense's plan for the integration of National Guard and Reserve components in the roles they play in combating WMD. The plan calls for the services to provide equipment, operations, and exercises, and sustain a reserve component response force that will support civil authorities in managing consequences of the use of weapons of mass destruction by terrorists. The goal is to improve the nation's ability to respond to a WMD incident with crisis and consequence management. The Reserve and National Guard can provide support in several key areas, including aviation operations, search and rescue, engineer support, transportation equipment, explosive ordinance, mortuary affairs, and medical support. Another key support provided by these components is decontamination units located in the more populous states.

An important program that is provided by CBDCOM is the Domestic Preparedness Chemical and Biological Help Line to assist first responders in providing the most current information relevant to a specific emergency. The United States Navy also lends support to counter the threat of a WMD event with Program 38. The Office of Naval Research and Technology carries out this program with a small cadre of personnel who are dedicated to biological, chemical, and radiological defense measures. Program 38's lead unit, Detachment 106, is comprised of specialized personnel to assist in problems of an unexpected nature. But the main contribution of Program 38 is providing a "reach back" resource that responders can tap into to better assess a situation and formulate the best action to take.

Notes

1. *World War I*, S.L.A. Marshall, American History Library, Houghton Mifflin Co., p. 167.
2. Chemical/Biological Terrorism Briefing, Jane's Information Briefing, October, 1997.

3. *Chem-Bio Handbook*, p. 15, Jane's Information Group, Alexandria, VA, 1998.

4. Congressional Quarterly Researcher, January 31, 1997 taken from the CIA, Business Executives for National Security, Congressional Quarterly, Inc.

Incidents

Kidnapping

7

Kidnapping as a Weapon

Kidnapping is another favored weapon in the arsenal of terrorists. The crime can be used as a fundraising device in the form of ransom payment, for extortion by trading the release of the victim for some specific goal or action, or simply as a publicity event to thrust the kidnappers' organization and cause into the headlines and onto television screens. Kidnapping has been especially favored by terrorists groups in Italy, Ireland, Central and South America, and the Middle East. Second generation terrorist groups also tend to make frequent use of kidnapping. These are groups who may trace their origins to political causes or ethnic or national freedom efforts, but have since lost their ideological orientation — though not necessarily the rhetoric — and have become merely self-indulgent criminal terrorists.

In Colombia, narcoterrorist gangs have been engaging in wholesale kidnapping, seizing large numbers of victims from the same company or group of companies. After certain sums are paid, a few victims are released and more ransom demanded. In Africa, large numbers of United Nations personnel have been captured and held for ransom by rebel forces. Ransom demands include everything from supplies to the removal of U.N. troops from a certain territory. In India, a nationally popular film actor was kidnapped by a dissident group in order to force the government to yield to its demands.

Risks Involved

Kidnapping falls somewhere between bombs/bombing incidents and hijacking/hostage-taking in the degree of risk involved for the perpetrators. Terrorists planting bombs, because of the availability of inexpensive timing or delay devices, run very little risk of being identified or apprehended. Hostage-taking and/or hijacking, on the other hand, is an action designed to precipitate a confrontation during which the terrorists will identify their cause and organization. It is also likely that each member will be identified individually.

This was demonstrated most dramatically on September 13, 1987, when the FBI, after extensive investigation, was able to identify a Lebanese man,

Fawaz Youonis, who was involved in a Jordanian hijacking incident in which two Americans were killed. On the promise of women and drugs, he was lured to an undercover U.S. ship in international waters in the Mediterranean in what is popularly referred to as a sting operation. He was arrested and brought to the United States to stand trial. He was convicted and sentenced to 30 years. This confirms the operational belief that those involved in hijacking and hostage incidents run a good chance of being captured or apprehended, if the incident comes to a peaceful conclusion, and wounded or killed, if it comes to violent end.

The risk for victims is the opposite. Hostage victims are rarely killed by the perpetrators because they have more value alive than dead. Kidnappers, on the other hand, often intend to kill their victims from the outset, having dug the hole or bought the quicklime even before abducting the unfortunate victim.

Differences between Hostage-Taking and Kidnapping

It is important that persons working with or within the criminal justice system are able to distinguish between hostage-taking and kidnapping. Kidnapping is the surreptitious taking and holding of a person or persons for the purpose of achieving some personal or organizational gain. In the case of terrorists, that gain may be strictly monetary, or it could be to force some course of action or to obstruct some course of action on the part of a government, a governmental agency, a private corporation, or some other group or organization. In all instances, a secondary goal of the terrorists is to attract media and public attention to themselves.

Kidnapping exposes the terrorists to a lesser risk, primarily because this type of incident lacks the confrontational aspects of hostage situations. The kidnappers have mobility and anonymity unless they choose to make their identities known. Except for the ransom note or telephone call, no one has any idea who or where the perpetrators are. Neither is there any way of knowing, in fact, whether or not they actually have the victim. For this reason, the kidnap victim is always in very grave danger.

Also, it is not unusual for a successful kidnap investigation to grow into a hostage situation before the incident is concluded. This is exactly what happened in Ireland when members of the Irish Republican Army kidnapped Jennifer Guinness of the Guinness brewery family, in April of 1986. Police tracked the culprits to a cottage in the countryside where they were holding the woman. Once the location of the victim and the perpetrator became known, it was obviously possible for a confrontation to take place between the perpetrators and the law enforcement investigators. In hindsight, the agencies investigating the abduction should have notified their tactical units during the early stages of the investigation, because it appeared that apprehension or confrontation was an inevitable consequence. This information should have been communicated to the tactical commander, which would have helped him or her move personnel to more practical or convenient locations. These locations, of course, should have been clandestine enough that they did not call attention to the number of armed personnel being assembled. The heiress was released April 8, 1986, following the siege. We discuss more on the differences between a hostage victim and a kidnap victim in Chapter 11.

In spite of media and popular use of the word hostage to describe various foreign nationals, and sometimes fellow citizens, abducted in Lebanon, Colombia, and other nations around the world, these incidents are more often kidnappings. This is because there is no confrontation between authorities and abductors. A kidnap victim is held hostage. The difference lies in knowing the whereabouts of the perpetrators and their victim in the latter instances, and their unknown whereabouts in the former.

Uses of Kidnapping

Kidnapping, like bombing, is often used to make a statement or register a protest. The victim may be symbolic (i.e., associated with a government, corporation, or organization that is somehow associated with the wrong side of the kidnappers' cause), or the victim may be virtually unknown to the public but still valuable to a government, corporation, or other organization and thus might have high ransom value.

It is difficult to determine why kidnapping has not been used to a very great extent by terrorists and radicals operating inside the United States. Most likely, U.S. terrorists have alternative means of achieving publicity aims and raising funds. In addition, the mystique of the FBI's success in tracking down kidnappers may serve as a deterrent.

In Europe, Middle East, Latin American, and Pacific Rim countries, kidnapping may be a more popular terrorist tactic because there are fewer publicity opportunities for terrorists to call attention to themselves. As for fundraising, banks in most countries are much more security conscious than in the United States, where the banks are very consumer oriented and emphasize customer service over security. In addition, outside the United States, relatively fewer opportunities exist to rob armored cars or retail establishments with large amounts of cash.

Types of Kidnappers

Kidnappers can be grouped into four categories:

1. Criminal
2. Professional
3. Political
4. Confrontational spouses or emotionally disturbed persons

Criminal

Criminal kidnappings are committed by persons attempting a one-shot effort at extracating a large sum of money from the family, friends, associates, or employer of a wealthy or well-connected individual. Kidnappings falling into this category include the Lindbergh baby in the mid 1930s; the December 1968 case involving Barbara Mackle, daughter of a wealthy Florida real estate developer; the abduction of Reg Murphy, the publisher of the Atlanta Constitution newspaper; the 1978 incident involving an entire bus full of school children in Chowchilla, California; the January 1987 case of Stephen Small, the heir to a publishing fortune in the Midwest; and three cases in 1992 involving the abduction of a 10-year-old girl by a child molester on Long Island; and the kidnappings of Exxon oil executive Sidney J. Reso in New Jersey and wealthy clothing manufacturer Harvey Weinstein, also in New Jersey.

All of these were kidnappings motivated by criminal intent and perpetrated by amateur criminals. There are those who believe the Lindbergh baby was dead by the time he left his parents' yard, or not long afterward. Barbara Mackle, abducted from her college dormitory, was buried in a box buried two feet below ground level, given two ventilation pipes, a small amount of water and a small, battery-operated fan. Acting on a tip, authorities located and rescued her after more than three days. The California school children were buried in a truck trailer. Only because the bus driver was able to dig his way out were the children rescued and the perpetrators apprehended. Stephen Small was not so fortunate, for although his kidnappers provided air vents, water, and a light, he was dead by the time police got to him.

In a more recent case, on April 29, 1992, Reso was kidnapped from his car while still in the driveway of his home, by a former police officer who was working in a security position at Exxon, Arthur Seale and his wife, Irene (Jackie) Seale. This was done after a tremendous amount of research into the habits of the victim. Reso was subdued and immediately placed in a large wooden box that had been constructed just for this purpose. The box was loaded into a rented van. Reso was held in that box, above ground, at Secure Storage, a self-store facility, until May 3, 1992 when he was found dead by the kidnappers when they came to feed him. They buried his body in a shallow grave. They could have walked away with almost complete certainty of not being detected or apprehended. Instead, their greed for the ransom contributed to their apprehension by the FBI. They were eventually convicted and incarcerated.

On August 4, 1992, Weinstein, a well-liked maker of men's formal wear, was kidnapped as he left the diner where he ate breakfast every day. A few weeks prior to the incident, two brothers, one a former employee of Weinstein's, had found a sump manhole in a secluded area off a parkway along the Hudson River in New York City. After finding the location, they decided kidnapping and selected Weinstein. He would be held there undiscovered for almost two weeks. During the ransom drop, the perpetrators were apprehended and the detectives, who had been given the approximate location, spent a considerable amount of time before locating the victim.

December 29, 1992 through early January, 1993 on New York's Long Island, pedophile John Esposito held a 10-year-old girl prisoner. He had constructed a virtual prison cell under his driveway with an entry shaft through a closet that was so secretive the police, executing search warrants, missed the entrance on two occasions. When the pedophile was arrested as a material witness and incarcerated, he told his lawyer (who was about to leave on vacation) that he had the child secreted in the cell. He realized the child might die of starvation. Esposito would eventually lead the police to the location and unlock the mysterious entrance of rugs, linoleum, cement cover, and block and tackle. The girl was alive and well.

The common trait in all these cases is that the perpetrator or perpetrators have the option of producing the victim if they have to in order to provide veracity to their claims, or to walk away from the whole incident if they get cold feet or the police investigation gets too close for comfort.

Professional

Professional kidnappings are carried out by a more-or-less organized group that uses kidnapping as a source of revenue. The Mafia in Sicily and other parts of Italy, guerrilla groups in Latin America, and the Irish Republican Army have all operated in this way. Quite often the victims are employed by or are principals of large, usually foreign, corporations who are kidnapped in the hope that the company will pay a huge ransom. One American oil company did pay $14 million to ransom one of its executives who was kidnapped in Latin America. One of the distinguishing characteristics of a professional kidnapping is that the victim is almost always returned alive. As professionals, these kidnappers expect to keep doing business and maintain their credibility by releasing victims in exchange for ransom. Professional operatives do not always limit their activities to people, abducting and holding for ransom everything from valuable racehorses to priceless artwork.

Among the areas where professional kidnapping is prevalent is the island of Sardinia off the west coast of Italy. Here the per capita rate of kidnapping is the highest in the world. Criminal groups in Sardinia research the financial resources of potential victims, and ransom demands are scaled according to the family's ability to pay. The amount is high enough to make the enterprise worthwhile, but still low enough that the family has little trouble meeting the demand. If there is an initial resistance to meeting the demand, a finger or ear of the victim may be severed and sent to the family as an inducement to pay the ransom.

A curious side effect of the success of the Sardinian kidnappers, on the one hand, and the political kidnappings of the Red Brigade in the 1970s and 1980s, was that the Mafia became active in trying to organize the kidnapping industry on mainland Italy by streamlining procedures and codifying behavior.

Political

Political kidnappings are designed to create incidents which put pressure on governments or political parties, and are usually conducted by terrorist gangs adept at exploiting the accompanying media coverage. The kidnappings can be accomplished with either long-term or short-term gains in mind. In Madras, India, on August 3, 2000, there was a political kidnapping of the popular film star Rajkumar by Tamil kidnappers who were led by a man named Veerappan. In addition to demands for amnesty and $12 million, the abductors also included political demands such as referring territorial disputes involving Tamil Nadu to the International Court of Justice and making Tamil the sole language used in schools in the Indian state of Tamil Nadu.

Long-term kidnapping has been used to a large extent by Islamic fundamentalists in Lebanon who have at various times kidnapped Americans, British, French, and West German nationals and held them for long periods of time, stockpiling them, so to speak, to be used as bargaining chips at some future time. It has been reported that Libyan leader Muomar Khaddafy would attempt to buy kidnap victims from Lebanese-based terrorists. Most victims of political kidnappings have been released in order to effect specific propaganda ends, although a number have been killed for the same purpose.*

Short-term political kidnappings include such notorious crimes as the abduction and murder of Italian politician Aldo Moro by the Red Brigade;

* The effectiveness of this tactic was demonstrated in 1988 when the French government, in order to win release of three French nationals being held in Lebanon, agreed to at least three conditions. According to published reports, the French government would repay Iran $300 million on a billion-dollar loan secured in 1974 from the Shah Mohammaed Reza Pahlavi; review the sentences of Iranian guerrilla teams jailed in Paris in 1980 for attempting to assassinate the Shah's last prime minister, Shahpour Bakhtiar; and release Tunisian Fouad Ali Saleh who was in jail awaiting trial in connection with bombings in Paris in 1986 which left 13 dead and 250 injured.

the kidnapping and killing of Hans-Martin Schleyer, head of the West German Federation of Industries, by the Baader-Meinhof gang; and the kidnapping of U.S. Army Gen. William Dozier in Italy.

The Moro kidnapping was a classic terrorist operation. Moro was head of the ruling political partly in Italy and in line to possibly become president of the country. On March 16, 1978, after Moro attended Mass as usual, he was sitting in the back of his limousine reading a newspaper en route to Parliament. His driver and bodyguard were in the front seat, while an Alfa Romeo with three security agents followed. As described in the book *Political Terrorism*:[1]

> Just before crossing the Via Stresa, a white Fiat sedan with diplomatic license plates cut in front of Moro's car, forcing the driver to brake hard. His escort car ran into the back of his car. The passengers in the white Fiat leaped out of their car as if to see whether their car had been damaged, then drew pistols and shot Moro's driver and bodyguard, killing both instantly. Four men in Alitalia uniforms, who were standing on the corner as if waiting for a bus, now drew automatic weapons from their flight bags and fired at the Alfa Romeo, killing all three policemen. Moro was dragged from his car, unharmed, and thrust into a waiting blue Fiat. A blonde woman wearing a scarf and a man had been watching the operation with interest. Now they climbed into a car and smoothly formed part of the convoy of three escape vehicles. The entire episode took 30 seconds.
>
> A few minutes later, a woman standing on her balcony overlooking Via Casale de Bustis, a road barred to general traffic, watched as two cream Fiats with a blue Fiat in between, paused at the padlocked chain while a blonde woman calmly cut the chain with long-handled clippers and returned to her car. That was the last ever seen of Aldo Moro alive.
>
> …That morning false bomb reports had diverted police to Fiumicino airport and the Piazza Cavour; the telephone system of Monte Mario was mysteriously put out of action for fifteen minutes after the attack; the man who sold flowers at the intersection where the kidnapping took place had wakened that morning to find the four tires of his small station wagon slashed and had not come to work; the diplomatic license plates of the decoy car were found to have been stolen from the Venezuelan embassy over a year before; and the getaway cars were equipped with police sirens.

Although Moro was held for 54 days and wrote more than 50 letters during his captivity before being killed, the terrorists failed in their goal of preventing the trial of 49 members of the Red Brigade and winning their releases from jail. Likewise, the abduction and murder of Hans-Martin Schleyer failed to win terrorists what they said was their stated goal: the releases of jailed members of the Baader-Meinhof gang.

The General Dozier kidnapping proceeded even worse, as far as the terrorists were concerned, for he was rescued, somewhat beleaguered but otherwise unharmed, mainly through the cooperation of various Italian police agencies and U.S. armed forces intelligence units. (One of the reasons kidnapping occurred with such frequency in Italy during the 1970s and 1980s was the organizational chaos created by interagency squabbles among various units handling the Red Brigade, as well as other terrorists and kidnappings. It is a negative case in point on the importance of pre-incident interagency liaison). The treatment of General Dozier offers another insight into what terrorist kidnappers will do to a political victim. During his incarceration, the general was kept in a tent that had been pitched inside an apartment, all in an effort to disorient him. He was also forced to wear headphones, through which loud music was blasted at all times, so he would be unable to pick up ambient sounds which might help him identify his location or his captors.

Domestic

Disputes involving spouses sometimes escalate into kidnappings. Statistical data indicate that there are more than 3000 cases of parental kidnapping of children when the other spouse has been awarded legal custody. In some instances, the marriage is between persons of significantly different cultures with conflicts and difficulties exacerbating normal marital differences. Often children in such cases are removed from one country to another. In many cases, there are no reciprocal agreements and marital disputes are considered so low level in importance as to be lost in diplomatic channels.

Abductions of infants from hospital maternity wards are most often carried out by persons with an emotional disturbance, such as a woman who either never had a child or had a child who died. The motivation in these cases may be understandable, but the action is still illegal.

Post-Cold War Political Kidnapping

For a long time, political kidnapping was mainly a Latin American phenomenon, with a few isolated incidents in Europe. Colombian terrorists were among the most adept. When selecting targets, they would conduct thorough financial analyses and background checks of potential victims and their connections, family or business. They would look not only at banking information, but also check tax returns to determine the amount of ransom to be demanded. By the 1990s, with increased interest by tourists and businesses in Asian and Pacific Rim countries, kidnapping became a means to support the political aims of new dissident groups. Many of these groups were comprised of former military people and so-called freedom fighters who were no longer able to make a living or support their families. Other kidnappers were members of radical religious groups or rebel factions looking to have colleagues released from jails and prisons.

Private Industry's Role

Private industry and private security companies can play major roles in effectively combating terrorist activity with regard to kidnapping. The single most important responsibility is to train executives and other key or sensitive individuals in the corporation about how to avoid becoming a kidnap or hostage victim. This falls under the larger umbrella of hardening the target as discussed in Chapter 2.

A second major important consideration is the formation of a Crisis Management Team which includes not only terrorist-related incidents but other crises as well, such as natural disasters and industrial accidents. Although there may be some overlapping, it does not mean that the same individuals will bear the same responsibilities in each category. For example, in a kidnapping, many decisions will have to be made based on little information or fragmented information at best, rather than the usual detailed analysis.

There are many private organizations, such as insurance companies, that hire specialists to negotiate ransom prices down. Control Risks and Risks International are two such companies, in addition to The Ackerman Group, Kroll Associates, and the Pinkerton Group. There are also many other businesses and individuals who serve as crisis managers. These private sources, who charge substantial fees, nevertheless have ever-growing client lists, in part because their analyses can be blunter than those of government agencies like the State Department, for example. Government agencies, admittedly or not, are influenced by treaties or trade agreements or both, and may hesitate to publicize dangers for Americans traveling or working in certain countries or regions. The common experience has been that terrorist kidnappers will ask for the moon, but they are willing and fully expect to negotiate down from there. The official policy of the U.S. government is that it will not negotiate with terrorists; however, in diplomatic language, talking is not the same thing as negotiating. Neither will the U.S. government pay ransoms, but it may very well assist a family in paying ransom. An incorrect way of dealing with kidnappers was carried out by a Canadian businessman in 1999 when he actually exchanged himself for an employee who was being held by a South American gang.

In addition to the grand schemes of kidnap prevention and international negotiating strategies, there are the small, detailed items to consider in establishing a terrorist defense plan. One seemingly insignificant item on the checklist should be that all public or pay telephones around a company's building and facilities are surveyed. Those phones with good or full views of the building should have their phone numbers recorded, because they could be used to make bomb threats, monitor police activity, and conduct general surveillance on the comings and goings of key individuals in the event they receive emergency phone calls. This information, coupled with the cooperation of the local telephone company, can be invaluable to law enforcement personnel working on a case. With the proliferation of telephone companies and services, in addition to the large number of cellular telephone and other wireless instruments, not to mention prepaid calling cards, the possibilities that are available to perpetrators have grown tremendously. However, covering the basics, such as local pay phones, is a good place to start.

The Police Role

When a kidnapping is reported, it is preferred that marked police cars or police officers in uniform not respond. Kidnappers usually include in their ransom demand a warning not to notify the police. Well-organized kidnappers have had homes and businesses under surveillance just to see whether the police have been called. Such surveillance is more likely to occur when terrorists are involved, because those groups are more likely to have a bigger and better organized cadre than most amateurs perpetrating a criminal kidnapping.

Noting the exact time of a ransom call can be important. Sometimes the local phone company can "dump" its billing computer, although this can be expensive, and go backward from the telephone on which the ransom call or other communication was received in order to determine where the incoming call originated.

In dealing with kidnappers or hostage-takers, there is a significant difference between being the individual cop and being the government. It is unimportant if an individual police officer is embarrassed, but it is a major concern should the embarrassment be visited upon the government of the United States or Germany or Colombia or any other country. Police in countries where there is a national police force have to balance compassion and strength when dealing with their own citizens. Civil rights must be respected, even if the individual is rebellious or a notorious criminal. In dealing with outside terrorists or those who would tear down the country, however, a harsher stance must be taken, with appropriate precautions so the government does not appear to be repressive. The objective is to avoid being pushed into an extreme position, as urban guerrillas have been counseled to do.

Police Response to Residence or Workplace of Victim

Who the first responders will be may very well depend on how the report of the incident comes to the attention of law enforcement. Most persons will just call 911 or some other emergency number, and in the panic and excitement may not indicate correctly the description and extent of the crime. It is important that dispatchers are trained and aware not to send uniformed members to the location if it appears to be a kidnapping. If the call comes from a business executive or a family member who has been briefed on the potential vulnerability of the victim, they should be directed to the unit designated to handle kidnap investigation. The designated investigators will be mindful of their response procedures. That is why it is important for agencies to designate who will be responsible for kidnap investigations, pre-incident, before it goes down.

The initial actions of the Kidnap Response Team to the residence or workplace of the kidnap victim will set the pace and may very well affect the outcome of the investigation and the safe recovery of the victim. Many such victims come from affluent or influential families or both. It is not uncommon for the responding officers to be somewhat in awe of the people and the opulent surroundings of their homes or offices. When the officers arrive on the scene, they must have a take-charge attitude as well as compassion. With the use of checklists to cover the various procedures to follow and tasks to be accomplished, the officers will not have time to be bullied or overly impressed by the principals. While it is natural to have compassion for a mother or father who seems to have lost a child, later investigation may implicate either or both as suspects. However, there may be other instances where the victims come from less affluent backgrounds and live or work in less luxurious circumstances, or come with questionable backgrounds, i.e., drug dealing, gambling, etc. These families, too, must be accorded proper and effective service.

When responding to either the residence or the workplace of the victim, the response team should have unmarked and otherwise nondescript vehicles. If none is available, the response team should park at some distance from the location and walk, to not raise suspicions of accomplices who may be keeping an eye on the location. Of course, the geography of the location can affect how the residence or workplace location is approached.

Response to the Kidnap/Extortion Threat

It is not unreasonable for the family, friends, or associates of a kidnap victim to request verification that the person is actually being held. More often than not, this request will be met. When the first report of kidnapping reaches the business associates, family, and friends of the victim, there is a sense of disbelief, quickly followed by fear and panic. These are part of the tactics kidnappers employ. They want a quick, emotional response to their demands. The first realization should be, however, that it is quite possible the victim is already dead. Or, if no request is made for verification, the victim may be dispatched as a matter of convenience. It is always wise to request to speak to the victim. Any pretext is acceptable, including the guise that it is assurance that ransom payments will be made to the correct individuals. In addition to verifying that the victim is being held and is still alive, speaking on the telephone helps keep the line of communication open longer, which may prove useful in a subsequent investigation. Even when verification is accomplished with videotape or a Polaroid photograph, where the victim holds up a newspaper to indicate the date, various opportunities present themselves for the gathering of information, as well as evidence for future prosecution.

The decision whether or not to pay ransom is strictly up to the family, business, or to whomever the demand has been made. Neither the local police nor the FBI will advise one way or the other. If the decision to pay is made, however, most law enforcement agencies will do what they can to assist in accumulating the funds and dropping off the ransom payment. If a large sum of money is involved, be mindful that the perpetrators or some independent criminal might rob the people moving or holding the ransom. In the case of Exxon executive Sidney Resso, the oil company had actually delivered $18.5 million in cash to his home. After it had been there almost a day, someone called attention to the lack of security for such a large sum and eventually an FBI tactic team was assigned to protect it.

In international kidnapping, terrorist or otherwise, it is the policy of the U.S. government not to pay ransom to anyone. There have been instances, however, when unofficial logistical assistance has been rendered by government agencies.

"Do Not Contact the Police"

A warning is often given, along with the ransom demand, not to contact the police. Unfortunately, there is no guarantee the kidnappers will not harm the victim even if the police are not contacted. A case in point: In April, 1984, a successful young New York restaurateur named Ernesto Castro was kidnapped. Later, he telephoned his family and said to his brother Benny, "They have me kidnapped, they want ransom." At this juncture another voice broke in and said, "thirty thousand," and specified a drop site. The second voice warned, "the money, no cops, or your brother will be killed." Brother Benny made the drop without notifying the police. As instructed, he waited at a nearby pay telephone. After five hours and no contact, he gave up; 48 hours later, the police notified Benny that they had found Ernesto's body with two bullet wounds in the head.

When kidnappers initiate contact, whether a ransom demand or other demands are made, there are procedures which, if followed, can be helpful to investigators. These include

1. Note the exact time, or time as closely as possible, that the notification is made and whether it is by telephone or a hand-delivered communique.
2. Request to speak to the victim or ask for some other verification to assure that there is no hoax involved.
3. If the notification is made via telephone, note as much information as possible, i.e., the exact wording of the message, the tone, pitch, and other qualities of the caller's voice including accents, speech impediments, or other distinguishing characteristics, as well as background noises such as car, train, or plane sounds, bells, whistles, machinery, etc. At the very least, such information could help pinpoint the telephone locations from which the calls were made.

Hoax

A bogus kidnapping can be carried out by strangers or by members of the alleged victim's family. Devious persons may attempt to make a quick score if they know a prominent or key individual (i.e., a prime target) will be out of touch for a relatively long period of time, be it six to eight hours or one or two days. One such hoax was perpetrated by the niece of a wealthy banker and her ne'er-do-well boyfriend who knew that the aunt had changed plans and was not in a position to inform her husband or other relatives. The niece and her friend then called the bank and demanded a substantial ransom, but an amount that was small enough for the bank to have on hand in cash. The bank's director of security had good pre-incident liaison with the local Kidnap Task Force, and the two perpetrators were apprehended before the aunt returned home.

Another kidnap hoax involved a young boy named Etan Patz who had disappeared from his New York City home. On the third anniversary of his disappearance, a call was made to the Patz home saying "information about the disappearance" of the boy could be had in return for a payoff. The Kidnap Task Force was mobilized and in a short time apprehended the would-be extortionist who had no information at all concerning the whereabouts of the boy. To this day, decades after young Patz's disappearance, there has been no evidence that he is dead, nor that he is still alive.

Prevention Tactics

The most important factor in combating kidnapping and extortion is prevention. Obviously, if a person is not abducted, the family or company need not be concerned about meeting ransom demands. By the same token, if a company's products are secure, tamperproof, and never adulterated, there is little need to worry about extortion threats.

A key to personal kidnap prevention is awareness — awareness of physical surroundings whether on the road or at home. All too often when a person (who by nature of occupation, nationality, or business affiliation) is a potential target of terrorist action, he or she still remains oblivious to danger signs. When traveling abroad, it would be wise to check into the possibility of local political unrest, or perhaps dates and anniversaries which are of significance to political minorities. As with virtually everything in the area of security and defense, there are no 100% guarantees that anything anyone does can prevent a kidnapping or hostage situation. Individuals who considered themselves targets or who are associated with target organizations can vary daily routines so that predictability cannot be used to the terrorists' advantage. When traveling, direct flights are preferred to those with stopovers or a change of planes. U.S. airlines are the preferred carriers, other than on flights to the Middle East, where the more secure airlines tend to be El Al and those from neutral first-world nations. Once in the plane, a window seat in the middle of the cabin will insulate the occupant both physically and psychologically from terrorists during a hijacking. Aisle seats, bulkhead seats, and those in the front and back of the plane provide the perpetrators with a direct line of sight and provide easy access should they want to make an example of someone.

Many individuals, corporate executives or otherwise, upon accepting a high-risk position, should take the time to prepare a personal profile folder containing information that could assist authorities in verifying an alleged or reported kidnapping. The folder should include a photograph, biography, telephone numbers, a medical and dental history, optical prescriptions, information on club and organization memberships, and similar information that could help prove positive identification.

It is equally important for a person in a high-risk position to prepare his or her family for the possibility of a kidnapping. Terrorists, who are seeking publicity as much as anything else, have made the media, particularly television, an integral part of their planning, strategy, and tactics. There is no question that in some instances, the kidnappers had done research into potential victims' families to determine whether they would be effective in pressuring the victim's employer or the government to comply with the demands of the captors. Terrorists will also callously manipulate a victim's family and associates by using them to deliver messages or lobby on behalf of the demands. Terrorists, through the wording of their messages, also will try to divide public opinion, so that whatever course of action the authorities take, a significant portion of the public will be opposed to it.

In a kidnap situation, unlike a hostage situation, time is on the terrorists' side. With a small group of loyal operatives in on the act, there is little chance of the perpetrators being apprehended.

What the Individual Can Do

High-risk individuals should prepare a personal profile. This should include sensitive information on how and where the individual can be contacted to minimize the possibility of a hoax being perpetrated. Obviously, it is very important that the profile folders be sealed and secured, to be opened only if the individual becomes a kidnap or hostage victim. If the individual leaves the company, the file should be returned still sealed and unopened. In addition, the person's residence should be equipped with as many security devices as practical, given the degree of risk and the funds available for prevention measures. Telephone procedures should be instituted to establish a pattern of check-ins and verifications. Codes should be employed, but they must be kept simple enough for family members to understand.

Despite whatever prevention measures are taken, an abduction could still occur. In order to minimize day-to-day complications for a kidnap or hostage victim's family while they go through the ordeal of waiting for the return of a loved one, there are a number of things that can be arranged ahead of time. These include

1. Making all checking, savings, and other bank accounts joint accounts
2. Drawing up a checklist of all bills which must be paid regularly, whether weekly, monthly, quarterly, or annually
3. Arranging to have salary deposited directly to the bank to facilitate the family's ability to carry on
4. Executing a power of attorney to a dependable relative in the event both husband and wife are taken
5. Maintaining a backup supply of prescription drugs, eyeglasses, and other medical or personal effects which may be needed on short notice

What the Family Can Do

An individual who is deemed to be a high risk kidnapping or hostage victim should make an agreement with immediate family members to accept the support of the employer, close friends, and other relatives. This may even include a promise by the family to return home immediately in the event of an abduction overseas. Such an arrangement will provide some comfort for the captive, who then will need to be concerned only with his or her own survival. The family should observe basic security procedures traveling to and from their residence. Telephone service should be switched to unlisted numbers to lessen the amount of crank or harassing calls. Travel plans should be kept confidential.

One Man's Ordeal

A classic example of how one high-risk individual hardened the target, was still kidnapped, but managed to survive the ordeal involves Sir Geoffrey Jackson, the British Ambassador to Uruguay, who was kidnapped January 8, 1971.

As recounted in his book *Surviving the Long Night*, Sir Geoffrey[2] was aware that he and his embassy were under covert surveillance by persons later identified as Tupamaros, the Marxist guerrillas active in Uruguay at the time. Jackson began taking precautions to protect himself and his family. He varied his daily routine, taking different routes to work, and using a number of vehicles. Although he was eventually taken, his efforts did force the terrorists to use more time, manpower, money, and vehicles than they had originally planned. A less well-financed group might have abandoned the effort. Realizing he was a high-risk target, Sir Geoffrey had also arranged with his wife that in the event he were kidnapped, she was to pack two suitcases, one for herself and one for him, which should be left in the foyer of their residence. Lady Jackson was to leave the country immediately for the United Kingdom and then proceed to their cottage in the country and have it painted. Knowing she would comply, this relieved Jackson of any concern for his wife and he was able to concentrate on his own situation and how to survive it.

What the Corporation Can Do

A company with even the slightest possibility of being a terrorist target should develop an internal policy on kidnapping. The policy should include the creation of a Crisis Management Team, and provide for alternate members in the event of emergencies involving permanent members. By virtue of their key decision-making positions within the company, the CMT should contain the chief executive officers, the chief financial officer, and the heads of the legal and security departments. Among the CMT's considerations should be

1. Who should be given protection? Be mindful that every employee is important. Which executives should be given what kind of protection, and to what level does family coverage extend?
2. Who should determine when to implement the CMT plan? The major consideration here is whether or not a hoax is involved.

3. The establishment of awareness conferences for executives and their families, to explain the company's policies. This will also provide an opportunity to define the reasons for requests for biographical profiles, pictures, etc.
4. Whether or not to provide assistance in securing offices, residences, and vehicles.
5. Establishing support procedures for families, should an abduction take place.
6. How and for what time period salary should continue to be paid in the event of a prolonged kidnapping or hostage incident.
7. Determining that the company does, in fact, have the authority to pay ransom, vis-à-vis stockholders and the Internal Revenue Service, as well as guidelines for when, where, and how much ransom will be paid.
8. Developing a plan for securing the actual funds and paying a ransom.
9. Establishing liaison with federal, state, local, and foreign authorities who may become involved in the event of a kidnapping.
10. If the abduction takes place outside the United States, a local negotiating team (LNT) would be onsite, maintaining close communication with the CMT at its base. The LNT should be made up of those who know the local people, laws, and customs. This might be where professional kidnap negotiators would work from as well.

These are but a few points to be addressed by the CMT. The use of pre-incident role playing will give members the opportunity to make mistakes in order to see who might function better in specific roles. It also provides a forum to examine the actions, or inaction, which might become the crux of future litigation should an incident ever occur.

On Becoming a Victim

Certainly the best tactic to employ upon becoming a kidnap victim or a hostage is to be well coached in the pre-incident psychological preparations discussed in defense planning in Chapter 2. Should a person not have the advantage of that training, the first thing to do is control fear and anxiety levels. The word hope has been developed into a mnemonic aid for the four attributes most helpful to a captive: humor, optimism, patience and energy.* Another strength captives must have is courage, the courage to maintain self-respect even when terrorist captors try to torment and demoralize their victims.

* This concept was developed by Morehead Kennedy, an American diplomat who was among the hostages held for more than a year in the U.S. Embassy in Teheran, Iran, during 1979–1980.

Notes

1. *Political Terrorism, Volume 2, 1974–1978*, Lester A. Sobel, Facts on File, New York, 1978, pp. 209–215.

2. *Surviving the Long Night*, Sir Geoffrey Jackson, Vanguard Press, New York, 1974.

Bomb Incidents

8

The Mechanics

In Chapter 3 we discussed bomb threats and other types of bomb incidents, building evacuations, and bombers and their motivations. Here we look at the mechanics of conducting searches for bombs, recognizing explosive devices, and the mechanics of explosions. Regardless of the advances terrorists make in constructing explosive devices, the methods of conducting a search remain fairly constant.

Search Overview

There are four types of searches that a security professional or law enforcement officer typically conducts:

1. The building search, where the premises may or may not be occupied at the time the search is conducted
2. The search of a suspicious vehicle
3. The VIP or pre-incident security bomb sweep of locations or vehicles or both
4. The use of explosive-detection canines

Unless extenuating circumstances exist, two general rules should always be followed when conducting a bomb search:

1. All searches should begin from the outside and gradually work inward to the interior.
2. Once inside, start with the lowest level and work upward, unless the search is in the basement of a building, where the converse is true, begin at the entry level and search downward from there.

The operative philosophy here is to never let an explosive device get between the searchers and a point of egress.

Building Searches

Traditionally, building searches usually were conducted as a result of a bomb threat notification being received, but currently, many searches are done as part of routine security procedures, particularly where sensitive personnel or locations are involved. Targeted buildings for the most part are multistoried structures or large, sprawling buildings, including schools, transportation facilities, government facilities, commercial office buildings, tourist attractions, and in some cases, private residences. Less frequently, searches may be conducted at safe houses used by fugitive radicals and terrorists, suspected bomb factories, or even major drug trafficking locations that may be booby-trapped. When private industrial or corporate buildings are the subject of an anonymous bomb threat, a search will often be conducted by the company's security personnel or a volunteer employee search team, assisted by law enforcement personnel.

Exterior Searches

The number of teams or individuals required to properly search the exterior portion of any location will depend on the size of the building, the area of the grounds, and the degree of experience of the searchers. A general rule for exterior search team assignments is that about 25% of the total personnel involved on each team should be assigned the task of conducting the exterior search. This task will be greatly reduced if explosive detection dogs are available, but the key factor is still the size of the exterior area.

The initial search should be concentrated on the area closest to the building and extending out from the building line for a distance of about 20 to 25 feet, depending upon the physical layout. Special attention should be given to shrubbery, window ledges, loading docks, waste containers, entranceways, and any indication of loose ducts, ventilation grills, freshly dug dirt, or anything else out of the ordinary. Search time can be reduced and safety enhanced by a regular program of maintenance that includes keeping the area free of unnecessary obstructions and shrubbery well-trimmed, removing accumulated trash, and generally reducing the chances of providing a hiding place for an explosive device.

Interior Searches

The interior of a building should be divided into two distinct segments for searching:

1. Areas to which the public or other outsiders have general access
2. Areas within the building which have a restricted access or to which access is limited in any way

Public access areas are most vulnerable to the covert placement of an improvised explosive device and, therefore, should be searched by the most experienced and best-trained members of the search team. Public access areas include lobbies, restrooms, unlocked maintenance and utility closets, hallways, fire or other stairwells, and reception and storage areas. Areas where outside delivery or other vendors have access should also be considered public access areas for search purposes.

Restricted access areas are places where the public does not have regular access and which are usually under employee observation, supervision, or control. Even though these areas are supervised, they may still be vulnerable to bomb attack by determined terrorists willing to attempt penetration by posing as repair technicians, messengers, and the like. The U.S. Navy was reminded of this when the U.S.S. Cole entered the port of Aden in Yemen and an explosives-laden skiff, apparently part of the harbor fleet helping to moor the ship on a refueling call, was able to approach the vessel to inflict considerable damage. Seventeen sailors were killed and more than a hundred others injured. The members of the search team assigned to restricted areas should be those most familiar with these areas because they would be aware of an item or object out of place or out of the ordinary. It is here, then, that nonsecurity personnel will be more helpful in staffing search teams.

A word of caution. When employees or volunteers are used in conducting a search for IEDs, it should be an "eyes only" search. Searchers must refrain from probing or physically disturbing any areas or objects of a suspicious nature or which otherwise cause concern. Training must stress that the search team members are concerned only with locating the obviously out of place item or package that is deemed suspicious. A suspicious package should not be touched or moved under any circumstances. Further examination should be conducted only by a trained bomb technician.

Search Teams

Search teams organized within private companies or organizations, such as businesses and schools, should be formed on a volunteer basis. Security personnel may be automatically included if the bomb search duties are specified as part of the job description when the individual is hired. The size and composition of the search team will depend upon a number of factors, including the location and size of the facility to be protected, the type and number of employees, the professional capabilities of responding public safety agencies, and the company's vulnerability to terrorist activity.

The voluntary nature of the search team cannot be emphasized enough, because nonvolunteers are likely to conduct inadequate searches. In assembling a search team, the assistance of the personnel director or human resources manager is vital. This individual can be very helpful in screening potential candidates. It is also important that first- and second-line supervisors and managers realize and understand the reason for using nonsecurity personnel in certain threat situations. These supervisors should also be made familiar with the eyes only restrictions that are placed on search team members.

Setting Up a Program

It should be anticipated that nonsecurity supervisors and managers who do not want their personnel exposed to danger or taken away from their primary duties may show resistance. As a result, the security manager may want to establish an orientation program for supervisors and managers to explain the training and utilization of search team members. The orientation should stress the benefits to the company of a search team and its importance in cutting down on lost time during a bomb threat. The traits to look for when screening for search team members include

1.   Level-headedness and the absence of gung-ho bravado which may lead to brash or foolish acts
2.   Willingness to accept training and instructions along with a demonstrated ability to follow established guidelines
3.   Familiarity with the sections of the building/facility/location that require searching
4.   A reputation for thoroughness and completion of assigned tasks

In many companies, especially those located or headquartered in suburban areas, a pool of employees with backgrounds that include volunteer firefighting service, auxiliary or past police experience, or military experience should be sought out, as should members of the existing fire brigade, if the company has one. In selecting personnel for search teams, employees with established track records with the company should be given preference over new or entry-level employees. Again, it must be stressed to each individual searcher that any search will involve an eyes-only, hands-off approach.

Surprisingly, supervisory and management personnel often do not make effective search team members. This is in part because they are used to giving orders rather than taking them. They also may not be broadly familiar with the day-to-day operations of the company, spending a majority of time in the area of their expertise. They also may be reluctant to search dirty, out-of-the-way areas. In addition, such personnel may be difficult to locate in an emergency as a result of the company's primary demand on their time and/or location.

Alternative to Search Teams

If a volunteer search team program is not feasible, all employees should be used to search their own work areas to determine if anything is suspicious there. Although this actually may be the fastest of the search methods, it has a number of drawbacks. First, all employees have to undergo some kind of training in what to look for, how to search, and how to react to suspicious packages. All employees are also potentially exposed to danger should an explosive device actually be planted. Additionally, a search team still must be employed to look through public, exterior, or other areas where no employees are ordinarily assigned.

Mechanics of the Search

Whether a search is being conducted by police officers, security personnel, or employees at the location, the mechanics of the search are the same. The search team should be divided into subteams, or units, of two persons each, with members deciding among themselves how they will divide the labor, such as who will handle the reporting and what search pattern will be utilized. The search pattern can be a grid, a circular or ever-enclosing spiral pattern, a pie-wedge, or other geometric design. No pattern is necessarily better than any other, although on occasion, the layout of a particular area may dictate a specific search pattern. Whatever pattern is employed, the most important thing to remember is that the search must be systematic, thorough, and include all confined spaces. A person familiar with the area may, with a quick eyeballing be able to determine if anything is strange or been tampered with. The next thing a team should do upon entering a room is initiate an audio check. To accomplish this, the team members simply remain silent and listen for any background noises. To enhance the searchers' concentration on listening, they should close their eyes and stand quietly in one spot. The searchers should try to identify each sound and its source (e.g., air conditioning, fluorescent light buzzing, constant-run machinery, traffic, or other exterior noises that filter into the building). All equipment and machinery that can be shut off should be, in order to reduce the amount of ambient sound. This will make it easier to recognize the sound of a timing device ticking away, should an actual bomb have been planted.

Searching a Room

Under normal circumstances, the starting point for a room search is the entranceway. The search team should follow whatever search pattern was selected, remembering that although speed is important, thoroughness is more so. Safety is the most important factor of all. Searchers must always remember not to disturb anything that appears unusual, and not to touch anything that is in the least suspicious. In searching a room, the searchers should mentally divide the room into three horizontal layers or sections. Searchers should be moving their eyes and heads left to right, back and forth, and *not* up and down. The up-and-down movement is the easiest way to miss something of importance, because the searcher will tend to be moving. The first horizontal zone of search is from the floor to the waist, following the general rule that searches are conducted from the outside in and from bottom to top.

The floor-to-waist layer, or zone, is the area where improvised explosive devices are most likely to be placed. Once this zone is cleared, the searchers should concentrate their efforts on the layer comprising the waist to the top of the head. The third segment — which may require standing on desks, chairs, other office furniture, or a ladder — includes the area from the top of the head to the ceiling. Under certain tactical conditions, the areas may be consolidated into two. This might occur where the room has virtually no hiding places along the walls, such as in conference rooms or windowed dining rooms.

A fourth search zone is the plenum, or that area above the acoustical tiles or false ceiling. This step is not required if an observable ceiling is permanent; if this step is required, it is usually the most difficult and time consuming to complete. To conduct a search of a drop ceiling, remove a ceiling tile in each corner of the room and, standing on ladders, have first one searcher, then another, sweep the area with a flashlight, outlining objects in the light's path. If the area is cluttered with wires, cables, or storage articles, if there are pillars blocking vision, or if the ceiling is particularly large, the plenum search will have to be accomplished in smaller sections. Throughout the search, eye and head movements should be from left to right, back and forth, and *not* up and down.

As the search progresses and sections of the building or individual rooms are completed, this information should be relayed to each search coordinator or command post so that the progress of the search can be monitored and recorded. It is most important to convey this information in order to track time, especially when a deadline has been specified by the threatmaker. It is also important to keep track of the search time so that in the event a search is progressing more slowly than anticipated, additional searchers can be added when the plan is critiqued and updated on the basis of actual performance. The time factor is also important in determining whether or not to keep evacuated personnel in the area or to send them home for the remainder of the day.

Common Bomb Placement Locations

Over the years, terrorist operatives have penetrated security defenses to place explosive devices in a wide variety of target locations. In some instances, these bombs have been placed outside the targeted building, causing glass and minor facade damage. There have been times, however, when exterior bombs were powerful enough to cause major structural damage. On other occasions, IEDs have been placed inside a critical area of the targeted facility. More typically, however, IEDs placed inside a building are secreted in places with relatively easy access. The most common placement locations include

1. Restrooms, particularly women's restrooms, where devices have been placed in trash receptacles, behind toilet bowls, and in false ceilings or ceiling air vents.
2. Lobby areas, particularly reception areas where heavy traffic can mask a terrorist's or bomber's moves. Favorite locations include behind and in planters, under couches or chairs, or just inside the main entrance doors.
3. Upper floors of multistoried buildings, particularly in hallways, fire exits and stairwells, restrooms, and adjacent to or in elevator shafts.
4. Fire stairwells, also open by law, are easily accessible and lightly traveled.

Precaution

When conducting a search for an explosive device, the searchers must be constantly on the alert for booby-traps and other antidisturbance devices which may be affixed to the IED or incorporated in the device's firing system. These include trip wires and similar action-activated initiating switches. The importance of eyes only cannot be overemphasized as the primary caution in conducting a search for explosive devices.

Vehicle Searches

Motor vehicles are routinely becoming subjects of bomb searches. Such a search can be prompted by an anonymous bomb threat, as part of a VIP, executive protection or pre-incident search, as a routine security search at entrances or restricted parking areas, or as the result of finding a suspicious vehicle on the premises. The same principles guiding a building search can be used in a vehicle search. The search starts on the outside and proceeds to the inside. Once inside the vehicle, the search is conducted from bottom to top, including the use of mirrors or optical-fiber scoping devices for the undercarriage. These can be the same types of long-handled mirrors or scopes used in interior searches for checking under and behind heavy furniture and equipment.

There are two primary methods in which passenger cars and other vehicles are used in bomb attacks. The first involves the placement of an explosive device in a vehicle with the intent to kill, maim, or otherwise injure intended targets within. In other situations, the vehicle is used to conceal a large amount of explosives or an IED. The trunk areas usually are used for this purpose. The use of car bombs is a method of delivery particularly favored in Western Europe and the Middle East.

In almost all cases, the actual explosives will be out of sight, so any searches of suspicious vehicles should be conducted by a qualified public safety official. The role of a private security professional should be limited to the identification of the suspicious vehicle. However, if the search is of vehicles in executive protection programs, professional security personnel are usually the ones to conduct the vehicle search.

Antipersonnel Car Bombs

This type of device is typically wired to the internal electrical system of the vehicle and is initiated by the actions of the driver or passenger or by remote means. Usually the explosives are placed under the driver's seat or in the engine compartment, often adjacent to the firewall. Typically, no more than two or three pounds of high explosives are required to do extensive damage to the automobile and most certainly kill the occupants of the car. Although an action switch is the most common type of detonating device in vehicle bombs, the use of remote-control devices is becoming more frequent. Because of the prevalence of action switches and command-detonated devices, vehicle searches should be conducted only by persons with extensive training in search operations. If a vehicle search must be done, steps to follow are

1. If time permits, do a background check on the vehicle to determine if the owner or regular driver(s) might be targets and why. The check also should determine who has regular access to the vehicle, and why the vehicle is suspected of having an explosive device within it or explosives hidden inside.

2. An external search must be completed prior to entering the vehicle. This involves searching not only the exterior of the vehicle itself, but also the area immediately surrounding it. Things to look for include obvious tampering with doors, hood, or trunk area; evidence of tape, wire, or other foreign matter on the outside of the vehicle; impressions in the ground of footprints or any sign that a jack may have been used to raise the vehicle; and any signs that dirt or other material has been dislodged and knocked to the ground as might occur if a device had been placed on the underside of the vehicle.

3. The search of the vehicle's exterior should proceed very carefully, insuring that nothing causes movement, jarring, or shaking of the vehicle. The use of a hydraulic or other type of jack in conducting the search should not be considered. To reduce search time, a long-handled inspection mirror is ideally suited for checking the underside or, if available, a scoping device utilizing optical fibers. If nothing suspicious is found, the interior search can begin.

4. Gaining entrance to the interior of the vehicle should be attempted remotely rather than manually, if possible. The opening of all compartment doors — hood, trunk, doors, glove compartment, etc. — should be done with remote devices, which should be part of any search team's basic equipment. The first interior area to inspect is the engine compartment. Because the battery under the hood is an ideal source of power for a concealed explosive device, it is the logical place to start. Beginning the interior search in the engine compartment allows for clearing any connection that might be affixed to the vehicle's electrical system. Once the engine compartment has been cleared, other areas such as the trunk and seating may be addressed.

Vehicle-Borne Explosive Devices

In the past several years, the use of vehicle-borne IEDs has increased significantly (Figure 8.1). These bombing attacks have usually occurred in areas where security operates in a business-as-usual atmosphere. In this country, the World Trade Center in New York City, and the Murrah Federal Building in Oklahoma City sustained extensive damage when large explosive devices were delivered in vehicles. Overseas, the 1983 attack on the U.S. Marines' barracks in Beirut, Lebanon, involved the largest IED ever used in a terrorist attack. It is estimated that the truck-borne device used approximately 15,000 pounds. of high explosives and propane gas in the attack. There were 243 killed in the suicide bombing. In the October 2000 bombing the U.S. Navy destroyer U.S.S. Cole was attacked within Aden harbor in Yemen, resulting in the deaths of 17 sailors. The attackers used a small Zodiac dinghy

Figure 8.1 A reconstruction of the vehicle-borne IED used in the Oklahoma City bombing. (Courtesy of F. Guerra.)

loaded with an estimated 300 pounds of high explosives. Because of lax observation of security procedures, the dinghy was allowed to approach the ship in broad daylight. Another example of operating in a high-risk area was the U.S. Air Force personnel housed in Khobar Towers in Saudi Arabia. The structure was adjacent to a public thoroughfare and on March 22, 1997, a tanker truck filled with explosives detonated in front of the building, virtually destroying it. Nineteen were killed and 200 injured.

Aircraft Searches

The extensive use of privately owned aircraft makes it imperative to include these craft in any executive protection program that requires bomb sweeps to be conducted in the general course of business. Once again, the search of the aircraft should be conducted in the same manner as other types of searches, from outside to inside, and preceding along the same lines as automobile and other vehicle searches. An additional security concern in the case of aircraft should be the search of baggage and other items, such as catered foods that are loaded on board. Food caterers and cleaning and maintenance services should be subject to background checks. In protecting an aircraft against a potential bomb attack, there is very little margin for error because a small quantity of explosives can bring an aircraft down.

Pre-Incident VIP Search

The VIP (very important person)-related bomb sweep, also called a pre-incident sweep, is handled in much the same manner as a search following an anonymous bomb threat. Searchers, who conduct the sweeps of meeting rooms, vehicles, public areas, or other locations in advance of an appearance by anyone who is a possible target of a terrorist attack, should be particularly alert to the use of action switches or command-activated devices. Often, searchers will not have the luxury of much time between the start of a search and the arrival of the VIP. Also adding to the difficulty of this type of search is that searchers are combing unfamiliar locations, making it easy to overlook small changes. Areas of concern should be those where the VIP is most vulnerable, namely, hotel rooms, dining rooms, or public pathways taking the subject from one point to another. Special emphasis should be placed on areas where trip wires, pressure switches, or similar devices can be hidden. In order to speed up searches, the use of explosive-detection canines should be considered. In recent years, a number of private security firms have added dogs to their arsenal of search equipment. As an example, a number of financial institutions with global interests and headquarters or other facilities in New York's downtown financial district use privately owned canine patrols on a daily basis to sweep incoming packages and bulk deliveries.

Explosive-Detection Canines

Although canines have been an important part of police work for years, especially in the patrol and detection function, the use of dogs for specialized searches such as narcotics and explosives is still on the increase. Because of the increasing call for bomb-detection dogs in the private sector, a number of security agencies now provide canines on a contract basis. Any business or organization contracting for such services should thoroughly check the credentials of the contract agency, if only for the numerous liability issues surrounding the use of such programs. Using canines to detect explosives received a major boost in 1972 when the federal government awarded the University of Mississippi a grant to study dogs as bomb detectors. The first dogs the study produced were used in New York, Los Angeles, and Baltimore. Although the dogs are extremely reliable, it must be remembered that they are just another tool for the bomb technicians. Of course, canines cannot be expected to be foolproof, either. Dogs are used to assist search operations and to detect the existence of explosives in suspicious packages.

Maintaining a bomb-detecting canine program can be an expensive and time-consuming project. There are training cycles, rest and work periods, and the physical care of the canine to consider. To maintain adequate coverage, more than one dog and handler will be needed, adding to the expense. If dogs fit into a department's or company's needs, there are numerous private firms available for training and related services. An organization contracting for such services must thoroughly check the credentials of the contract agency, for again, numerous liability issues surround the use of canine detectors, not to mention reliability and possible subversive intentions. According to many canine practitioners, the best dog is one that is trained for solely one task. This means that a dog is best used for only explosives, and not cross-trained for narcotics or other scent work.

Dogs used in bomb-detection work are usually trained on the reward system. When a dog locates something, or to use the handler's phrase, "makes an indication," the dog is rewarded with a biscuit, a short play period, or some other style of positive reinforcement for its efforts. Since a search is a bit of a game for the dog, it must find something on every search to keep its attention on the search. To accomplish this, the handler carries a "plant" to be placed every so often to assure that the dog finds something. Even with this approach, the dogs quickly lose interest in searches and begin to lose their effectiveness after about 20 or 25 minutes. After a short rest period, the search can resume if sufficient time exists.

What a dog actually reacts to when sensing certain explosives has been the subject of some debate in the field. Much of the debate relates to what makes up the sense of smell and how the sense actually functions. One theory holds that molecules of substances vibrate at different rates, with pungent substances having a quite different rate from stable substances, and that it's to the vibration rates of the molecules are that the dog actually reacts.

A somewhat different theory proposes that there are seven primary odors, just as there are three primary colors, and that each of the primary odor molecules has a distinct geometric shape. Receptors in the noses of dogs (and humans, for that matter) have cells corresponding to the various shapes of the odor molecules, and eliciting the appropriate or associated smell response.

Whatever the reason for their behavior, bomb-detection canines are a valuable tool for the bomb technician and are especially useful for pre-incident sweeps involving corporate executive security.

Suspicious Packages

Once a bomb threat has been received and a search begun, the first, last, and most important rule is DO NOT TOUCH. As part of their training, searchers should be kept informed of current trends among terrorist bombers, such as how deliveries of IEDs have been masked. Over the years, terrorists have secreted devices in containers designed or specifically chosen to blend in with the surroundings of the targeted site. Containers used in the past include boxes of long-stemmed roses, lunch boxes, takeout and delivery containers from fast-food chain restaurants, and similar everyday items. In incidents where antipersonnel devices were involved, the bombmakers have been especially ingenious. One such incident involved a Hammas terrorist, Yihya (The Engineer) Ayyash, who was assassinated in 1995 (reportedly by Israeli agents) when operatives were able to secrete a small IED into his cellular telephone. Given such examples, it behooves search teams to be composed of individuals with a keen working knowledge of an assigned area so that they can ascertain very quickly what does and does not belong. Items become suspicious packages when there is no one who can account for a specific thing to be in that particular area, especially when a bomb threat has been received or if the facility previously has been the target of a threat.

When searchers discover something they feel is suspicious, the immediate area should be vacated quickly. When the searchers are out of the immediate area, the command post or search coordinator should be informed of the situation. The suspicious item should be considered, and thus treated as, an explosive device. Only after the item is positively identified as harmless or innocuous (such as an identifiable backpack or tote bag being left behind), or the item has been examined and cleared by a qualified bomb technician, should the search resume. The searchers and others involved in a bomb incident operation should be aware that a secondary explosive device may also be present. Several terrorist groups have done this in the past, particularly the Irish Republican Army (IRA) in Europe and the Puerto Rican group FALN when it was active in the United States. The primary purpose for planting a secondary device is to kill or maim any emergency personnel who have responded to the scene. These secondary devices are usually only a short distance from the initial explosive device.

A suspicious package should never be disturbed in any way, and this includes bomb-suppression items such as bomb blankets over the device. A bomb blanket is strictly a tool for the bomb technician. If used improperly, it may cause a premature detonation of the explosive device. If hasty damage-control functions are to be performed, they should be limited to venting the area (opening doors and windows) and shutting down any utility feed that may be in the immediate area.

Identifying Improvised Explosive Devices

Several different types of improvised explosive devices are used by terrorists. You do not have to be a qualified bomb technician to recognize the types of

Figure 8.2 Improvised hand grenade. An empty soft drink can be refilled with BBs and a high explosive and become a deadly, easily thrown hand grenade.

IEDs, explosives, and firing devices that are commonly available. The great majority of IEDs used in terrorist attacks are of fairly simple construction, utilizing either an electrical or non-electrical firing system. Generally, IEDs will contain these components:

1. Explosive main charge.
2. Firing or initiating system.
3. Delivery system (package, container, or vehicle in which the IED is placed). IEDs can also be delivered utilizing firing systems such as homemade mortar tubes and rocket launchers. (See Figure 8.2.)

Explosives

As defined by the Military Explosives Technical Manual, "an explosive produces an explosion by virtue of the very rapid, self-propagating transformation of the material into more stable substances, always with the liberation of heat and almost always with the formation of gas."[1] Explosives can be solid, such as trinitrotoluene or TNT; liquid, such as nitroglycerine; or gaseous, including elemental hydrogen or oxygen. The solid explosive is used most often in terrorist operations. Explosives are further categorized into two major classifications: high explosive and low explosive.

Figure 8.3 Smokeless powder. Relatively easy to obtain, smokeless black powder is a common filler used in improvised explosive devices, particularly bombs.

The major differences center on three characteristics:

1. Burning rate. A low explosive generally has a burning rate of under 3200 feet per second (fps), while a high explosive has a burning rate in excess of 3200 fps.
2. Container. A necessity for using a low explosive, it can be galvanized pipe, cardboard cartons, or similar items. Conversely, a high explosive needs no container to achieve detonation.
3. Firing techniques. A low explosive requires only the introduction of heat, flame, or spark to achieve initiation. A high explosive needs the introduction of another high explosive, called the primary explosive, to produce sufficient shock to achieve initiation.

Low explosives are generally classified as propellants and are used in small arms and ammunition. Among the more common low explosives are smokeless powder, black powder, and nitrocellulose powder (Figure 8.3). To achieve detonation, the powder must be enclosed in a vessel that contains the expanding gases until a sufficient force is built up and the explosion is achieved. Such powders are a common filler in pipe bombs and similar IEDs. Low-explosive powder is generally manufactured through mechanical blending where raw materials are reduced to a fine powder and mechanically mixed together. A bonding agent may be used to form a paste which is then dried, reduced to small pieces, and ground to the desired degree of fineness.

High explosives are designed to shatter or destroy the intended target. They are available in a wide range of detonating velocities (burning rates) from 3300 fps for ammonium nitrate to 29,900 fps for HMX. The faster the burning rate, the greater the shattering effect. The lower the rate, more of a pushing and heaving effect is obtained. High explosives are generally considered compounds rather than mixtures, because the combustibles and oxidizers are molecularly blended. Some high explosives are more sensitive than others. These are used as initiating charges and are considered primary explosives, while the less-sensitive explosives are classified as secondary explosives. Common primary explosives are

1. Mercury fulminate is an explosive that appears in crystalline form and is white when pure, but usually has a brownish-yellow or gray tint. It is extremely sensitive to shock, friction, or heat, and accidents during manufacture are not uncommon. This explosive is used in detonators; fires in the range of 13,400 to 21,100 fps.
2. Lead azide is a crystalline, cream-colored compound with a high ignition temperature, and is less sensitive to shock, heat, and friction than mercury fulminate. It is used for major caliber-based detonating fuses and point detonation fuses as well as a number of other detonators and has a burning rate of 13,400 to 17,000 fps.
3. Lead styphnate varies in color from yellow to brown and is extremely sensitive to fire and heat; when in a dry state, even a small charge of static electricity may cause a detonation. Firing at 17,000 fps, lead styphnate is used as a component in primer and detonating mixtures.
4. Tetracene is a pale-yellow explosive that burns around 13,000 fps and is extremely sensitive to flame, producing a heavy black smoke. Due to its low detonating velocity, it usually is combined with other explosives.
5. Diazodinitrophenel (DDNP) is a yellowish-brown powder that is less sensitive to impact than mercury fulminate and lead azide, but more powerful upon detonation. DDNP is usually mixed with other explosives and used as a priming mixture.

Secondary explosives include

1. Trinitrotoluene (TNT) is a solid cast explosive that is a yellow crystalline substance with a high brisance, or shattering effect, and is well-suited for cutting steel, breaking concrete, and similar demolition work. Primarily a military explosive, it is issued in $^1/4$-, $^1/2$-, or 1-pound blocks for demolition work and as a filler in bombs and artillery ammunition. It is used as a standard in measuring other explosives, with an index of 1.00, and has a burning rate of 22,500 fps (Figure 8.4).

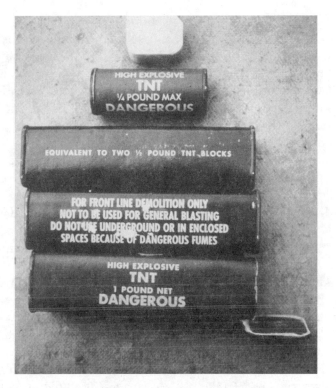

Figure 8.4 Trinitrotoluene. TNT manufactured for the military comes in a variety of sizes and shapes.

2. Nitrostarch is closely related to nitrocellulose, and is less sensitive and less powerful than TNT. It was not until early in the 20th century that it was possible to produce it in a stable form. Nitrostarch is similar to the straight and ammonia dynamites except that nitrostarch is used in place of nitroglycerine. It is white in color, burns about 16,000 fps, and is used as a base charge in grenade and mortar ordnance.

3. Tetryl is a clear-to-pale-yellow crystalline material with a very high degree of shattering effect (brisance), has a burning rate of 25,800 fps, and is sometimes used as a booster and in blasting caps.

4. Cyclonite (RDX) is an extremely fast-firing, white crystalline solid with a high degree of brisance, used in detonating cord, bursting charge in shells, blasting caps, and in the manufacture of C-4. RDX has a high degree of stability in storage and is considered one of the most powerful of the military explosives.

5. Composition B, or cyclotol, is a product of combining 59% RDX, 40% TNT, and 1% wax. It has a very high detonating rate, 26,000 fps, and is known for its shattering effect. Composition B is used as a filler in military-shaped charges.

6. Composition C-4 is one of the best known of all the military explosives. It is made of 91% RDX and 9% plastic binder, keeps its plastic form from −20°F, and will not leak oil up to 170°F. Because of its high brisance and insensitivity to shock, C-4 is used as a combat-issue military explosive. C-4 burns at a rate of 26,400 fps. Factories in what was once Czechoslovakia produced a version of this substance, called Symtex H, which was reddish to orange in color and used by terrorists in both Western Europe and the Middle East.

7. Flex-x is another type of plastic explosive that is used as a cutting charge. This flexible explosive is waterproof and insensitive to shock, with a burning rate of 23,000 fps.

8. HMX is one of the most powerful explosives made today and can produce a high degree of shattering; white-colored with a firing rate of 29,900 fps, it is often mixed with TNT in the manufacture of high-blast munitions.

9. Ammonium nitrate is a white crystalline substance, but may be dyed to other colors. It is used in military cratering charges because of its pushing and heaving effect due to a low-detonating velocity of 3300 to 8900 fps. Ammonium nitrate-based explosives are a favorite of terrorists who improvise them for use in vehicle-borne explosive devices.

10. Picric acid is highly explosive in a crystalline state with a burning rate of approximately 19,000 fps. The Japanese used picric acid as a base explosive during World War II. It is available in a powder configuration that is used in various dye tests under laboratory conditions. When stored for a long period of time, picric acid can become extremely unstable and sensitive to shock and friction. When the chemical comes in contact with lead, it forms lead picrate, a sensitive and violent explosive. Bottles of unstable picric acid are routinely found in school chemistry labs, presenting another challenge to bomb technicians.

11. PETN is an extremely powerful explosive used extensively in detonating cord, blasting caps, and ammonium primers; this explosive is white in color and has a detonation rate of 27,200 fps.

12. Tetrytol is light yellow to buff in color and a high explosive that is used primarily as filler in artillery shells and bursting mines. It is similar to TNT and tetryl, firing at 24,000 fps. It is also used in demolition satchel charges.

Common commercial explosives include

1. Dynamite was developed by Alfred E. Nobel as a substitute for the highly volatile nitroglycerin. It is the most widely used explosive in the world. Dynamite can be manufactured in a variety of sizes, ranging

from .50- to 50-pound cartridges. Originally, the explosive was made with a train of nitroglycerine or other sensitive explosive, along with other energy-producing ingredients mixed with an inert binding material. Today, the nitroglycerin has been replaced largely by ammonium nitrate. Military dynamite contains little or no nitroglycerin, nor does it absorb or retain moisture. It is much easier to use and store than the commercial variety and is generally used in noncombat construction projects. There are so many formulas for commercial dynamite that there are no agreed-upon standards for color, firing speed, or size.

2. ANFO (ammonium-nitrate-fuel oil) was developed for commercial use in the 1950s employing "prilled" rather than crystallized ammonium nitrate. The explosive is prepared with 94% prills and 6% No. 2 fuel oil and detonates at a very low speed, which produces an excellent pushing and heaving effect. ANFO, whether improvised or manufactured, is the terrorist's explosive of choice for large vehicle-delivered explosive devices. ANFO is not cap sensitive and requires a heavy booster charge to detonate it.

3. Water gels, also called slurry, were introduced in the late 1950s, and are composed of ammonium nitrate, TNT, water, and a gelatinizing agent with a bonding agent. This explosive is used primarily for quarry blasting because of its concentration of strength.

Explosives used in improvised devices include

1. Powder. Virtually any type of explosive can be improvised by those with the training and access to the proper chemicals. One of the most popular explosives to use in improvised devices is black powder, frequently found in pipe bombs fashioned by young experimenters.

2. Improvised plastic explosives. Knowledgeable bombmakers and terrorists commonly manufacture their own explosives. A mixture of easily obtainable potassium chlorate, ground very fine, and petroleum jelly, can be detonated with a blasting cap.

3. Fuel-oxidizer mixes. There are almost an infinite variety of improvised fuel-explosives that can be made by a determined bomber. Some of these mixtures are difficult and dangerous to manufacture, others are fairly simple. Raw materials for the devices are regularly found in areas where there is agricultural, mining, and quarrying activity. Improvised mixtures of ammonium nitrate and fuel were used in both the New York World Trade City and Oklahoma City federal building bombings. These explosives require booster explosives to achieve detonation.

Of the secondary explosives discussed, the majority are used in military applications. The same criteria that make certain explosives acceptable for military use also make them attractive to terrorist organizations. These include

1. Relative insensitivity to shock, heat, and/or friction
2. Good shattering effect
3. Convenient shape and size for handling, storage, and placement under combat conditions
4. Manufacturable from readily available raw materials
5. Usable under water

Initiation Systems

A low explosive needs only a spark, flame, or friction to be initiated, whereas a high explosive requires the introduction of an explosive shock to achieve detonation. This shock is usually accomplished through a detonator or blasting cap. The blasting caps are of two varieties: electric or nonelectric. Blasting caps generally consist of a metallic sleeve containing a small amount of primary explosive and measuring approximately $1/4$ inch diameter by 2 to 5 inches in length, depending on design and intended use.

Electric blasting caps are detonators designed to function when an electric source, such as batteries or generating equipment, is available (Figure 8.5). Electrical impulses from these sources are transmitted through leg wires, which initiate the base charge. These caps will function with the application of a very small electrical charge and with low amperage. In addition, they come in a wide range of time delays, from instantaneous to a delay of several seconds.

Nonelectric blasting caps are small metal cylinders, closed at one end and containing a small amount of primary explosive as a base charge. They are designed to function when a small spark or flame is introduced to the base charge, usually from a burning length of safety fuse. This fuse transmits a flame of uniform rate in order to provide a time delay prior to detonation. The fuse usually consists of a train of black powder encased in a waterproof covering, measuring approximately $1/4$ inch diameter, which provides a fairly constant burning rate from 35 to 45 seconds per foot. Burning rates may vary with manufacturers, climate, or other such factors. A sample length of fuse would be test-burned to establish a burning rate for the particular items prior to actual planting of the device. Fuse colors may vary from highly visible, colorful shades for commercial use to olive drab for military use.

With low explosives or propellants, only an introduction of a spit of flame, heat, or spark is required to initiate the mixtures. A favorite initiator

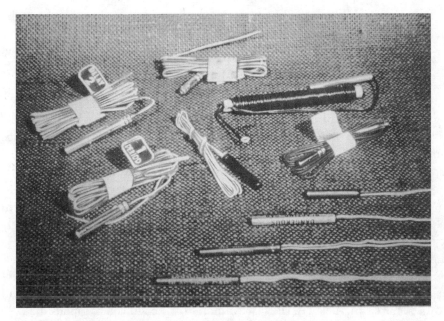

Figure 8.5 Blasting caps. By themselves, electric blasting caps are easy to obtain and may seem relatively harmless, but are powerful and must be handled with extreme care.

in IEDs utilizing smokeless powder and an electric firing system is common photographic flashbulbs. These flashbulbs come in a variety of sizes and shapes and can be modified for use in IEDs. In addition to being widely available, these flashbulbs can be triggered with virtually any commercially purchased 1.5- or 9-volt battery. Not only will they initiate propellant powders, but they also work very well with an assortment of incendiary materials.

There are other initiators commonly used for, and found in, IED construction. Among them are

1. Hot, or bridge, wire elements that consist of a wire bridged across the ends of the two leg wires carrying the current. This bridge wire, being less resistant than the leg wires, will heat up and glow quickly when power is applied, thus initiating the charge.
2. Electric squibs or "matches" that function much in the same way as an electric blasting cap, but lack the explosive main charge.
3. Any type of safety, firework, or other improved nonelectric fuse capable of transmitting a flame or spark.

There are three primary methods for firing systems utilized in the construction of IEDs, and each has its variations.

1. Time delay, provided by electronic or mechanical timers, fuse, or by the use of chemicals
2. Action, a mechanical system that can be fired by an individual pushing, pulling, or applying pressure
3. Command, which functions by electrical or radio signal

All three types of time-delay options have been used by terrorist operatives. The choice of system depends more on personal or group preference and availability of materials than on the performance advantage of any one option. Improvised versions of various time-delay options can be simplistic or sophisticated.

Mechanical time-delay devices include everything from an altered alarm clock to long-delay miniature electronic circuitry. Time delay is limited only by the power source the bombmaker can provide. Mechanical time delay is still common among bombmakers, who frequently employ such time pieces as alarm clocks, wristwatches, and kitchen timers in a wide variety of electrical circuitry hookups. Unless a very large action is planned, terrorists tend to use short time-delay devices, with many of the IEDs being placed at the target within an hour of detonation. When a timepiece is used in a mechanical firing system, it may be altered in several ways to provide time delay. Among the more common methods are

1. Using the hour hand to achieve a time delay of up to 12 hours, or the minute hand for a delay of up to 59 minutes
2. A stem-wound watch where the mainspring is used as a contact, thus increasing the potential delay up to 36 hours or more
3. Using a mechanical alarm clock winding stem as the contact point

As more advanced technology becomes available, i.e., printed circuits, miniaturization, programmable timing devices, and similar sophistication, more timing options exist for bombers, which can result in detonations being set far in advance, days and even weeks ahead of time.

Chemical delays are used effectively in both incendiary and explosive devices, including those employing high explosives. Chemical delays are not used as frequently as mechanical delays, because the measurement is neither as exact nor as accurate. The delays may be either improvised or manufactured, the latter usually being prepared for the military. The most common of these is the delay fuse M-1, usually referred to as a time pencil. There are foreign-manufactured equivalents with different nomenclature. The M-1 has an effective time delay from as little as two minutes to as much as 23 days, although the longer the delay the less accurate the timing device will be. Terrorists have made extensive use of chemical delays, especially improvised

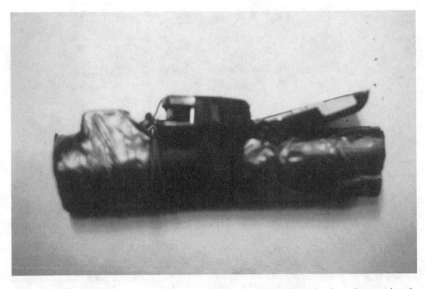

Figure 8.6 Pipe bomb pictured above is the type used in the bombing of Atlanta abortion clinics. (Courtesy of F. Guerra.)

chemical delays employing acid solutions. Hydrochloric and sulfuric acids are the most common because they are easy to obtain through legitimate sources. In addition, gasoline, lye, and other common caustic substances can be used as chemical initiators and delays. In the 1970s, the FALN used chemical delay timers and initiators in their bombing campaign in and around New York City.

Time delay fuses are commonly encountered with nonelectrical systems, the most common being safety fuses. Although the safety fuse is designed for use with nonelectric blasting caps, it can be used in the initiation of low explosive powder and propellants. This type of delay initiating system is commonly used in the construction of pipe bombs (Figure 8.6). Although there are a number of safety fuse manufacturers, the chief differences among the brands are the types of exterior waterproofing and color-coding systems employed for easy identification. Military issue is generally olive drab in color. Improvised burning-type fuses can be made from such readily available materials as cotton string which has been impregnated with black powder or drinking straws filled with a smokeless powder mixture. Easily found manufactured items that can be used as safety fuses are fireworks fuses and those used to initiate model rockets.

Action switches are set off by the action of an individual, either the person planting the bomb, the targeted individual, or a person tampering with the device. They are often referred to as booby traps or anti-tampering devices. There are four types of action switches:

Figure 8.7 Mock-up of a pipe bomb that was used by the Unabomber in his long-running bomb campaign. (Courtesy of F. Guerra.)

1. Pull release, which is designed to function when tension on a wire is severely decreased by pulling or yanking. These switches come in a variety of configurations specifically manufactured for military use. The most common item in improvising the switch is an ordinary spring-type clothespin, which also can be used for a press-release or pressure-applied switch. The action switch is used primarily in anti-personnel devices, particularly letter and parcel bombs, such as those crafted by the Unabomber (Figure 8.7).

2. Pressure-application switches are designed to initiate a device through the release or application of pressure or tension. There are a wide variety of these switches available, particularly for military application in mine warfare. Pressure switches are also easily improvised. These types of switches are of particular concern for a searcher undertaking a VIP or pre-incident sweep.

3. Tilt switches are usually found on devices fired by an electric circuit. The switch functions when tipped, tilted, or jarred in any direction, or in a single, predetermined direction. The most common is the mercury switch, which has numerous mechanical and electrical applications, and is available at virtually any electronic components store. These switches also are easily improvised using glass tubes, ball bearings, and other common items.

4. Command detonation is a method employed when a bomber wishes to activate a device at a precise, but undetermined time, such as when an

individual walks or drives past it. Command detonation can be achieved by electrical ignition or radio transmission. Radio-fired explosive devices are becoming more frequent in terrorist bombings, particularly in the Middle East. The drawback with firing a radio-control device is that line-of-sight with the target is required. The ETA, the Basque terrorists in Spain, make frequent use of radio-detonated IEDs. Electrical control of a command detonation is the more traditional method, because it is routinely employed by demolition teams in legitimate work. It is accomplished simply by introducing an electrical charge into wires connected to the explosive charge, using either batteries or handheld generating equipment manufactured for that purpose.

Summary

Searches for bombs are of three types: building, vehicle, and VIP or pre-incident. The three general rules to be observed are

1. Search teams should be composed of two-person units to assure that a proper and thorough search is conducted.
2. Searches should be conducted from outside, working toward the inside and, once inside, working from bottom to top.
3. Searchers should never touch or disturb suspicious packages; suspicious packages should be handled only by qualified bomb technicians. Certain searches, particularly those involving VIPs, should be conducted by trained searchers, augmented where possible by canine detection teams.

Recognition of improvised explosive devices is made difficult because IEDs can be can be secreted in almost any type of container. Those who planted the device do not want it to be detected; hence, those defending against their use should take nothing for granted. Explosives are generally classified as either high explosives, both primary and secondary, or low explosives, also called propellants. Among the most common high explosives covered were commercial dynamite, C-4, TNT, and PETN, a military explosive. Initiators of IEDs can be either electric or nonelectric. The major types of firing systems described are time-delay (mechanical, fuse, chemical), action (pressure-activated, pull-release, or tilt), and command (electrical or radio).

Notes

1. U.S. Army TM-9-1300-214/11A-1-34, Military Explosives 11/67, Department of Defense.

Hostage Incidents

What Is Involved

Dealing with hostage incidents means setting up communications with the hostage-takers. Also, a command post must be established and a support system created for the one person actually dealing with the perpetrator(s): the hostage negotiator. Though only one person should be speaking directly with the perpetrator, he or she will be closely backed up by a secondary negotiator. The No. 2 will listen to both sides of the negotiations and will feed the primary negotiator appropriate intelligence as it is passed up to the point of negotiation. He or she also will act as insulation to permit the primary negotiator room for concentration. There also will be a person who acts as coach and who will monitor both the primary and secondary negotiators and feed intelligence through the backup to the primary. The coach will coordinate the efforts of those gathering information and intelligence. While all this is happening, more intelligence-gathering should be ongoing in order to formulate a negotiating strategy and tactics.

Communicating with the Hostage-Taker

We already have learned in Chapter 4 about the physical and mechanical parts of establishing communication, such as the use of bullhorns, telephones, etc. Equally important — possibly more important, really — is what kind of stance the negotiator is going to take in dealing with the hostage-taker, or if it is a group, with the leader or spokesperson.

For law enforcement agents dealing with a hostage situation, a conservative approach is probably the safest. Police officers might not be much of a help in making the situation any better but, most assuredly, no one wants to make the situation worse. Being conservative does not mean being inactive or taking no action whatsoever, but neither is there any reason to rush into action. Certainly, it takes time to gather as much intelligence as possible. Once that intelligence begins to filter in, it should be weighed so that a negotiating strategy can be formulated.

Probably the first decision to be made is whether to take a hardline or softline stance. Few would question that the State of Israel probably has the hardest line anywhere in dealing with terrorist hostage situations. Exaggerating only slightly, it is said that hostage-takers confronted by the Israelis are given about 10 minutes to come out with their hands up or they will be brought out with their feet up. However, this policy certainly has not stopped acts of terrorism from being perpetrated against Israel.

On the other hand, the so-called softline approach to dealing with hostage-takers has critics, too. The New York City Police Department, for example, has been accused of dealing too softly with hostage-takers. One judge reportedly said that in New York if you were robbing a bank and things went bad, all you had to do was grab a few hostages. Then, the NYPD would help you pack the money and drive you to the airport. The exaggeration here is greater than it was in describing Israel's hardline approach.

The differences between hardline and softline approaches and the arguments over which is preferable are not as important as what will achieve the desired outcome in the hostage situation. Will the hostage(s) be harmed? Will a martyr be created? Will the stakes be raised in a sequel or imitative incident?

The policy and approach of the NYPD, for example, does not encourage imitative or copycat actions. Generally, when hostage incidents end and the perpetrators surrender, they are taken away to a city hospital where they are given a cursory physical and psychiatric examination by a mental health professional. The physical examination is made to preclude any allegation of beating or other police brutality, while the psychiatric examination determines whether there is a mental health problem. If there is, the subject can be treated. If no mental health problem is apparent, the subject can be returned to the criminal justice system and a defense plea of insanity is almost certainly precluded. This approach helps prevent imitative copycats, since people want to emulate heroes, not persons with mental problems.

The whole question of martyrdom is based upon putting tremendous value on the cause for which one gives his or her life. The fact that such martyrdom now is often associated with Islamic fundamentalist terrorists does not mean that others before have not been so motivated. As far back as the Crusades, Pope Leo told Christian crusaders that if they died in the service of the Cross, they were assured a place in Heaven.

The Making of a Hostage Incident

In order to know how to negotiate, what attitude to adopt, and what stands to take, it is necessary to understand what goes into the making of a hostage incident staged by terrorists. Dr. Brian Jenkins of the Rand Corporation, a research group located in California, coined the phrase "the theater of terror." The perpetrator is the star of the production, that is, the leading actor. The police are the supporting cast, the hostage is the co-star, and the public, the rest of the world, if you will, is the audience. The vehicle used to make this presentation is the hostage-taking. This is what attracts an audience and what draws media attention, which, in turn, creates an even larger audience. Whether the incident is local (with news coverage), or global (with worldwide satellite coverage), the incident reaffirms Shakespeare's observation that "all the world's a stage."

The publicity value of holding hostages can almost never be underestimated. A person who is ignored by society, by the bureaucracy of government, or by friends and neighbors can become the center of attention, the No. 1 attraction in town, simply by taking an unsuspecting person, even a relative, hostage and holding the police at bay with the mere threat of doing bodily harm.

A classic example of this involves one Anthony Koritsis in Indianapolis, Indiana, who felt he had been cheated out of his life savings by a financial company. He did not demonstrate his anger by simply storming into the company offices and shooting the principals. Instead, he purchased a shotgun, cut down the stock, and sawed off the barrel. He affixed a wire noose to the end of the barrel. He then went to the financial company's offices and forced the manager to put the noose around his neck. Koritsis then proceeded to parade the man through the streets of Indianapolis, finally wending their way to Koritsis's previously booby-trapped apartment where he held the manager hostage for many, many hours. Eventually, after receiving a promise of immunity from the state attorney general, Koritsis held a press conference with the hostage still in a noose at the end of shotgun. Koritsis was able to manipulate the media — all the major television networks provided coverage, as did local television stations, numerous print reporters, and photographers. Finally, after forcing the hostage to read a prepared statement, Koritsis did surrender. The grant of immunity, incidentally, was held to be null and void, but Koritsis was eventually found not guilty by reason of temporary insanity and was institutionalized.

Though the incident with Koritsis took place in the 1970s, another event happened years later in Hawaii when a disgruntled former employee by the name of John Miranda returned to his former place of employment and shot and wounded a supervisor. He then forced another employee, who normally would not have been in the office, to place around his neck a wire that was attached to a shotgun. After a few hours of talking to the media and negotiating with police, Miranda forced the employee down an outside stairway. The two pirouetted in a macabre dance in the company parking lot, surrounded by police who could not fire at the perpetrator for fear of hitting the hostage. After setting a series of deadlines, Miranda told his captive to count down from 100 and then he would fire. When the count reached 13, the hostage spun around and tried to grab the gun. It was now away from his head. Miranda fired but missed. The police fired and didn't miss. The hostage was saved.

Nearly every day we see the principle of theater being applied in international terrorist operations, whether perpetrated by dissident Sikhs, the Islamic Jihhad, or any of the too-numerous-to-mention national, political, or ethnic groups using terror as a political weapon.

While we examined, in Chapter 4, the expropriation of media attention during the 1972 Olympic Games by terrorists of the Black September organization, an even more effective example of media manipulation was effected by the Symbionese Liberation Army operating in the United States during the 1970s, one of whose members was pardoned by outgoing President Clinton in January 2001. The SLA was a group that probably never had more than 12 active members, but managed to lead the media and general public into thinking that it was in fact a large, well-organized army. This was the organization that staged the highly publicized abduction of Patricia Hearst, heir to the Hearst publishing fortune. The SLA demand that the Hearst family distribute food to the poor, and the subsequent distribution of food caught the attention of the whole world. Journalists reported how some United Nations officials were calling for an investigation into the plight of the Symbionese people, because their liberation army had been pushed to such extremes for attention. The name Symbionese, of course, is related to symbiosis, a biological term describing the relationship of two dissimilar organisms living in an association that is beneficial to both (as opposed to parasitism).

The Announcement

If a person were holding one, two, or more persons hostage and no one was aware of the situation, there would be little value in continuing to hold hostages. Because hostage situations are designed to influence authorities or obtain something of value, the perpetrators do not want anonymity. They want an audience. Not unlike the old circus parade through town to herald the arrival of the greatest show on earth, hostage-taking perpetrators may stage a robbery, crash a bus through a fence, or fire a couple of gunshots in order to bring attention to themselves. Only then can they move on to the next step, the position of power.

This is why, in planning negotiating strategies, it is so important to have all of the information and intelligence possible about the incident: who, what, when, where, how, and why. How was the announcement made? Was anyone hurt in the takeover? How many perpetrators are there? What weapons do they have? How many hostages? Where are they located? What are the demands, and how logical are they? It is important to note, however, that logic does not necessarily set the value or seriousness of the demands. Another question that should be answered quickly is whether any demands were granted by those individuals first responding to the announcement. All of this information will assist in securing the safest possible outcome.

Reaction of Law Enforcement Professional

Hostage negotiation is based on the theory of cognitive dissonance which, explained in everyday language, means that something is worth whatever someone is willing to pay for it. This is the principle involved in the pricing of objects sold at auction, whether art or antiques or racehorses. What was last paid for the object, or similar object, sets the basis for the new price. What is the highest price that can be paid for anything? A human life! So if someone is willing to give his or her life for a cause, others will evaluate that particular cause in a similar manner. Making a martyr out of a hostage-taker will only encourage imitation. Negotiation offers the optimum chances of recovering the hostages alive, while at the same time providing the least opportunity for creating a hero or martyr of the hostage-taker(s).

There are certain principles that have been gleaned from our work in hostage recovery. One of these is that it is in neither the hostage-taker's nor law enforcement's best interest to have a situation become violent. The hostage-taker knows that ultimately the police will win. Although there could be temporary setbacks for the police, if it comes to an all-out confrontation, the authorities have the equipment and manpower to eventually overcome any violence that the perpetrator(s) can muster. This leads to the obvious conclusion: hostage situations are really not as delicate as many observers tend to think they are. If a hostage-taker truly intended to kill his or her victim, the police would be there investigating a homicide rather than dealing with the dynamics of hostage negotiation. On the other hand, hostage-takers must be regarded as potential killers. If pushed to a point where they must demonstrate power and control, they may resort to violence.

Criminal Role

There are roles played by both the criminal and the police. Many times, the criminal role is to play the unbalanced person, the crazy, if you will. This is especially true if there are two perpetrators. One will speak with the authorities in a rational manner, usually warning that he doesn't know how long he can control the other, apparently more irrational culprit. The other will be just that, apparently and overtly irrational, unstable, and volatile. If the perpetrator is alone, he may do things such as seeming to play Russian roulette with himself or the hostage. Depending upon how extreme the response of the negotiator or authorities is, the more or less likely the hostage-taker is to engage in these actions. However, total disregard of such actions could provoke a demonstration of power; therefore, some slight acknowledgment of power will placate the hostage-taker's ego.

Police Role

The police also have a role to play. They have been called the good daddies of society, and the mere presence of a uniformed officer many times can calm the anxieties of the public in a crisis situation. It is not uncommon for two persons in a fender bender traffic accident to leave their vehicles in the middle of the roadway to await the arrival of a police officer. It is as though once the officer surveys the situation, everything will work out all right. Simply exchanging driver's license information and insurance company data is all that is required and all the officer will do upon arriving at the scene (often delayed because the accident participants have left their vehicles in the middle of the roadway).

What officer, when donning a uniform on the first day on the job, has not looked in the mirror and believed that he or she could make a difference to the public waiting to be served? It is no surprise, then, that most police officers become action oriented. When they get to the scene of an incident, they are usually under the gaze of a crowd that has gathered, and many times feel the need to do something. Usually, this starts with moving back the crowd, an action not always appreciated by the curious onlookers. At a hostage or barricade situation, the first things the officers should limit themselves to are containing, evacuation, and intelligence.

Containment

Generally, containment is a physical exercise, although there is also a psychological component to the activity. First and foremost, however, is physical containment, keeping perpetrator(s) within the smallest area practicable. A locked or wedged door creates a barrier that cannot be opened or moved by the perpetrator yelling or threatening. It is preferable that the police prohibit, or at least restrict, the movement of the hostage-taker and the hostages, because a mobile situation is usually not in the best interest of law enforcement personnel or the hostages, although there may be times when going mobile produces a tactical advantage for the authorities.

Containment also has its psychological aspects, i.e., in the initial stages of the incident, not trying to converse with the perpetrator and letting him or her get over panic and calm down in order to assess the situation. Often this is all that is needed to bring an incident to a safe conclusion. On the other hand, it is possible that police actions could provoke a violent reaction, particularly if the perpetrator has power over the situation, or worse, intends to commit suicide. Often, such individuals do not have the wherewithal to pull the trigger on themselves and will kill or otherwise harm a hostage in order to draw police fire, which has been termed "suicide by police." This behavior was discussed in Chapter 7.

Evacuation and Intelligence

The orderly evacuation of innocent persons is important to preclude injury or death or the possibility of the perpetrator taking additional hostages. The hows of evacuation were covered earlier. The gathering of information as quickly and accurately as possible will greatly affect the outcome of any hostage situation, be it terrorist or otherwise. However, intelligence, no matter how accurate, becomes valueless and useless unless communicated to the appropriate individuals.

Why Police Do the Negotiating

A hostage-negotiating situation and the employment of hostage-recovery methods obviously involve the use of certain psychological principles and techniques. This leads to the question as to why mental health professionals or others trained in psychology are not involved in the negotiating and why police officers are used instead. The answer revolves around the environment in which mental health professionals work. More often than not, a person using the services of a mental health professional is either a voluntary patient paying good money per session, or is an institutionalized individual in a hospital or prison who is required to see a therapist as part of a legal obligation or rehabilitation program (Figure 9.1).

The patient will usually see the therapist one or two sessions a week for anywhere from three to six months. During that time, the mental health professional will learn a great deal about the patient, such as likes, dislikes, emotional needs, and feelings about people and situations. The mental health professional may or may not have a lasting impact upon the subject. In an active hostage or barricade situation, there is no such expansive time luxury. The police officers at the scene must deal with an immediate crisis, albeit one of uncertain duration. Police officers are trained in, and experienced at, dealing with situational occurrences whether an accident, burglary, assault, rape, murder, or similar on-the-spot situations. There are also some pragmatic

HOSTAGE NEGOTIATOR CHECKLIST

The Purpose of this checklist is manifold:

1. To gather information about the incident and its participants thus aiding in the application of psychological tact. The Who, What, Where, When, How, and Why, briefly indicated, starts your Intelligence.

2. To ensure that the Intelligence is disseminated to and exchanged with all who require it. REMEMBER, COMMUNICATE.

3. To prepare this format permitting all actively engaged to evaluate what has occurred and how to proceed accordingly. REMEMBER, TIME IS ON YOUR SIDE.

4. To assist with covering the basis of the negotiations and to psychologically prepare you to enter and conduct purposeful negotiations with the subject(s).

5. Properly prepared, you will better cooperate with the Emergency Service Unit personnel in assisting the Area Commander. REMEMBER . . .SLOW IT DOWN. . .

Figure 9.1 Hostage negotiator checklist. The use of checklists kept on a clipboard will help the primary negotiator, secondary negotiator, and their backups keep track of people and activity.

reasons for using police officers rather than mental health professionals, or others, as hostage negotiators. There are, in shear number, more police officers than mental health workers. Also, police work around-the-clock. In the end, it is easier to teach police some basic psychological principles than to teach mental health workers basic police techniques.

The early models for police hostage negotiators were detectives who by virtue of their street experience in interviewing and interrogating had empirically discovered many psychological principles. This practical experience was then reinforced with theoretical, academic, and clinical approaches provided by mental health professions. Police hostage negotiators are not dealing in long-term therapy, but rather are applying a kind of psychological first aid. For those who are critical of not using mental health professionals, the analogy can be made with emergency medical situations during which a police officer applies first aid only to stabilize a situation until medical professionals can be utilized. Examples are treating severe bleeding, cardiopulmonary resuscitation, or artificial respiration.

NEGOTIATOR CHECKLIST

What:

A. What occurred:
   (emotional dispute)
   (crime, i.e., robbery)
   (political terrorism)

B. Time of occurrence: date _____ day _____ time _____

C. Who called Police Department:

D. Time notified: date _____ day _____ time_____

E. From where: scene _____ telephone _____

F. Injuries: Yes   No.   Describe
   1. Hostage   ____   ____   _____
   2. P. D.   ____   ____   _____
   3. Perpetrator   ____   ____   _____
   4. Other   ____   ____   _____

G. Contact with suspect:
   1. When
   2. How
   3. By Whom
   4. Anything promised

H. Contained:
   (P.D. deployed)

I. Weapons (what):
   1. Verified

J. Number of suspects _____

K. Number of hostages _____

Where (location):

A. Suspects
B. Hostages
C. Police
D. Floor plans (separate sheet)
E. Containment (separate sheet)
F. Observation posts (number on sheet)
G. Entrances, exits (indicate on sheet)
H. Telephones (indicate on sheet)

Communication (how) [radio (frequency), telephone, field phone]:

A. Police to Police (frequency) _____
B. Police to suspect   bullhorn _____   face to face _____
   telephone _____
C. Command post to operations unit _____
D. Other _____

Figure 9.1 (continued)

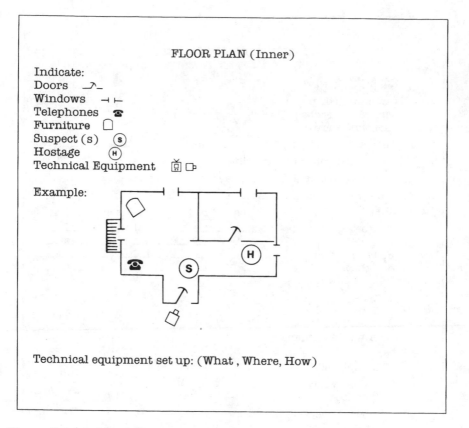

Figure 9.1 (continued)

This is not to say that nonpolice personnel cannot be successful negoti-ators. There are cases when a mother, other relatives, or clergymen have been successful. An occasional success should not, however, be the criterion for use. Remember that often it is strained relationships with spouses, parents, or friends which precipitated or contributed to the incident. On numerous occasions, the appearance of a wife or mother at a hostage incident has resulted in the perpetrator becoming violent. This has led to both suicide and the killing of hostages. It is also best to have only one primary negotiator at a time, because multiple negotiators have at times created a competitive environment. The purpose of negotiating is to lead the hostage-taker on a path toward a specific course of action or solution. Anything that distracts attention from that goal is counterproductive. If a second person must speak to the perpetrator, for example, to combat fatigue of the primary negotiator, it would be best to have someone with a distinctly different voice so the hostage-taker does not feel a trick is being played. If one negotiator is making no progress with the perpetrator, then it may be a police decision to use a

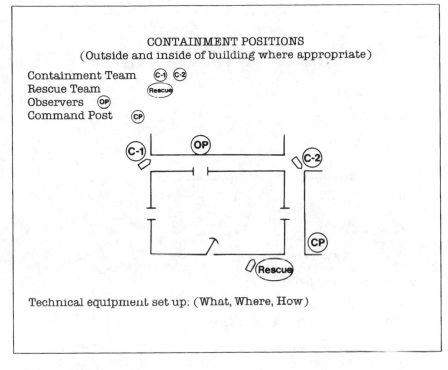

Figure 9.1 (continued)

different negotiator in order to change the pattern. If things are going well, however, the introduction of a second voice would only complicate matters.

Post-Incident Crisis Intervention Teams

In the past few years we have seen a proliferation of mental health professionals and social workers who are available to respond to locations of terrorist or hostage incidents, multiple homicides in public places such as schools or office buildings, or other locations that were scenes of some kind of horror. Examples of this include the survivors of the bombing of the federal building in Oklahoma City; students, parents, and teachers connected to the Columbine High School shootings in Littleton, Colorado; as well as the multiple homicide at the Wendy's fast food restaurant in Queens, New York, in the spring of 2000. The same principles of post-traumatic stress disorder that people may experience after surviving devastating floods, earthquakes, tornados, airplane crashes, and bus and car accidents also are experienced by those affected by urban terrorism. The counseling offered helps first to recognize the pattern and symptoms of the disorder, and then to overcome

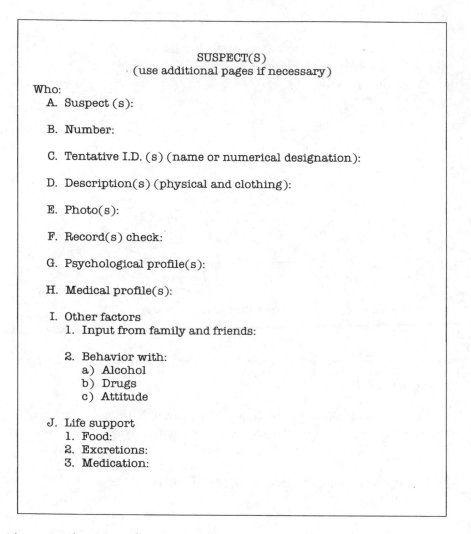

SUSPECT(S)
(use additional pages if necessary)

Who:
  A. Suspect (s):

  B. Number:

  C. Tentative I.D. (s) (name or numerical designation):

  D. Description(s) (physical and clothing):

  E. Photo(s):

  F. Record(s) check:

  G. Psychological profile(s):

  H. Medical profile(s):

  I. Other factors
    1. Input from family and friends:

    2. Behavior with:
      a) Alcohol
      b) Drugs
      c) Attitude

  J. Life support
    1. Food:
    2. Excretions:
    3. Medication:

Figure 9.1 (continued)

the fear, confusion, and the stigma that once was attached to seeking or receiving treatment or help. (See Chapter 12.)

Controlling the Environment

Controlling the environment has two meanings, referring to both the physical environment (light, temperature, noise, the view outside, access, and egress, etc.) and to the atmosphere in which the negotiations are conducted (including things such as initiating communication, controlling the discussion, and regulating the pace of negotiation). Once control of the environment has been established, its manipulation becomes a viable option in the negotiator's tool kit. Raising or lowering the temperature, controlling the amount of light, raising or lowering the amount of outside noise, even odors such as cooking smells or the scent of perfume can be used to influence the situation.

Manipulation of the environment should be done as unobtrusively as possible, in increments that are not readily noticeable. A sudden change could provoke a violent response, because a hostage-taker might interpret the change as an attack. Conversely, a gradual raising of the temperature in the room might be discerned only after a period of time. The perpetrator's reaction, if there is any at all, would likely be in the form of a complaint to the negotiator, who then would be in a position to offer assistance to remedy or at least alleviate the situation in exchange, of course, for some concession by the hostage-taker. Bargaining chips are hard won and must be used judiciously.

There are situations, however, in which manipulating the environment can have negative consequences. There has been concern, for example, that hostage-takers might have police scanners or other equipment obviously requiring a power source. This could be a reason to deprive them of electricity. If this is the decision, however, it must be done in a manner that does not induce panic. There was a situation in 1986 when the deprivation of electricity by Pakistani authorities during the hijacking of Pan Am Flight No. 73 was accomplished in such a manner that it put the hostage-takers in a panic situation, contributing to the loss of hostages' lives in the ensuing gun battle.

One of the most effective instances of environment manipulation took place in West Chester, Pennsylvania where the millionaire heir of the duPont chemical fortune, John duPont shot and killed a former Olympic wrestler who served as a caretaker on his estate. When police responded to the estate, duPont retreated to his mansion and barricaded himself there. It was known that duPont had all kinds of exotic and powerful firearms, including an armored personnel carrier. Any attempt at an assault would be extremely dangerous to officers. The subject was contained and negotiations commenced. The talks went on for two days in rainy and cold weather. The police were even castigated by the media, some saying it was duPont's money and influence that prolonged the negotiations and kept the police from going in after him. However, it was a correct decision on the part of the incident commander not to risk the lives of his officers against heavy weapons just for expediency and possible overtime pay considerations. After fruitless negotiations, it was ascertained that the heating boilers for the main house were located in an outbuilding. Members of the tactical team shut down the boiler and the cold weather soon permeated the house. When the subject, speaking with the negotiator, commented on the cold, the officers told the subject to go to the basement to check it out. The subject stated that the boiler wasn't in the basement but in an outbuilding, something the negotiator knew but kept to himself. The negotiator told duPont that the only way to check was to leave the weapons in the house. He agreed and when he went to the outbuilding unarmed, the tactical team was there to take him into custody without having to fire a shot.

Dynamics of Hostage Negotiation

Negotiations (or even simple two-way discussions) have been broken down into win–lose, lose–win, and various other configurations, depending upon the results of the talks (Figure 9.2). We always have viewed a hostage-negotiating situation as a win–win dialogue, meaning that both parties get something they want out of the situation. This is preferable to a win–lose approach where one party obtains satisfactory results and the other is unhappy, displeased, or possibly humiliated. Avoiding this latter outcome is as important in the area of international terrorism as it is in the field of international diplomacy.

Part of the dynamics of negotiations utilizes a frustration–aggression equation. Frustration is considered a negative factor in life, as in situations in which a specific goal or end cannot be achieved and frustration results. Not that all aspects of frustration are negative, for it is an important part of the learning process and is the driving force behind ambition. If an infant

Words and Phrases

Note: be non-judgmental, encourage taking, and deal with feeling
1.   First, I'd like to get to know you better.
2.   Could you tell me about it?
3.   I would like to hear your side.
4.   Could you share that with me?
5.   I guess that's pretty important to you.
6.   Tell me about.
7.   That's interesting.
8.   I see.
9.   Is that so?
10. Oh.
11. Uh huh.

Figure 9.2 Verbal communication. The exact phrasing of statements by a negotiator to a hostage-taker can be extremely important to avoid misunderstanding and misinterpretations. Nonjudgmental words and phrases are preferred.

had everything he or she could possibly want, there would be little reason for the child to learn how to grip, how to talk, or how to cope by manipulating the people and things in the larger world.

As that child grows and develops, he or she moves from learning how to cry in a certain way to be fed, to learning that something out of reach can be obtained by crawling or standing up. The desire–frustration–solution process continues throughout our lifetimes. However, as we know, at times there may be some things that appear to be attainable but remain just beyond reach. In the frustration–aggression equation, the presumption is that if a person is sufficiently frustrated, this will lead to aggressive behavior, whether it is a big kid taking a toy away from a smaller child or an adult pounding on a countertop looking for service in a store. Most people, however, do not move into aggressive behavior as long as they believe there may be a remedy for the source of their frustration.

In an effort to eliminate frustration from a hostage situation, the negotiator must eliminate the word no from his or her working vocabulary. Rather than saying no or using negatives, replace them with such phrases as "let me see what I can do," "I'll work on it," or "I don't know, let me check that out." Even when the request cannot possibly be granted, such as one for weapons, never use the word no. Were the response to a request no, this could close off the option of problem-solving and force the subject into the aggressive behavior part of the equation. Aggression in these situations can be focused in either of two ways: internalized or externalized. Carried to logical extremes, internalized aggression could result in suicide, externalized aggression to murder. The dynamics are interchangeable; suicide and homicide are two sides of the same coin (Figure 9.3).

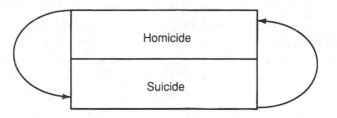

Figure 9.3 Internalized vs. externalized aggressive behavior. Suicide is internalized aggression. Homicide is externalized aggression. Aggression, like love and hate, is a two-sided coin, and it is difficult to predict which type of behavior a perpetrator will exhibit. Sometimes it is both: if homicide does not satisfy, a suicide may ensue.

Persons who could commit homicide could commit suicide and vice versa, as strange as that may sound. Many persons who have committed homicide, when incarcerated, hang themselves in their cells. Experienced homicide detectives, when faced with a list of three or four possible suspects of apparently equal culpability will research whether any of the suspects has a history of suicide attempts or a series of self-destructive incidents such as driving off the side of a road, driving into a wall, and similar one-car accidents.

A Note on Weapons

When gathering information and intelligence, it is important to note that the use of a checklist is important. It permits an orderly gathering of information. It is also helps to know who contributed what. For example, whenever a statement or allegation is made that the subject has a weapon or a device, even if it is not displayed, the assumption must be that this weapon or device does exist and appropriate tactics used to counter it until contradictory information can be verified from the contributor or source, or can be discounted from other sources. It is best to operate on a worse-case scenario basis.

Saying "No"

When we say a negotiator should never say no, this does not mean there are no no-nos in hostage negotiations. There most assuredly are, and here are four of them:

1. No exchange of hostages. No person — not the negotiator, nor the first responding officers who make the initial contact with the hostage-taker, nor any volunteer — should be exchanged for a hostage or otherwise sent into a hostage situation. Even if a hostage slips out undetected, that individual should not be allowed to reenter captivity, regardless of pleas or circumstances. There is no circumstance that would justify such action. First, there is no guarantee that any deal struck with the perpetrator will be honored. Second, any hostage, or all hostages, may be killed. No one has a right to send a person into such a situation. Even a police officer should not be sent in because cops remaining on the outside will lose their objectivity. Just as doctors do not perform operations on members of their own families, police officers can be emotional and may use different criteria and judgment when another officer is involved. Once a person is a hostage, he or she cannot be a negotiator. There will always be a time when the subject will say something like, "You want me to trust you, then you gotta trust me. Take off your gun and come in here like a man and sit down with me." Under

no circumstance should a negotiator be permitted to go inside. This should be distinguished from what is called face-to-face negotiating, as we discuss later. A negotiator must always leave an avenue of escape. Though I am aware of a few instances where negotiators have violated this principle and have succeeded, the luck of that incident may not carry over to all cases. Last, from a strictly pragmatic point of view, allowing a person to enter a hostage situation and become a hostage leaves the police open for vicarious liability court action should that person be killed.

2. No weapons. Do not give the hostage-taker a weapon. The one he has may be bogus or may not work. Even if the weapon has been fired, it may have jammed or there may be no more ammunition. There was a case several years ago where a security guard surrendered his gun, figuring there was no harm since the hostage-taker was already armed. The sad fact was he had only a starter's pistol that fired blanks and was not really armed until he had the security guard's gun. Again, picture the scene in court with you, the police officer, on the witness stand admitting that it was your gun that was used to kill a hostage, that the lawyer's poor, demented client had not even been in possession of an instrument of death when the situation started. Does the negotiator say no when a hostage-taker demands a gun? Of course not, delaying language is used. "I don't know, I'll have to check on that," or "I'll work on it, let me talk to my boss," would be appropriate responses. Never say no and never give a perpetrator a gun.

3. No prisoners released from jail or prison. Once prison doors swing open, this will only encourage others to try the same tactic to free their comrades. Even in hostage-taking situations in prison disturbances, most prisoners know they cannot get out. There are no demands for escape, but rather for better conditions, tastier food, more recreation, longer family visits, etc. They want to save face after taking hostages, so they have to demand something. Have there ever been hostage situations where prisoners have been freed? Not in the United States although it has happened elsewhere. The West Germans were ready to free domestic terrorists in their jails during the hostage incident at the 1972 Munich Olympics. Several years later, Salvadoran President Duarte released some prisoners when his daughter was kidnapped and held hostage by rebels. He ran two risks. First, he could have wound up with a dead daughter and some free anti-Duarte terrorists running around the country. Second, he encouraged others to attempt kidnapping members of his family, even after he moved them to Florida. It is difficult to be objective when your own family

is involved; however, in this case Duarte had a greater responsibility to his people and his country.*

4. No special nuclear materials should leave a facility. Whether it is a weapons facility, a nuclear power plant, or some other source of fissionable material, special nuclear material should never be given to terrorists. The amount involved may not be enough to construct a nuclear weapon, but when combined with dynamite or other conventional explosive, it can make a very hazardous dirty bomb. From the standpoint of the federal government, police may use deadly physical force to protect nuclear material; that is how potentially disastrous the material is regarded.

Another never to remember for hostage negotiators is to never leave yourself without an avenue of escape. Do not position yourself in such a way that if the hostage-taker decides to make a break for it, the hostage negotiator will be unable to head for cover. One other admonition, which is covered in more detail later, is never take the weapon from the hand of a surrendering perpetrator; there may be a change of heart at the last instant. Have the individual leave the weapon inside or send it out. If it is a gun, have him unload it if he intends to give it to a hostage to bring out.

The Art of Negotiation

Negotiations are conducted in order to avoid confrontation, which almost invariably leads to violence. The question of confrontation in a hostage situation is a perplexing one for most law enforcement agencies. No one wants to be responsible for precipitating violence, yet police cannot sit back and watch as the bodies of hostages are being thrown out of a building one by one. The determination must be made, however, whether these killings are made during a panic reaction on the part of the perpetrator, on a deadline, or perhaps for some other reason. When people are killed on a deadline, this evinces the workings of a depraved mind and may indicate that an assault is the necessary alternative, if only to save the lives of the remaining hostages. If, however, a person has been killed during the initial takeover, it might be the product of a panic reaction. Though this death would not be excusable, it could be understandable and not rule out negotiation as the option. Therefore, though it may appear arbitrary, we will make an assumption that anyone killed prior to our establishing contact with the perpetrator is the product of a panic reaction. We could, therefore, negotiate.

---

* Ines Guadalupe Duarte Duran was kidnapped September 10, 1985, and after her father freed 22 political prisoners, was released October 24, 1985.

Courses of Action

Before negotiations begin, or at any time during the negotiations when the talks may get bogged down or the perpetrator's actions indicate a depraved mind, three courses of action remain open to the incident commander, and are discussed at greater length in Chapter 12:

1. Rescue
2. Sharpshooters
3. Chemical agents

Rescue. The Rand Corporation conducted a study of hostage situations throughout the world. One of its findings was that out of a thousand hostages killed in various incidents more than 10% were killed during rescue attempts. That is a high rate and underscores the need for serious consideration before the decision is made to go in on a rescue. In considering a rescue, the CID triad (communications, intelligence, and discipline of firepower), as discussed in Chapter 4, comes into play. It must be determined beforehand how many perpetrators there are, what kind of weaponry they have, their exact locations inside the building, who they are, and what they look like (beyond description of their clothing) in addition to how many hostages there are (Figure 9.4). Useful, and absolutely essential, is information on whether or not there are any booby traps. Lacking such intelligence, the possibility of booby traps must always be considered.

Rescue attempts present special problems. In spite of lessons learned earlier, mistakes are made in assault attempts to recover hostages. In 1986 in Malta, Egyptian commandos stormed an Egyptian airliner that had been hijacked by Palestinian terrorists. In the rescue attempt, 58 hostages died during the assault and only 12 of them, it was later determined, had been killed by the terrorist hijackers from the Palestinian Liberation Organization (PLO). The classic hostage rescue case, although it does not involve terrorists, occurred at Attica State Prison in upstate New York in 1971. In that situation, 11 hostages died, one as a result of injuries sustained during the takeover by inmates. The other 10 died several days later during a direct assault by various law enforcement agencies — national guardsmen, state troopers, corrections officers, and police from local municipalities. The cause of death was gunshot wounds; however, it was later learned that the inmates who were holding the hostages had no firearms. A prudent person would have to assume that the would-be rescuers brought about the deaths of the hostages. The lengthy civil litigation involving the Attica inmates was not completed until the summer of 2000. The corrections officers and their families had been urged to settle their lawsuit shortly after the incident, and it has been said by some critics that they were forced into settling for the good of the agency.

Hostage No._____

PHOTO
(Polaroid)

Name _____
Verified by_____How_____
Address _____
Verified by _____

DESCRIPTION (circle)
Male / Female   W/B/H/O/Other_____
Age (5 year brackets)_____D.O.B._____
Height_____Weight_____Build_____
Clothing_____
_____
_____

Participation (customer, relative) etc._____
_____

Causation_____
_____

Injuries_____

Occupation_____

Psychological profile_____
_____
_____

Medical profile _____
_____
_____

Other_____
_____

BEHAVIOR
Alcohol_____
Drugs_____
Attitude_____

LIFE SUPPORT
Food_____
Excrements_____
Medication _____

Figure 9.4 Biographical sketches. Forms should be created for recording intelligence about both hostages and their captors. It is important that two formats — one horizontal, one vertical — are used to help maintain the distinction between suspects and victims.

Suspect No. _____

Name (if known) _____
Verified (Who) _____ How _____
Address _____
Verified (Who) _____ How _____
Record check: Neg./Positive _____ Verified _____
Major offenses _____
Occupation _____ Role _____
Organization (if appropriate) _____
Psychological profile _____

Medical profile _____

Tale or incident _____

BEHAVIOR
Alcohol _____
Drugs _____
Attitude _____

LIFE SUPPORT
Food _____
Excretions _____
Medication _____
Others: _____

PHOTO
(Polaroid)

DESCRIPTION (circle)
Male/Female   W/B/O/H/Other _____
Age _____ DOB _____ (if known)
(5 year group, 30-39 if unknown)
Height _____ Weight _____ Build _____
Clothing _____
_____
Weapon _____
_____

Figure 9.4 (continued)

The Surrender and Suicide Ritual

For the perpetrator of a hostage situation, there are four perceived options:

1. Escape
2. Surrender
3. Suicide
4. Homicide

For two of these options, a subject will go through a ritual. The ritual preparations for both suicide and surrender are similar and may be difficult to differentiate. Many hostage-takers feel they will be killed when they come out. No matter what crime or action may have created the hostage incident, most perpetrators perceive that if and when they come out, they will be killed, shot, or beaten. Violent police/action television shows and movies have helped create such an image in the minds of emotionally charged persons who when they become hostage-takers feel they will be punished, and fantasize about how this punishment will be administered.

Although many hostage-takers expect punishment, and even death, they want to look good. They know family and friends will be there; the media, too. So as part of the ritual, they will primp and preen, or at least make themselves look presentable. The perpetrator is saying, "It's all over now; the end is near." The only question is whether the end will bring surrender or suicide. The police don't know. The negotiator can only guess. The perpetrator himself may be uncertain up to the last second.

The negotiator must be aware of his own body language. This helps determine how the individual will come out. He has to know that the negotiator is in control, so it is incumbent upon the negotiator not to look nervous, confused, or disorganized.

In setting the stage for a surrender, the word surrender should not be used, but instead phrases such as coming out, or meeting half way are employed. The negotiator should soothe the subject, telling him to take his time, explaining to him what to expect (there will be a few other officers with me, etc.), painting a verbal picture that conveys the sense that the negotiator will protect the perpetrator from any harm.

Even though the negotiator will meet the subject half way, under no circumstances should the negotiator place himself or herself in the position of not having immediate cover available. Care should be given in coordinating the apprehension with the tactical team. By giving the subject direction, he can come out without adding any danger to the apprehension team. This will also obviate the need to apply force. We have seen where the subject came to the door, unloaded his gun, and surrendered his weapons. He expected to be interviewed by the media. Instead, the subject was thrown to the ground, three or four officers piled on top and forcibly handcuffed him. If they had told him to turn around and place his hands out, the same control of the subject could have been accomplished. The importance of tactical discipline in the final apprehension was demonstrated when a man who had been holding his wife and child hostage decided to surrender to police. He said he had been influenced by the careful apprehension of his brother during another hostage situation four states away three weeks earlier.

Thought Interruption

Although suicide and surrender rituals may appear similar, one critical indication of a suicide is the disposing of worldly possessions. When this occurs, a person contemplating suicide can sometimes be dissuaded.

An incident illustrating the suicide ritual took place in the finished basement of a suburban home. The subject had stabbed a man in the chest and, at the approach of responding police, took hostage his common-law wife's 6-year-old son and the wounded man's 20-year-old girlfriend. Negotiators progressed to the point where the mechanics of surrender were being worked out. Upon hearing his mother's voice at the scene, the hostage-taker requested that the negotiator (who was now negotiating face-to-face, blocked by furniture, since the weapon involved was not a firearm) pass along his money to his mother. This was followed by the perpetrator's jewelry and keys, as he explained he would have no need for them in jail. Before emerging, the subject washed his hands and face and put on a clean shirt. He then walked with the young boy toward the darkened rear of the basement. A few moments later, the child returned carrying a folded knife: the weapon with which he had been held captive. Responding to the beckoning police negotiator, the lad explained that the perpetrator was fixing a lamp. Within seconds, there was a large bright blue flash from the darkened rear of the basement. This was followed by another flash and the sound of a body crumpling to the floor.

The negotiator and backup tactical team entered the area and found the subject grasping two hot wires of a dissembled lamp. The quick disengagement of the lamp's plug and application of CPR techniques revived the subject.

There was another case in which a man was holding his infant child hostage on the roof of a building. After a long and tiring confrontation with the police, the man leaned over the edge of the roof and began emptying his pockets, indicating who should get his money, his keys, jewelry he was wearing, etc. Disposing of his worldly goods was a catharsis of sorts. Although it was the middle of summer, the negotiator asked if he thought it was going to snow. The man stood upright and asked the negotiator, "Snow? Are you crazy?" The officer quickly corrected himself and asked about rain. The man's thought pattern had been broken. Suicide was no longer foremost in his mind. Eventually he gave up the baby unharmed and surrendered.

Never Take a Weapon from the Hand of a Surrendering Perpetrator

No matter how sincere or well-intentioned a surrendering hostage-taker may seem, *never* take a weapon from his or her hand. It may all be a trick, or there could be a last-minute change of heart. Even if the weapon is offered handle-side toward you, it could be swung around swiftly in one last violent act. It may even be that the perpetrator wants to commit suicide, but cannot pull the trigger. Death can usually be assured by killing a police officer out in full view of all the tactical people with their guns drawn. The appropriate course of action is to have the perpetrator throw the gun out, give it to a hostage (unloaded to prevent any further confrontation), or leave the weapon inside. Throwing the weapon out of a window would be the last resort because certain weapons can fire and may injure someone accidentally. Remember, even if a weapon is recovered, use caution because there could be more weapons available to the perpetrator.

Special Qualifications

Occasionally, there may be demands to match the race or sex of the negotiator and hostage-taker. There is no reason to match black negotiators to a black perpetrator or white to white. The police must control the situation and use the best negotiator available. Language, training, and ability are the criteria. Communication is the key. The ability to take criticism, even ridicule, is important, because hostage-takers will often test a negotiator by hurling invectives. A negotiator cannot be thin-skinned, for a perpetrator will do everything he can to test the negotiator, just to see who is in control. The hostage-takers are trying to determine if the negotiator really cares about them.

Women police officers have often been successful negotiators, especially in instances involving young girls. It has been observed, however, that the insults male perpetrators direct toward female negotiators often become explicitly sexual. An officer might say, "I'm here to help you." The perpetrator might respond by saying the only way she could help was to have sex with him.

There are a number of other factors to consider when designating a negotiator, such as the cultural background of the hostage-taker. It may be unthinkable for him to surrender to a woman. On the other hand, a female negotiator might have an advantage because the perpetrator may think he is pleasing his mommy or doing the woman a favor, that he is being charming by surrendering.

There are no hard and fast rules on matching a negotiator with a particular situation. This is a commander's decision. The perpetrator will eventually have to talk to whomever is the negotiator, or he speaks to no one. As hard-nosed as that might sound, remember that the perpetrator initiated the hostage-taking in order to get an audience and announce his message. Eventually, he will speak to whomever is available.

Post-Incident

Post-Blast Environment

Getting Back to Normal

In earlier chapters, the various components of pre-incident planning relative to a bombing attack were discussed. In the following pages we expand upon the subject as it relates to the consequence phase of a bomb attack. As indicated before, even the best defense can be penetrated by a determined foe. The manner of attack, and its resulting severity, as well as how sufficiently the target is prepared to meet the challenge will determine how quickly a building, worksite, or other location will be able to return to normal operations. In the public safety arena, the response will be only as good as the trained personnel responding to the incident and the degree of pre-incident liaison planning with the private sector.

The Incident

A bomb attack involving an improvised explosive device can occur at any time, day or night. The blast may happen outside or inside and in any type of weather. The damage caused by the device, even with a small amount of explosive used, can be devastating. Even if a location was not the intended target, collateral damage caused by the blast can be quite substantial. In the Oklahoma City bombing over a hundred businesses sustained damage in some shape or form. Even if a facility is spared physical damage, the infrastructure of the surrounding area, e.g., public utilities, may not be functioning and travel for the public so restricted that employees cannot get to the workplace (Figures 10.1 and 10.2).

First Responder

The most important individual in any emergency situation is the first responder. Whether the first responders are private security, concerned civilians, or trained emergency people, assisting the injured is the paramount concern. Although injuries may be extremely severe, victims must be removed from the immediate area to provide proper medical care. Since blasts caused by explosive devices vary in type and the area of destruction affected, a general rule to follow is that the threat of fire or secondary explosions is an immediate

Figure 10.1 Rescue and evidence recovery operations at the Murrah Federal Building in Oklahoma City. (Courtesy of F. Guerra.)

Figure 10.2 Close-up of the type of destruction of the Murrah Federal Building that challenged both the rescuer and investigator. (Courtesy of F. Guerra.)

concern. Exposed electrical wires, ruptured gas lines, and similar hazards can precipitate further damage and injuries. There have been occasions when a secondary improvised device has been secreted a short distance from where the original bomb attack was carried out. A search for secondary explosive devices should be made as soon as the injured are removed from the area.

Where there is sufficient personnel on the scene, the search can be conducted simultaneously. Secondary devices are generally placed and timed to explode only a short distance away, thus targeting the responding emergency personnel.

The site of any bombing is handled like any other crime scene and appropriate procedures should be followed. There are basic investigatory steps to be taken in dealing with any crime scene from which physical evidence can be collected. It is extremely important that the crime scene be safeguarded against all unauthorized entry, because in any explosion the evidence is likely to be small and fragmented. Evidence in this state can be very easily mistaken to the untrained eye for unimportant refuse and discarded in a rush to clean up the site.

To properly safeguard the scene, it must be properly defined. This may be a very large area, such as in Oklahoma City, making it very difficult initially to control. In this case, the rescue effort lasted several days, making evidence recovery a more complex task. In smaller explosions the task is simplified. The first step is to locate the spot where the device actually detonated; this is called the seat of the explosion and should be pinpointed exactly. From there, all fragments usually radiate in a 360° circle, depending on the physical location of the device, e.g., if it is out in the open or in a concealed area. The placement of the device will dictate the fragmentation pattern, i.e., the path the majority of fragmentation followed. The crime scene proper should include the area where the furthest piece of physical evidence could be found. The area comprising half again that distance should be marked and designated as a restricted area for only those on official or legitimate business. Safeguarding the crime scene may under certain circumstances be difficult to control, such as cases of large explosions, like Oklahoma City, where the devastation covered a wide area and huge throngs of people were drawn to the scene. In high profile cases, a heavy media presence can be expected and will add another dimension to an already chaotic scene.

Investigative Phase

Overview

The investigation of the post-blast or consequence phase of the incident should be conducted only by qualified investigators. If a large scene is being processed, searchers at minimum should be supervised by trained bomb scene investigators. In crime scenes involving the more common crimes, i.e., burglary, robbery, and homicide, physical evidence is usually readily discernible and may be developed through traditional methods of investigation. Although post-blast investigations make use of these techniques, much of the development of physical evidence requires a well-trained eye.

Figure 10.3 The water-filled bomb crater in front of the troop barracks, Khobare Towers. The building was virtually destroyed by a large vehicle-borne IED. (Courtesy of F. Guerra.)

Once the crime scene is secured and defined, the search for physical evidence may begin. As in all crime scene investigations, the recording process is very important and must be accomplished by using photographs, including video, sketches, and diagrams, as well as written reports. Once this has been completed, a preliminary search can begin.

Preliminary Search

Because after a bombing the physical appearance and characteristics of the scene have been drastically changed, it is important to gain as much information as possible about the pre-blast configuration of the location. This can be gotten through photos, floor plans, and technical drawings provided by the building owner or management company. Another good source of this information might be the architects who designed the building. Building engineers and maintenance staff should be on hand to help identify items in order to establish whether they are common to the area.

After establishing the search area, a search team or teams should be organized and the role of each member defined. The physical examination of a bomb scene should be undertaken only by trained bomb technicians and crime scene investigators. As indicated, it is important that the scene be properly recorded for a number of reasons, but it is most important to recreate the crime scene for further investigation. Remember, any charting should be accompanied by photographic images. (See Figures 10.3 and 10.4.)

Figure 10.4 The destructive force that was generated by the blast virtually destroyed the building. (Courtesy of F. Guerra.)

Seat of the Explosion

The "seat of the explosion" is the precise spot that the explosive device was placed and detonated (Figure 10.5). In theory, all the damage and debris will radiate from that point outward in all directions, including up and down. In reality, because explosive force is directive, it radiates at a 90° angle from the surface of the explosive. There are certain physical manifestations that cause the explosive force to follow the path of least resistance, which may dictate the pattern of fragmentation after an explosion.

The seat may or may not be located easily, and the location will be dictated by a number of factors:

1. The size and type of explosives used in the explosive device will determine the amount of destruction to the target.
2. If the target is a vehicle, aircraft, or ship and is totally destroyed, it must reassembled. This is especially difficult in dealing with aircraft bombings, such as Pan Am flight 103, popularly referred to as the Lockerbie bombing, where fragments were scattered over hundreds of square miles.
3. If the explosive device detonated inside a building or similar structure, a fair amount of material must be removed in order to locate the seat.

Figure 10.5 Seat of an explosion. The cratering effect created by a blast is called the seat of the explosion. In this instance, this seat was created by a high-order detonation placed against a building foundation.

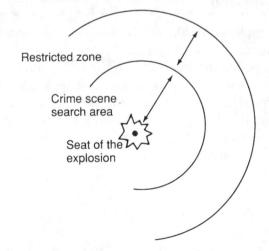

Figure 10.6 Crime scene. In a post-blast investigation, the entire area needing to be searched for bomb fragments is part of the crime scene and should be protected by a buffer zone around the perimeter to which access is tightly controlled.

In most cases, the experienced bomb scene investigator can get a feel of what occurred within a short time at the scene. The general area of where the device detonated is first located and will then become the focal and initiating point of the investigation. (See Figures 10.6–10.9.)

Figure 10.7 Overall photo of the damage to basement area of the World Trade Center. (Courtesy of the author's collection.)

Figure 10.8 Trade Center damage on a closer scale. (Courtesy of F. Guerra.)

Gathering Physical Evidence

When examining the scene of a bombing, one can expect to gather a huge amount of physical evidence for examination (Figure 10.10). Much of this evidence will fall into the category of general debris, while other material will

Figure 10.9 Trade Center damage on a ramp to the lower garage area. (Courtesy of F. Guerra.)

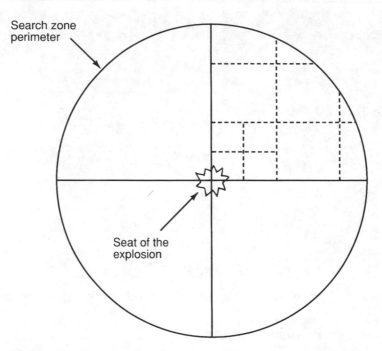

Figure 10.10 Post-blast search. The area needing to be searched following an explosion should be defined first by a perimeter, then divided into small segments which can be labeled in order to record each location where fragments are found.

have to be retained. Bigger items, such as masonry wall debris, ceiling tiles, wallboard, and lighting fixtures may have to be cleared first to get to the seat of the explosion. All evidence that is recovered at the scene should be classified as either "known items" or "unknown items". One of the more challenging aspects of the bomb-scene investigation is that no fragment or piece of evidence can be discarded automatically, because components in an improvised explosive device are limited only by the imagination of the bomb maker. In addition, items that may seem inconsequential or appear innocuous at the time of recovery may in fact be important evidence once all the pieces are put into place and fitted together. Often it is not easy to identify items or their uses because they may be greatly distorted or deformed due the force of the explosive.

Examining Fragments

The seat of the explosion and the immediate area surrounding it, once again depending upon the size and type of the explosive device, will usually yield the most productive evidence. Evidence recovered from this area is critical because chemical testing for explosive residue is best accomplished from fresh, uncontaminated pieces. Trace residue is not only found on recovered bomb components, but also from soil and masonry fragments as well. Such evidence should be placed in proper evidence containers and submitted to a certified crime laboratory. In the majority of cases, this type of residue is processed at either a Federal Bureau of Investigation or Alcohol, Tobacco and Firearms facility.

The search and investigation of a bomb scene are similar to an archaeological dig in that an attempt is being made to reconstruct a scene that has been greatly altered. For archaeologists, the alteration comes from time, natural forces, and perhaps disturbances by animals and humans. For the bomb-scene investigator, an explosive force of an undetermined magnitude altered the evidence. In both instances, the only solution is slow, methodical examination of every scrap of evidence, distinguishing the known from the unknown, the recognizable from the indeterminate, and segregating what could have been part of an explosive device from what is probably not.

Many fragments will initially be difficult to identify, and many will be suspect. Gears, wire, electrical tape, and similar fragments could easily come from technical and mechanical equipment generic to the area or be part of the explosive device. Eliminating this type of fragment as part of the explosive device could be accomplished by utilizing site engineers or other specialists familiar with area's equipment. This also applies to fragments of paper boxes, canvas tote bags, and other items able to secret an explosive device. In most cases, elimination or identification of fragmented wire, switches, etc. can be best accomplished with a manufacturer's assistance.

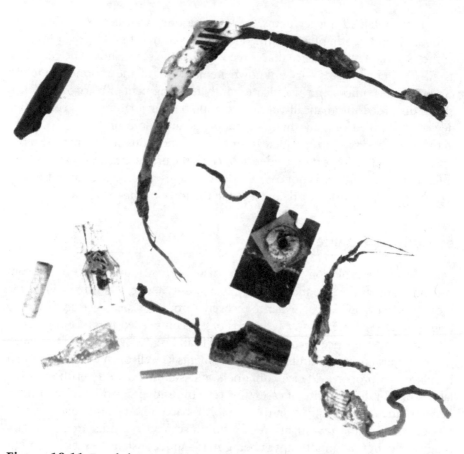

Figure 10.11 Bomb fragments. Typical fragments from an improvised explosive device that produced a low-order blast, in this case injuring one of the authors.

The investigation of vehicle bombs proceeds in the same fashion, identifying bomb components vs. those of the vehicle itself. Vehicle identification and type are extremely important because the recovery of vehicle identification numbers on key parts, ornaments that identify auto make, and other items will assist in suspect development (Figure 10.11).

Evidence Recovery

Again, the recovery of evidence is a slow and demanding activity. To be successful it takes a professional eye and a lot of luck. Once the large and obviously identifiable debris has been removed, the smaller debris around the seat can be examined. The best tried and true method is to sift the remaining debris through a variety of different sized screens until only a granular substance remains.

Figure 10.11 (continued)

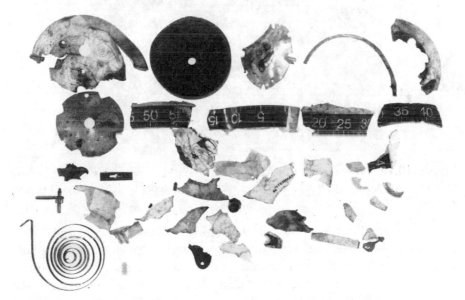

Figure 10.11 (continued)

Screens can be readily and cheaply made with 2 × 4 inch lumber constructed into rectangular boxes approximately 2 × 4 feet with wire mesh screening affixed to one side. Ideally, the sifting should begin with 1-inch grids, then move down to ¹/₂ inch and subsequently to ¹/₄ inch or finer depending on the situation. As a load of debris is worked through the sifting

Figure 10.12 Typical sifting operations at the scene of post-blast scene. Debris is being worked through a fine sifting screen into receptacle below. (Courtesy of F. Guerra.)

screen, the smaller pieces will fall through into a holding container. After examining the items that remain in the sifting screen and removing any suspected fragmentation, the remaining debris can be placed in containers and stored in a secure location. The debris that fell through the screen then will be processed through the smaller grid screens and the process repeated.

As the sifting proceeds, fragments that may be of investigative value should be closely examined, tentatively identified, cataloged, and properly packaged. Items that do not appear to be part of the explosive device should be retained in a separate and secure area in the event that future examination is required. Remember, none of the debris should be discarded until the physical examination is concluded without reservation. In addition, nothing should be discarded without appropriate prosecutorial permission.

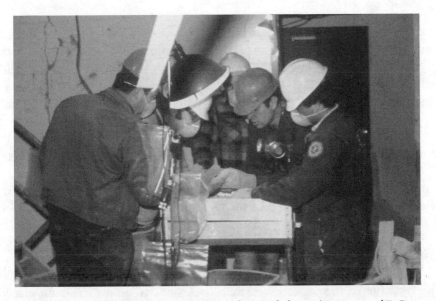

Figure 10.13 Closer view of the operations depicted above. (Courtesy of F. Guerra.)

It may take several rounds of sifting to assure that all meaningful pieces of the evidence have been recovered. In many cases, the investigation will be under pressure to complete an onsite investigation so that restoration of the target area can begin. In these cases, it may be required to move the recovered debris to another area where what may be a lengthy investigation can continue without disruption. However, the operation should not be moved until a thorough preliminary examination of the scene is completed and recorded.

There are certain advantages that a change of location may give to the investigator:

1. It allows the debris search to be completed without pressure to release the crime scene to the owners or operators.
2. It can provide sufficient space for the investigators to spread out the physical evidence for a more detailed examination.
3. It can protect debris from the elements and provide a secure location for the temporary storage of possible evidence.
4. It will allow the scene to be processed without external disruption from public or media scrutiny.

In almost all cases where prolonged sifting and search operations are going on, there is always the danger that the investigators will tire or become bored and possibly overlook important pieces of evidence. It is for this reason that searchers should be rotated in and out of the area if sufficient personnel are available. (See Figures 10.12 and 10.13.)

Physical Evidence

The amount of evidence and its relative importance is predicated upon the severity of the explosion and the secondary thermal effect. As a general rule, the larger the device, the smaller the fragments and the greater the area in which trace evidence will be distributed. When an explosion results in a fire, much of the nonmetallic evidence may be destroyed and the metallic evidence even more distorted. When searching for physical evidence, it should be remembered that the device's degree of complexity is strictly limited by the ingenuity of the bomb maker, but the fact is that most bombs are constructed in a fairly simple manner. Physical or trace evidence recovered from the scene of a bombing can be grouped into the three general categories discussed below (Figures 10.14, 10.15, and 10.16).

Container

The container is the package in which the explosive device has been placed and concealed and may include virtually any item.

Smaller devices can be secreted in common containers such as attaché cases, small pieces of luggage, shopping bags, and travel bags. Latches, catches, hinges, inner and outer case coverings from these containers, although severely fragmented and distorted, may be readily found by the trained investigator. In cases where pipe bombs are used, the size of the

Figure 10.14 Typical evidence recovered from a pipe bomb that was exploded with a low-explosive filler. (Courtesy of the author's collection.)

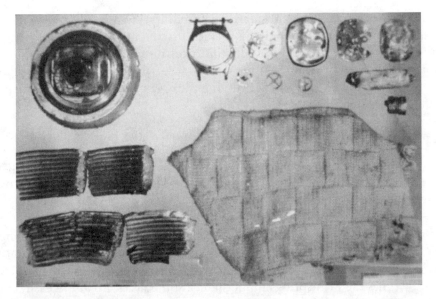

Figure 10.15 Pipe bomb evidence showing end-caps, cloth used to tamp powder into pipe. Lower portion of photo shows fragments of wristwatch used as a time delay. (Courtesy of the author's collection.)

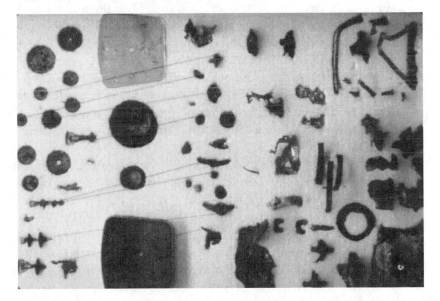

Figure 10.16 Fragments from a wind-up alarm clock used as a time delay in an improvised explosive device. (Courtesy of the author's collection.)

fragments will depend upon what explosives were used in making the bomb. The more powerful the explosives, the smaller the fragmentation. The body of the bomb can be plastic, copper tubing, or galvanized pipe.

Vehicles can also be considered a container in cases of large vehicle-delivered devices. Important items include ornaments, manufacturer's logo, and most significantly vehicle identification numbers. In addition to the main VIN number located on the dashboard, a number of major component parts are stamped with identifying numbers that will assist in tracing vehicle ownership.

Firing Systems

Physical evidence of the firing system will generally include fragmented mechanical or electronic timer-power units (TPU). Common items recovered in sifting operations include

1. Even in this electronic age, the most common timers used in bombings are small clocks, pocket watches, or kitchen timers. These mechanical timers will produce gears, and in older pieces, mainsprings. Many times the mainsprings in mechanical timepieces are found easily due to their flexibility and resiliency.
2. In addition to mechanical timers, an electrical power source is usually incorporated into the IED, with a storage battery the most common source of power. These batteries can range from the bulky type used in motorcycles to those small enough for use in hearing aids or musical greeting cards. Fragments commonly recovered are the outer casings, carbon interiors, and connector studs or plugs. A smaller device, or one utilizing low-explosive main charges, may leave substantial portions of the battery. In many cases, fragmented outer casings will be located in sufficient quantity to establish identity. Commonly used batteries are 9-volt transistors, A series, C or D cell, lantern, or similar items.
3. Time delay can also be accomplished in a nonmechanical manner, through the use of a commercial safety fuse, fast-burning common firework fuse, or an improvised burning fuse. Nonmechanical time delays have been used in several recent major terrorist bombings. The fuse must be of sufficient length to allow the bomber to escape unhurt, and it is not uncommon to have a significant portion thrown free of the blast site. In addition to the physical remnants of the fuse, there may be scorch and burn marks located in and around the seat. Fuse may also be used to ignite low explosive filler. In small explosions, firework fuse may have been used with traces of ash found around the scene.
4. The lack of any mechanical or burning fuse residue may indicate the use of a chemical delay element. This may result in the deposition of chemical trace material at the seat of the explosion, particularly when an incendiary type device is used. There are instances when

military-type chemical delay fuses may be encountered. In this case, metal tube fragments may be recovered. In most cases, however, the recovery of chemical delay fusing systems is difficult.

5. One of the more difficult portions of the explosive device to find is the actual detonator, particularly if a large quantity of high explosives was used. Fragments recovered from the scene may be from the outer shell and, if electrical caps are used, include the rubber waterproof grommet and pieces of the cap's leg wires. Locating and identifying portions of the leg wires can be vital, since manufacturers utilize color-coded systems for identification. In addition, crimps used to hold the waterproofing grommet and wires in place are identified by virtue of manufacturers' different designs. In nonelectrical systems, the blasting cap fragments are almost impossible to recover, unless the explosive functioned in a low order manner. As indicated, fusing fragments in nonelectric firings may be recovered easily, more so than electric leg wires. Blasting caps are not the only types of initiators that may be used in an IED, especially if a low-explosive main charge is used. Common initiators employed in these systems are electric bridge wires, photo flash bulbs, or just the spit of flame from a length of fuse.

6. The recovery of evidence at the scene of a bombing may indicate that booster charges may have been used to enhance the power of the main charge. These boosters may include volatile materials such as propane (added by attaching portable tanks to the device).

Equipment

Equipment that should be on hand when conducting a bomb scene investigation or brought to the scene by prior arrangements includes portable lighting, tripods, or other stands on which to mount lights, because electricity to a bombed building or area frequently is cutoff or electrical fixtures may have been destroyed in the blast. Handheld lighting is a must, along with extra batteries. A portable generator along with temporary string lighting would be best of all.

Prior to beginning or early on in the search, floor plans, electrical diagrams, furniture floor plans, HVAC system diagrams, and even recent photographs of the target should be obtained. These are necessary to reconstruct the blast scene and to identify physical evidence.

Containers of various sizes, from 55-gallon drums and large boxes for temporarily discarded debris, down to airtight canisters for transporting and storage of evidence are needed. In addition, a variety of plastic and paper bags should also be available for evidence retention. Personal safety items should include hard hats, work gloves, safety glasses, dust masks, and jumpsuits with high visibility markings.

Group area safety items such as first-aid kits, brightly colored and high-visibility tape for defining restricted areas, fire extinguishers, rope of various lengths and sizes, and large plastic or canvas tarpaulins for temporary cover or for protecting portions of the crime scene from contaminating factors are necessary. Hand tools such as screwdrivers, pliers, hammers, wood saws, adjustable wrenches, pry bars, shovels, rakes, pre-built sifting screens, wheelbarrows, and sawhorses on which to hold sifting screens are needed.

Post-Blast Investigation Process

The investigation will lie initially at the feet of the first responding law enforcement agency. The first step is to determine whether or not the explosion was caused by a bomb or accidental causes. Once it is decided that an explosive device caused the explosion, the investigation can remain a local level or fall to federal jurisdiction.

If it is a suspected terrorist attack, the Federal Bureau of Investigation will assume the lead agency role. The Explosive Unit – Bomb Data Center provides onsite explosives-related technical support in crisis situations to federal, state, local, and international law enforcement agencies. This unit responded and directed the processing of the crime scene and examination of the forensic evidence from the Oklahoma City bombing, the Unabomber bombings, the World Trade Center bombing, as well as a number of other high-profile terrorist attacks. In a nonterrorist situation the Bureau of Alcohol, Tobacco and Firearms will point the investigation. If the mails are involved in the delivery of any explosive device, the U.S. Postal Inspectors office will assist in the investigation. It should be noted that most bombings in the United States are nonterrorist related.

Case Studies

The following are some examples of major bombings that have occurred in the past several years and brief descriptions of the difficulties with which bomb investigators had to contend.

Pan Am-103 Bombing — December 21, 1988

The bombing of Pan Am Flight 103 over Lockerbie, Scotland, was a crime scene of the most challenging proportions. After taking off from Heathrow Airport, as the plane reached an altitude of 31,000 feet a bomb exploded, strewing debris over 50 square miles, and killing 259 people on the plane and 11 on the ground. The main wreckage plowed a 155-feet-long furrow in the ground, with the nose of the aircraft landing almost four miles from Lockerbie.

Because the aircraft was an American carrier and 189 people onboard were Americans, the United States offered any assistance that might be required to solve the bombing. In the end, personnel from the United Kingdom, the United States, France, and Canada participated in the investigation. The scope of the case was enormous: more than 15,000 people were interviewed and somewhere around 180,000 pieces of evidence were examined. A break in the case occurred when a man discovered a T-shirt that had a piece of timer attached to it. Along with other evidence recovered, the investigative team was able to ascertain that a bomb using Semtex explosives was detonated by means of a timer. The improvised explosive device was secreted in a Toshiba radio-cassette player inside a brown Samsonite suitcase. A high-ranking Libyan military officer was convicted of being involved in the bombing during a trial that ended early in 2001.

As of this writing two suspects from Libya are on trial at the International Court in the Hague.

World Trade Center — February 26, 1993

Early on a Friday morning, a bomb blast ripped through the parking garage of the landmark World Trade Center killing six people, injuring as many as 700, and setting off a national terrorist alert. The explosion ripped through three levels in the parking garage and started a fire that sent smoke spiraling through the twin 110-story towers of the complex. Even though the amount of damage was massive, a key piece of evidence was quickly recovered. In the world of the bomb investigator, it was an example of getting lucky early. NYPD Bomb Squad detectives quickly were able to retrieve a portion of the delivery vehicle containing a key identification number that allowed rapid tracing of the vehicle. This break, coupled with the fact that those who carried out the bombing were not really the sharpest, allowed for a quick closing of the case. This massive investigation involved thousands of pieces of evidence that required examination and lab analysis. The investigation indicated that a van containing approximately 1200 pounds of improvised fertilizer-and-fuel-oil explosives was detonated using a simple time fuse.

Oklahoma City — April 19, 1995

At 9:02 a.m. a massive truck with an improvised explosive device detonated in front of the Alfred P. Murrah Federal Building in Oklahoma City. This bomb attack, the worst act of terrorism in U.S. history, was made against a target in a location that least expected it. The massive explosion caused a collapse of a majority of the building, and killed 168 people including 19 children. The detonation of the Ryder truck used to transport the estimated 4000-pound explosive device blew out the support columns of the nine-story building to collapse almost half the building. The crater in the street measured 30 feet long, 8 feet wide, and 3 feet deep. Local law enforcement and public safety officials were totally unprepared to handle such a devastating bombing. In reality, not very many communities would be able to deal with the massive destruction wrought by the event. The problem faced by the local government was tremendous.

Initial Response

1. Even though there was a massive explosion, there was no fire at the primary target location, but surrounding autos in parking lots were ignited. These fires emitted heavy smoke and made initial medical response difficult.
2. Another difficulty was bringing emergency vehicles close to the scene. The streets were clogged not only with responding emergency vehicles, but private cars of responding emergency personnel also quickly overwhelmed the area.
3. Although there were massive casualties, a public call for medical personnel brought such a response that there was almost one doctor for each victim.
4. The massive influx of emergency and specialized investigators from throughout the United States created a massive logistical nightmare. These individuals had to be fed, housed, and equipped for a prolonged investigation. In the days following the attack, search and rescue and investigative teams came from well over a dozen cities. During the investigation, the Red Cross and Salvation Army provided 24-hour service to support the operation.

The Investigation

1. The size of the crime scene was so massive that it required hundreds of police officers just to secure the scene. Eventually, the perimeter was expanded to include a 20-square-block area.
2. The FBI was charged with the criminal investigation, but the Oklahoma City Fire Department retained responsibility for the search and rescue effort. The recovery of physical evidence was a massive and complicated undertaking. Collateral damage caused by the explosion was extreme. Many buildings within 12 square blocks were severely damaged and in some cases collapsed.
3. Prior to processing the physical evidence, digging and shoring up of large portions of the building were required. There was also concern that asbestos and other hazardous materials, in addition the biohazards

resulting from the body fluids of casualties, were a threat to the responders. To deal with this particular problem a team from the Center for Disease Control was dispatched from Atlanta.

TWA Flight 800 — July 17, 1996

The destruction of TWA Flight 800 presented a unique challenge to crime scene investigators. The violent and immediate destruction of the aircraft had all the earmarks of a bomb attack against the aircraft. As any trained investigator knows, you build a crime scene around a theory, but you build your theory around the results of examining physical evidence. The media and public thought it was a foregone conclusion that a terrorist caused the tragedy. The problems of evidence recovery proved to be a challenge. The debris field was spread over a wide area of ocean, with debris being washed up on shore. In order to plot the field, the NOAA hydrographic survey vessel ship *Rude* scanned the ocean floor and found the primary wreckage fields of the aircraft, enabling Navy divers to recover crash victims and the flight recorders quickly. It took months of painstaking effort to recreate the aircraft before investigators were able to determine that an accidental center fuel tank explosion brought the aircraft down, although the theory of a missile take-down is still in play.

Hostage/Kidnapping Aftermath

11

The Dangers Involved

Kidnapping victims, as we have seen, are in grave danger primarily because their physical whereabouts and their captors are unknown, and the victims are usually the only ones who can identify their abductors. In addition to the physical danger, there is also a mental health threat. To this extent, there is a common threat to the victims of both kidnapping and a prolonged hostage incident. A kidnapping can evolve into a hostage situation should the police track down and confront the kidnappers, as happened in the Tiede Herrema case in Ireland.

On October 3, 1975, Dutch industrialist Tiede Herrema was kidnapped near the Forenka Steel Cord Factory in County Limerick. He was seized by former members of the Provisional wing of the Irish Republican Army, Edward Gallagher and Marian Coyle. The kidnappers demanded that the Forenka plant be closed and that the Irish government release three imprisoned IRA members. The steel cord factory was closed by its Dutch parent corporation, but the Irish government did not release any prisoners and refused to negotiate with the kidnappers.

Investigators eventually located the hideout where Gallagher and Coyle were holding Herrema, and on October 21, armed troops smashed in the front door. The kidnappers, however, had taken their quarry and retreated to the upper floor of the house where they were able to barricade themselves. A standoff ensued and the kidnapping became a hostage situation. Negotiations were conducted by a ranking police officer. During the course of the incident, food and changes of clothing were provided as part of the successful negotiations. Herrema was released on November 7. Although the Herrema kidnapping ended satisfactorily, sometimes the psychological states of both perpetrators and captives can frustrate police attempts to peacefully resolve such confrontations. Knowledge of what goes through peoples' minds in these instances can prepare authorities for the appropriate course of action.

The Immediate Reaction of Victims

The first reaction of most people when a kidnapping, hijacking, or hostage-taking occurs is one of disbelief; what is happening before their eyes is not really taking place. Soon enough, the realization begins to sink in and the body reacts. In some cases, blood may drain from a person's head and rush to the stomach, causing dizziness to the point where the person will pass out. An even more common reaction will be involuntary responses of the nervous system: pumping adrenalin into the bloodstream, rapid heartbeat and heightened pulse rate, tensing of muscles, perhaps heavy and rapid breathing, perspiration oozing out of pores, or even hairs on the back of the neck standing out.

The next response is one of acceptance. As the situation continues to unfold and events take on a pattern, there are several different reactions: the body may begin to tremble uncontrollably; sobbing may start; there may be a loss of control over bodily functions with the bladder or bowel emptying itself; or there may be a retreat into a catatonic state, perhaps even nodding off into sleep in order to escape from the reality of the situation. For those who remain conscious, there is usually some soul-searching or a guilt reaction for somehow placing themselves in the situation. As the captivity progresses, a number of different psychological states or emotional responses can be adopted, often with the victim alternating between two or more. One reaction is to adopt a festive mood, as in trying to make the best of a bad situation. Thoughts of escape or overpowering the perpetrators are bound to arise. Eventually, however, most people accept their roles as captives, realizing that they have no control over the situation. Once this sense of reason returns, they can begin to protect themselves from possible harm.

Long-Term Reactions

Once the why me reaction fades and the body returns to close-to-normal functioning, the victim is able to assess the situation in fairly rational terms and the whole incident takes on a different complexion. Long-term incidents are usually kidnappings, since even the best-planned hostage takings are not designed to last more than a few days at most. With long-term incarceration, the group holding the victim or victims may be well-organized, but this does not mean that they are professional. Any individual guard or member of the group may be highstrung, tense, or easily shaken — or all three. The captors may have, and often flamboyantly display, weapons that they do not know how to use properly. Even if the organization behind the abduction is a professional terrorist group, the individuals employed on the operation may be recent recruits specifically brought on to handle this particular incident. A typical tactic of such hired help is to intimidate the victim with threats, verbal abuse, and all too often, physical beatings and death threats.

The common factor in such incidents is isolated confinement, often with deliberate attempts to disorient the victim by shutting out ambient sounds, obliterating light changes from day to night and back to day, and the removal of wristwatches and marking devices for keeping a calendar of captivity time. For a person in such circumstances, the obvious strategy is to counter these efforts by marking time with sleep habits or by noting the routines of abductors, such as when there is a changing of the guard. The important thing to remember in such circumstances is not to intensify apprehensions and fears, but rather to wait, observe, and note. One of the most comforting thoughts — even though a twisted observation — is that if the captors wanted you dead, they would have killed you. The fact that you are still alive means you are worth more alive than dead.

The Family

In any long-term abduction, the family suffers as much as the actual victim. Whatever contingency plans that were prearranged should be implemented. If the abduction occurs overseas and the pre-incident agreement is for the family to return home, arrangements should be made accordingly.

There is a possibility the family will be subjected to abuse. The media, of course, will be intrusive and at times appear insensitive in the pursuit of information or a new angle to a story. More threateningly, terrorist kidnappers may try to use the family for propaganda purposes, getting them to make statements they might not do otherwise in the belief or hope that this will win release of their loved one. Terrorists will, as has been demonstrated, pit the families of the hostage or kidnap victims against their own government, which is the real target of the terrorist action.

After the initial period of emotional adjustment, the family should try to resume its normal lifestyle. The victim wants the family to function. The family should celebrate holidays, birthdays, graduations, weddings, births, etc., and record them on film, tape, or photographs so that when the victim returns, he or she can share these milestones. Not only are such celebrations therapeutic for the family, but they will also help the victim in readjusting to freedom.

Unfortunately, there can be situations which are irretrievable, such as the death of a loved one. During U.S. journalist Terry Anderson's captivity, in Lebanon beginning on March 16, 1985, his father died. Pleas to the kidnappers to release Anderson so he could attend the funeral fell on deaf ears. (Recently, Terry Anderson and some other international victims received court awards of monies from the governments that have supported international terrorism.)

Police Handling of the Incident

Upon verification of an abduction, standard operating procedure guidelines for a kidnapping should be implemented. Those assigned to investigate the

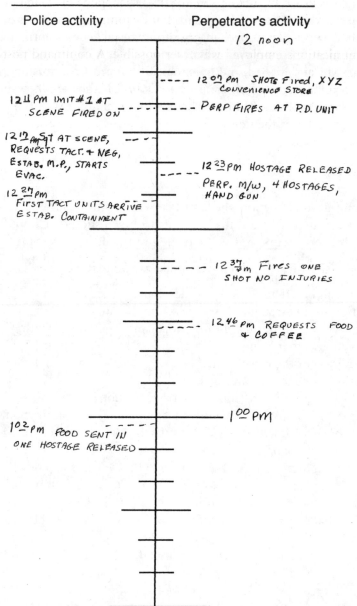

Figure 11.1 Time bar chart. A visual chronological record of events as an incident unfolds assists in quickly updating backups and supervisors. The left-hand side of the chart refers to actions of the police (i.e., activity outside of the hostage scene), the right-hand side to actions of the hostages or perpetrators on the inside. The axis is broken into a time scale that will vary depending on the length of the incident and the amount of activity.

case should be mindful that the victim's residence or place of business may be under surveillance by accomplices of the kidnappers. Plainclothes officers in unmarked vehicles should respond. Radio communications may also be monitored, so appropriate precautions should be taken and alternative means of communications employed whenever possible. A command post should be established and staffed, with appropriate procedures implemented and notifications made, as described in Chapter 14. The use of a time bar chart is helpful for rapidly orienting new or relief personnel (Figure 11.1). Half of the chart indicates the actions of the perpetrator, while the other half records the major activities of the police. The chart can be drawn on either a horizontal or a vertical axis, but the format should be consistent, at least through any one incident. Though originally used in kidnapping investigations, such a chart's usefulness in hostage situations became evident very quickly.

The Stockholm Syndrome

In hostage situations and kidnappings, an almost perverse association between captives and perpetrators sometimes develops. This is called the Stockholm Syndrome, a term coined by Harvey Schlossberg, a police officer psychologist and colleague who was with the New York Police Department. The Stockholm Syndrome derives its name from the reaction of the victims during a 6-day siege in a bank vault in Stockholm, Sweden. A lone gunman, trapped during a robbery attempt, herded a man and three women into the vault and then demanded and received the release of a former confederate who had been imprisoned.*

For almost a week, under the most intolerable conditions imaginable, the two men held off police. Without plumbing facilities, all hostages were required to relieve themselves into waste baskets. One of the women went through her menstrual cycle without sanitary napkins or tampons. Hostages were paraded to the vault door with a loaded gun held under their chins. They were tied to safe-deposit boxes with metal wire around their necks, so if authorities bombarded the vault with tear gas, the hostages would faint and collapse against the wire, choking to death. Eventually, police drilled through the vault, shot tear gas into it, and forced everyone out. As they fled, however, the four hostages encircled their captors because, they said, they wanted to protect them from possible harm by the police. Later, one of the women said she was in love with the bank robber and would wait for his release from prison to marry him.

---

* This was the first and most serious of the mistakes police made in handling this case. The release of an inmate from prison set a bad precedent. It also gave the bank robber help on the inside. The police couldn't employ time to their best advantage by wearing down the perpetrator because he now had the opportunity to rest.

Why? Because, psychologically, the captor has had life-and-death control over the victim and has allowed the victim to survive, earning a sort of everlasting gratitude. This is the ultimate in transference. Cruelty, it appears, only served to heighten emotional value for those susceptible to it. The pattern has also been called survival identification. The Dutch call it aggressor identification and note that it is hardly a new phenomenon. It occurred extensively amid the horrors of Nazi concentration camps, where some victims earned places of honor with the captors by emulating them and often outdoing the Nazis themselves in cruel treatment of fellow prisoners.

Transference

While the Stockholm Syndrome is an extreme form of transference, there are other types more common and less devastating. Transference is a term used by psychiatrists and psychologists to denote the identification by one person with another (Figure 11.2). This is the key to what develops between a patient and a psychotherapist, for example. In a hostage or kidnapping situation, the cause of the perpetrator may well become the cause of one or more of the hostages. As a result of such transference, it is unwise to accept uncorroborated intelligence from hostages. They may tell you something is happening or not happening because they think this is what the perpetrator wants to hear. Even released hostages may not provide reliable information because of transference. By the same token, police plans should not be divulged to hostages because there is the possibility they, in turn, will relay the information to the perpetrators.

Transference can develop between the hostage-taker or kidnapper and his victims, too, as well as between the negotiator and perpetrator. The only

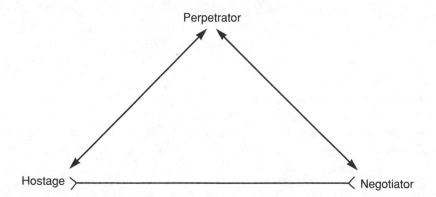

Figure 11.2 Transference. Transference is a relationship that can develop between the perpetrator and the hostages or between the negotiator and the perpetrator. Transference rarely develops between hostages and negotiators.

relationship in which transference is unlikely to develop is between negotiator and hostages, because there is so little interaction between them. In addition, the hostage perceives the negotiator as one of those prolonging the situation by not giving the perpetrator what he wants.

Transference is a coping mechanism, one that could well keep a hostage alive. The police — the negotiator, specifically — should do everything possible to encourage interaction between perpetrators and hostages. It is less likely that a perpetrator will kill a hostage when some degree of transference has developed. Some terrorist groups who have taken hostages have isolated a designated triggerman from the hostages just to prevent any transference from developing in the event one of them is to be killed. Another tactic used with only limited success by terrorists is to cover the hostages' heads with hoods in an effort to frustrate the development of transference between the hostage-takers and their victims.

Even when transference develops between the perpetrator and the negotiator, it is not necessarily a negative occurrence. The important thing is to control it so it doesn't get out of hand. The secondary or backup negotiator should monitor the primary negotiator so that he doesn't go off the deep end and almost fall in league with the perpetrator. Experienced negotiators may be aware of transference, but they cannot prevent it from developing. When people are in a crisis, they have to share that crisis with another human being, any human being. In a hostage-negotiation situation, both the negotiator and the perpetrator are in a crisis. In fact, it may even be said that transference is the magic that allows negotiations to progress.

Because of transference, it is best that the negotiator not be the officer making the arrest complaint, in the event an arrest is made. The negotiator may be reluctant to fully prosecute the case or may otherwise try to give a break to the perpetrator. A second reason for not having the negotiator be the complaining officer is that it might be perceived as stealing an arrest from the first responding officer. Ideally, the cop in the street should get the arrest, if for no other reason than he or she might not be so quick to call for help in similar incidents in the future. Instead, the officer may want to handle it alone, without proper equipment, intelligence, or backup. This could lead to injury or even death. It is also probably better not to have negotiators testify in court, if at all possible, in order to maintain credibility with future hostage-takers and to maintain the overall good guy image of negotiators.

When an Incident May End in the Use of Deadly Physical Force

There are two schools of thought about whether a negotiator should be told when the use of deadly physical force to neutralize a perpetrator may be necessary to recover hostages or when a sharpshooter will be used. The argument against telling the negotiator is based on the likelihood of transference. Because the death of the perpetrator is a very real possibility, the negotiator may give some indication of the impending assault or provide some warning to the hostage-taker.

The opposite tack, telling the negotiator that deadly force is going to be used, is designed to protect the negotiator's mental health. Imagine talking with a person and not be aware of the commanding officer's decision to use deadly physical force. Suddenly, after what may have been several hours of sharing the same space, the other person's head explodes like a watermelon from a sharpshooter's round. This would, in all probability, have a devastating effect on the negotiator. Knowing ahead of time what is about to happen makes the action easier to accept, particularly if it does, indeed, result in the perpetrator's death.

It is preferable to take the negotiator aside and advise him of the impending assault. If he feels he cannot handle the situation, then have him introduce a new negotiator to the perpetrator. Because transference has not yet had a chance to develop, the new negotiator should be able to handle the assault situation better.

Ransom: To Pay or Not to Pay?

Before any ransom payment is made, verification must be made to determine if the people making the demand are, in fact, holding the victim. The request — really, it should be a demand — to verify that the victim is alive and well will not be perceived as unreasonable by any kidnappers. Hoaxers, on the other hand, may object saying they are not being trusted and, as a result, the life of the victim may be in danger. In many instances, a code word can be exchanged with the verified kidnapper when future communications are initiated to insure that someone with cursory knowledge of the incident is not exploiting the circumstances for personal gain. On the first anniversary of the disappearance of a young boy named Etan Patz, a call came to the home of the parents indicating that the caller had information he would give the family for $10,000. Police were able to apprehend the callers. The ensuing investigation revealed the hoaxers knew nothing more than the anniversary date of the boy's disappearance.

While law enforcement agencies and police officers cannot advise one way or the other whether to pay the ransom, there are professional negotiators who can be engaged to handle the transaction. Such negotiators are usually engaged by businesses that have had an overseas executive kidnapped. Companies foreseeing kidnapping should establish pre-incident liaison. This means that security people within the organization should have, or have access to, people familiar with the geography, language, laws, customs, and different ethnic or religious groups from areas where such problems occur.

In some instances, negotiations by professional negotiators can decrease the amount of ransom payments. Obviously, the decision to pay or to yield or to make counter offers will either fall within the preestablished guidelines or will require approval of a company's crisis management team. If the ransom amount is very large or the money must be transported a great distance, there is insurance available to protect those funds. If the ransom is lost or stolen in transit, the payee could go bankrupt coming up with additional funds to meet the kidnappers' demands.

Making the Payoff

Once the decision has been made to pay the ransom, the next consideration is getting the money together. In a corporate context, arrangements must be made through the chief financial officer, who must authorize the outlay through the company's bank or banks. In most large cities, law enforcement agencies have arrangements with financial institutions to have available large amounts of cash in small bills, the serial numbers of which have been recorded or photographed. Corporate financial officers can usually arrange for a wire transfer of funds to cover the ransom monies.

In kidnappings involving individuals, the family or parties paying a ransom often will have difficulty in making their assets liquid in order to meet the demands. Once the decision has been made to pay the ransom, however, the police and law enforcement agencies will do what they can to assist. The specifics of how and where a ransom will be delivered are usually within the domain of the abductors, although counterspecifics can and should be made in an effort to assure the safe recovery of the victim.

The perpetrators usually will have done a good deal of homework and reconnaissance on the victim and family or company. It is not unusual for a particular individual to be specified as the courier for the ransom funds. Often, domestic law enforcement agencies will want to plant a small radio transmitter on the courier. This is more for the individual's protection than it is for the safety of the funds, particularly if the courier is redirected to another drop location after receiving telephone instructions. Now there are all forms of electronic gear that can be of assistance to keep track of the ransom courier, everything from infrared fireflies (thermo-packaging of the ransom) to the use of global positioning systems. Tailing can be accomplished by all sorts of vehicles, even aircraft. However, tailing a walking courier, or one who might be directed to public transportation such as a bus or subway requires investigators who have had training in this type of surveillance.

The surveillance teams following the courier should keep him or her in view, know what the person is wearing, and what he or she looks like, especially from behind. There may even be a hand signal or other sign so the courier can communicate with the surveillance team. Caution should be taken, however, to keep the tailing officer's identity and person out of the courier's view. There was one dramatic instance in which a father, acting as a courier, inadvertently revealed the identity of the tail team to one of the kidnappers making the pickup. There were no fatalities in the incident, but there was a great deal of anxiety and a felon fleeing with the ransom while the officers tried to regain their composure.

In some instances, law enforcement officers have been used to deliver the ransom. Their objectivity and training are usually very effective in assisting the investigation and eventual prosecution.

Proper packaging of the ransom can be used to assist in gathering physical evidence for eventual prosecution. The use of new untouched paper or even new kraft paper bags is very useful because they both hold fingerprints very well. Wrapping and taping the package so that the perpetrators must place their hands inside on the underside of a flap in order to open the package also will help in obtaining good fingerprints. In some cases, kidnappers will specify a certain type of receptacle, such as a briefcase or suitcase. In these circumstances, the container should be marked unobtrusively, with the mark being recorded on film or videotape. Another possibility is implanting an electronic device in the container, although if this is discovered by the perpetrators, it could result in harm to the victim.

When possible, the drop location of the ransom should be observed from concealed positions. If anyone retrieves the subject package or bag, that person should be followed, although not necessarily confronted, since the victim is still in danger. Several considerations need to be taken into account regarding confrontations, including the possibility of losing track of the pickup person or the inability to maintain a tail secretly. In both of these instances, it may very well be preferable to apprehend the person picking up the ransom package.

The Recovery

A kidnap victim may be returned alive in any number of ways. The easiest, and probably least traumatic, is for the victim to be released blindfolded on a deserted road or in an open field. The victim may be told to count up to 500 or more before removing the blindfold. During the countdown, there may be some trepidation, waiting for a bullet or some other life-threatening action. Another manner of return might be escape, or what appears to be an escape, as we have seen in Beirut, Lebanon, when abductors will sometimes offer no resistance or aid an "escaping" hostage.

A different ending to a kidnapping incident could result from a successful cooperative investigation, as we noted earlier in the Tiede Herrema incident in Ireland that developed into a hostage standoff eventually resolved successfully through negotiations. Care must be taken that once the location of the victim is ascertained, appropriate action occurs. Ideally, quick, aggressive, and decisive action can bring about the safe rescue of the victim.

If there is a question of whether the abductors are aware of the police presence and possible assault or rescue attempt, then it is probably better to deploy a containment force and treat the incident as a hostage situation.

Victimology

Victims of terrorist action include more than just those who were killed or injured in a bomb blast, or who were taken captive in a kidnapping or hostage incident (Figure 11.3). The families of those involved are victimized, as are the police officers who work the incident, particularly in hostage situations. Even the public at large can be considered victims because there is more to

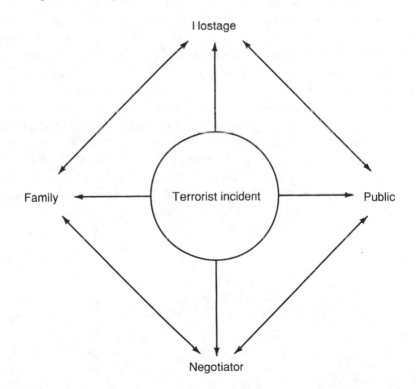

Figure 11.3 Victimology. All victims of a terrorist incident are not always immediately recognizable. The chart shows the lines and flow of relationships which develop in the aftermath of an incident.

be afraid of, and new regulations or procedures may be instituted, making everyday living just a bit more difficult. Traditionally, in the aftermath of such criminal acts as bombings, kidnappings, or hostage-takings perpetrated by terrorists, psychological examinations, psychiatric treatment, and social counseling have concentrated almost solely on the criminals, with little thought given to the mental health of victims or their families.

Historical Background

The guiding light, if not founding father of victimology is Dr. Richard Molders, a Dutch psychiatrist who participated in the negotiations involving the South Moluccans who took hostages in The Netherlands in the 1970s. Molders' principal American disciple is Dr. Frank Ochsberg, formerly of the National Institute of Mental Health. One of the first discoveries these victimologists made was that a victim's tribulations do not necessarily end with the termination of the criminal activity and the apprehension of the criminals.

Courses of Action

Some former captives will be eager to talk about their experiences, others may grow reticent and prefer not to talk, or even think, about it. Both types of individuals, however, need counseling and guidance. Post-incident counseling should be a total program involving a whole team, with initial debriefing interviews conducted by a law enforcement aide and a psychologist or psychiatrist. The victim should have a 24-hour phone number to call should problems arise at any time of the day or night. At least one other formal interview should occur, this one with the district attorney or prosecutor preparing the case against the perpetrators, at which the presence of a psychiatrist or psychologist may be helpful. One of the reasons for proffering official help is that former hostages or kidnap victims need to know that someone cares, and that someone in the system understands and is trying to help them readjust. This obligation is felt so strongly that the Dutch, for example, mandate such treatment for former captives. Talking about the incident and sharing the experience with others are generally a good idea. Many former hostages have indicated that they felt better after sitting down and writing about what had happened to them. This ventilating seemed to aid in getting their lives back on track. Media interviews, press conferences, and radio and television appearances pose another question. Certainly they can be part of the process, having a cathartic effect in relieving anxiety and other strong emotions. However, the danger exists that the victims or family members will grow comfortable with their new-found celebrity status, yet be unprepared for the inevitable letdown when the media's interest in the incident fades.

Immediate Post-Incident Reaction

Other than an overwhelming sense of relief, there is no universal reaction displayed by kidnap or hostage victims upon release. Some laugh, some cry, some do both. The closest thing to a typical post-incident reaction comes when someone has been killed during captivity. There is almost always a sense of guilt among surviving captives who wonder why they were spared and whether or not they could have done something to save the life of their dead comrade. Interestingly, at the time of the killing, when self-preservation instincts are running high, most captives are relieved that they were not the one killed, even while combating a new sensation of fear and apprehension at the perpetrators' escalation in violence. Only later does this sense of relief become a feeling of guilt and burden.

Longer-Term Reaction

Both the actual victim and his or her immediate family should be prepared to experience psychological trauma. There may physical trauma as well. Fear, anxiety, sleep disorder, depression, aggression, digestive disorders, or sexual dysfunction may occur. Somatic reactions such as skin rashes, blotchy skin, loss of hair, or any one of a number of other maladies may develop. There also seems to be some distinction between hostages of opportunity and hostages of designation. In many cases, captivity of hostages of opportunity is of relatively short duration, typically less than 24 hours. An example of how one family was affected by a kidnapping involved a bank vice president who was taken from his home by three masked gunmen. The banker and his family were watching television when there was a knock on the door. His 17-year-old son opened the door without bothering to check who was on the other side. True, the gunmen could have forced their way in, but the ruckus and commotion might have alerted neighbors or allowed a family member to escape and call police. The planned bank robbery was unsuccessful because of vault timing devices and the banker was eventually released unharmed. Afterward, his son required extensive psychiatric care to help him cope with the guilt he felt for putting his family in danger just by opening the door. For a long time afterward, the boy's mother experienced uncontrollable fits of crying. The man himself abandoned his banking career and found a job in another field.

Returning to Normal

However post-incident reactions manifest themselves, there are two important points to remember: these reactions are completely normal, and they will usually fade with time. For most people who have been held captive, this means that returning to the pre-incident lifestyle as quickly as possible is the best course of action. Getting back to the routine of a job, or resuming normal school or household duties, has the reassuring comfort of normalcy to it. Various studies of former captives indicate those who are not kept busy have the most difficulty. For example, of the 52 people held hostage for 444 days in the U.S. Embassy in Teheran, Iran in 1979–1980, the ones who had the most difficult period of adjustment were the Marines who left the service because their enlistments were up. The civilians who returned to work had an easier time readjusting.

Post-Incident Effects on Rescue Officers

The need for possible psychological assistance for officers involved in the rescue of victims of hostage situations and/or kidnappings cannot be under-estimated. We have personally observed and experienced the immediate effects. If right after the end of an incident the officers went directly home, many experienced severe bouts of insomnia, inability to eat or keep down food, and even sexual dysfunction. Two officers suffered heart attacks. Almost by accident, we found out that retiring to a bar or restaurant after an incident and spending an hour or two talking about the situation stopped the previously outlined symptoms from manifesting themselves. When relating this to our colleague, Dr. Harvey Schlossberg, he indicated that in actuality what we were doing was conducting a group therapy session, thereby providing a catharsis for any pent-up emotions. Perhaps this has worked well, because we have not gotten any further reports of those symptoms or any more dire effects of post-traumatic stress disorder (PTSD).

In other parts of the country and for other incidents, we have seen that when we speak of victims, we have to include many officers and rescue personnel. In 1987, an 18-month-old baby named Jessica McClure was rescued from an old well into which she had fallen some 20 feet. The entire country was riveted by televised reports during the 58 hours rescuers took to dig a parallel shaft before a slim fireman by the name of Robert O'Donnell wiggled down and freed the child. She was brought to the surface cold, tired, but very much alive. O'Donnell was hailed as a hero and was inundated by media coverage. After the media moved on, however, the hero had a downward spiral. In 1995, as he watched the rescuers and search crews looking for survivors in the Alfred P. Murrah Building in Oklahoma City, he told his mother that those rescue people were going to need lots of help, and that he didn't mean just for a couple of days or weeks, but for years. A few days later, April 23, 1995, O'Donnell took his own life.

One of the rescuers involved in the aftermath of the Oklahoma City bombing was NYPD Sgt. Terrance Yeakey. He assisted in rescuing four people before part of a floor collapsed and he fell two stories, injuring his back. A little more than a year later, and three days before he was to receive his department's medal for valor, Yeakey shot himself to death. Similarly, a police lieutenant in New Jersey, shortly after completing a 36-hour tour of duty in the command center directing the rescue of hundreds of people from flood waters caused by the remnants of a tropical hurricane, apparently took his own life. His stressors appeared to manifest themselves more quickly than those of the other officers.

Interviewing Victims

12

BY FRANK OCHBERG*

Whenever an investigator meets a survivor of traumatic events there is a chance that the interviewer will witness — and may even precipitate — post-traumatic stress disorder. Therefore, it is important that professional investigators (including grizzled veterans) anticipate PTSD, recognize it, and report it, while earning the respect of those interviewed. The recognition of PTSD and related conditions enhances not only an investigator's professionalism, but also the interviewer's humanitarianism.

PTSD is three reactions at one time, all caused by an event that terrifies, horrifies, or renders one helpless. The triad of disabling responses is

1. Recurring intrusive recollections
2. Emotional numbing and constriction of life activity
3. A physiological shift in the fear threshold affecting sleep, concentration, and sense of security

This syndrome must last at least a month before PTSD can be diagnosed. Furthermore, a severe trauma must be evident and causally related to the cluster of symptoms. There are people who are fearful, withdrawn, and plagued by episodes of vague, troubling sensations, but they cannot identify a specific traumatic precipitant. PTSD should be diagnosed only when an event of major dimension — a searing, stunning, haunting event — has clearly occurred and is relived, despite strenuous attempts to avoid the memory.

* Dr. Frank Ochberg is a pioneer in the study of victims of violence. A psychiatrist, Ochberg has worked with and studied victims of war, terrorism, domestic violence, rape, incest, and natural disaster in many countries. When American hostages were released from 444 days of captivity in Teheran, he was the expert commentator for ABC's, "Nightline" and "Good Morning America".

When human shields were held by Saddam Hussein, he helped organize a rescue mission by hostage wives. He holds adjunct professorships in psychiatry, criminal justice, and journalism at Michigan State University.

Intrusive Recollections

The core feature of PTSD, distinguishing the condition from anxiety or depression, is the unavoidable echo of the event, often vivid, occasionally so real that it is called a flashback or hallucination. The survivor of a plane crash feels a falling sensation, re-visualizes the moment of impact, then fears going crazy because his or her mind and body return uncontrollably to that harrowing scene. A victim of the "cooler bandit," whose modus operandi was to rob urban convenience stores at gunpoint and force the clerks into refrigerated storage rooms, had nightmares for more than a year.

There are important distinctions among traumatic memories. Some are clearly memories. The beholder knows this is a recollection, painful but not terrifying. Through time and (often) through telling and re-telling of the trauma story, the memory is muted, modulated, and mastered. It no longer has a powerful, disruptive presence. It is a piece of personal history. On the other hand, that personal history may burst forth into awareness and a trauma survivor may feel and act as though bombs are falling, a rapist is ready to strike, or the death of a loved one is witnessed again. (The loss of a loved one and the consequent bereavement is not, by definition, a source of PTSD, unless the death evoked images of terror or horror. Tragic loss is often an aspect of PTSD, but shocking imagery is not usually part of natural death.)

Some repetitive recollections include regrettable acts by the person with PTSD. A patient of mine killed a boy in Vietnam. It was self-defense, in combat, but indelible and inexcusable in my patient's overactive conscience. Guilt, crushing guilt, was a major component of his intrusive recollection.

Emotional Anesthesia: Constricting Life Activity

Numbing may protect a person from overwhelming distress between memories, but it also robs a person of joy and love and hope. While participating in a national PTSD research effort, I interviewed dozens of soldiers, decades after their service in Vietnam. To these veterans, survivor meant being no more than a survivor and considerably less than a fully functioning human being. Painful memories might have subsided. Anxiety attacks were tolerable. But the capacity for feeling pleasure was gone.

These victims were not necessarily sad or morose, just incapable of delight. Why bowl or ride horses or climb mountains when the feeling of fun is gone? Some marriages survived, dutiful contracts of cohabitation, but devoid of intimacy and without the shared pride of watching children flourish — even when the children were flourishing.

Numbing and avoidance are less prominent, less visible, and less frequent than the more dramatic memories and anxieties. Early on, most survivors of trauma will consciously avoid reminders and change familiar patterns to prevent an unwanted recollection. For example, some ex-hostages from a notorious train hijacking in the north of Holland avoided all trains for weeks. Some avoided only the particular train on which the hostage incident had occurred. Others took that train, but changed to a bus for the few miles near the site of the trauma.

Numbing and avoidance are adaptive to a point, then become a serious impediment to recovery. They can also mislead an interviewer of a survivor into seriously underestimating the severity of a traumatic event. There is a popular belief that victims of rape, kidnapping, and other violent crimes should be full of feeling, tearful, shuddering, even hysterical, after the assailant leaves. When feelings are muted, frozen, or numb, the survivor may not be believed. When testimony in court is mechanical and unembroidered, jurors may assume that damages were minimal or never inflicted. I have testified as an expert for the prosecution (and for the plaintiff in a civil suit) on several occasions to explain this phenomenon.

Victims may be numb or withdrawn or both and, therefore, do not come forward immediately. When they do they appear to untrained observers to be indifferent, unconcerned, and unharmed, when, in fact, they are in a state of profound post-traumatic stress. This dimension of PTSD includes psychogenic amnesia. Along with loss of emotional tone and limited life pursuits are holes in the fiber of recollection. For example, an opera singer, battered by her husband, could not recall the most serious beatings. She was ready finally to divorce him and she needed to testify in court at a settlement hearing. After several supportive sessions, including hypnosis, she remembered his choking, almost strangling her. Eventually, all of the memories returned, and she could joke, "He not only threatened my life but my livelihood! No wonder I put that out of my mind."

Lowered Threshold for Anxiety and Arousal

This is physiological. Unexpected noises cause the person to shudder or jump. The response is automatic and not necessarily related to stimuli associated with the original trauma. A patient of mine, a bank teller who was robbed, held hostage, then kidnapped, was not exposed to gunfire or loud sounds during her ordeal. But six months later, she was visibly startled and upset by the rumble of a train near my office.

It is as though the alarm mechanism that warns us of danger is on a hair trigger, easily and erroneously set off. A person lives with so many false alarms that he or she cannot concentrate, cannot sleep restfully, and becomes irritable or reclusive. A normal sex life is difficult with such apprehension. PTSD, therefore, impairs the enjoyment of intimacy, and this, in turn, isolates the sufferer from loved ones — the ideal human source of reassurance and respect.

Often, the anxiety takes familiar shape: panic and agoraphobia. Panic is a sudden, intense state of fear, frequently with no obvious trigger, in which the heart beats rapidly, respirations are quick and shallow, and fingertips tingle. There is light-headedness. There may be sensations of choking or smothering, and the person feels he or she is dying or going crazy or both. After a few panic attacks, a person will often suffer agoraphobia, avoiding places such as shopping malls and supermarkets, where an attack would be particularly embarrassing.

PTSD Is Not Always the Same

Thus, PTSD has not only a variety of dimensions and components, but vastly different effects and implications. Some trauma survivors are continually reminded of their victimization and experience relief when they tell the details to others. Some survivors are humiliated by their dehumanization or laden with guilt for harming another person. They refuse to discuss details. Some are dazed, moving in and out of trance-like states. Some are full of fear, hypervigilant, easily startled, unable to concentrate, wary of strangers. The syndrome may be evident soon after the trauma or may emerge years later.

Who Gets PTSD?

Most current research shows that the intensity and duration of traumatic events correlate positively with the occurrence of PTSD, but individuals exposed to the same extreme stress will vary in their responses. Heredity may play an important role. Just as some children are born shy and others exhibit a bolder temperament, some of us are born with a brain pattern that keeps horror alive, while others quickly recover. As a varied, interdependent human species, we benefit from our differences. Those with daring fight the tigers. Those with PTSD preserve the impact of cruelty for the rest of us.

I tell patients that there is nothing abnormal about those who suffer. It is a normal reaction to abnormal events. Anyone could develop PTSD given enough trauma.

Other Difficulties

Victims of human cruelty (as opposed to victims of natural disasters) experience additional emotional difficulties that are not listed in the official diagnostic manual and are not part of PTSD. Foremost among them is shame. Although violent criminals should feel ashamed, they seldom do. Instead, the victim who has been beaten, robbed, or raped is humiliated. This person has been abruptly dominated, subjugated, stripped of dignity, invaded, and made, in his or her own mind, into a lower form of life.

Who cannot recall being bullied as a child, forced to admit weakness, mortified by the process? As an adult, this shame quickly becomes self-blame: Why was I there? What could I have done differently? Why did I let it happen?

Self-blame may actually be a good sign, correlating with self-reliance and self-regard. But it may also be hostility turned inward, a relentless self-criticism and downward spiral into profound depression.

Hatred is another human emotional response to trauma with no reference in the diagnostic manual. On the path to recovery and possible forgiveness, victims of cruelty are entitled to hate their abusers. But survivors often do less hating than one might expect. Sometimes they are simply grateful to be alive. They may, ironically and paradoxically, love the kidnapper who could have killed them, but instead gave them life. This is called the Stockholm Syndrome, named for the bizarre outcome of a crime in Sweden in 1974 when a hostage-taker and a bank teller fell in love and had sex in the vault during a siege. Like Patty Hearst and countless others, the teller denied that her assailant was a villain, but responded passionately to his power to spare her life.

It is the Mothers Against Drunk Drivers who are MADD. The co-victims, the next of kin of the injured and dead, are more often the ones moved to rage and vengeance, if not hatred. Obsessive hatred is a corrosive condition, seldom the focus of psychiatric treatment, but of major concern to historians and journalists.

A Guide to Interviewing

A knowledge of post-traumatic stress disorder is vital to investigators in their understanding of the way victims experience emotional wounds, particularly wounds that are deliberately and cruelly inflicted. A relatively recent area of clinical science, traumatic stress studies, teaches us that victims of violence have several distinguishable patterns of emotional response. These patterns are easily recognized once their outlines are understood. Seeing the logic in a set of psychological consequences re-humanizes and dignifies a person who may feel dehumanized and robbed of dignity. A sensitive explanation of the traumatic stress response aids recovery. When we as a society pay attention to the victim as he or she heals, we are less likely to be consumed by hate and focused on perpetrators, thereby contributing to a contagion of cruelty.

Investigators can interview victims, understand them as multidimensional human beings and possibly, just possibly, reduce some victims' impulses toward vengeance in the process.

Timing

When interviewers seek a trauma survivor's comments soon after the event, they are very likely to encounter one or more of the emotional states mentioned above. As time passes, emotional composure will increase. But a distorted recollection is also possible, i.e., selective memory and competition from many other interviewers, each with a different agenda, each raising new questions in the mind of the person interviewed. Therefore, even from a psychiatric point of view, no formula for setting the ideal time for a post-traumatic interview exists.

Assume you have access to a clerk who was robbed at gunpoint an hour ago. She appears uninjured. You might begin, "Have you had a chance to discuss this with anyone else?" This tells you where this interview is in the predictable sequence of police investigations, insurance and management inquiries, and conversations with family, friends, and others, including reporters. It also allows you to follow up with questions about those discussions, if they occurred. An interviewee reveals a lot about conversational preferences, when given the chance. For example, he or she might indicate a desire to talk at length, to be brief and to the point, to learn about the incident from you or to get away from the scene — all in response to an open-ended question such as, "How was that previous discussion for you?"

Then you can set the stage for your interview, having assessed your subject's attitude and emotional state before he or she regards you as responsible for his or her feelings. Have subjects focus on how someone else made them feel.

Consider a very different interview. It is the one-year anniversary of a major catastrophe such as the Oklahoma City bombing and you are assigned to interview a survivor who now lives outside of Oklahoma in your small town. You telephone to arrange a meeting. This story, a year rather than an hour later, will deal with emotions throughout that year and on this anniversary date. The incident is less important than the impact of the incident on one individual through time. The interview may (probably will) cause vivid recollections. Do you mention this over the phone? Or do you assume that agreeing to be interviewed signifies a willingness to revisit painful memories?

The fact that this is an inquiry long after the event gives you more flexibility in arranging the time and place, meeting once or on several occasions. But you the investigator may be the cause of emotional injury, since this person was exposed to major traumatic stress and has reached some new adjustment state that you will disrupt. In a way, this is a more delicate, difficult situation.

Setting the Stage

Setting the stage is important regardless of the timing of an interview. A trauma survivor should be approached with respect, neither gingerly nor casually. This is a person who has witnessed and lived through a major event outside normal experience, someone who has something significant to share and who undertakes some re-exposure to traumatic memories by talking with you. If you convey respect for this situation, then you are off to a good start.

Consider the possibility that a survivor might be more comfortable at home or might want to be out of the family circle. Some might feel more secure with a friend or relative present. The clerk robbed at gunpoint would probably be encountered first at the convenience store. But if she had the authority to leave or to be joined by a friend, you might get more details, more spontaneity, than if you stayed at the scene of the crime. Of course, other professional deadlines might preclude taking an extra hour to learn about the emotional impact of the robbery on your witness/victim. Obviously, if you can remove someone to a comfortable, secluded place, the chance of interruption is reduced and concentration is enhanced.

Interviewing people as a Red Cross volunteer at disaster sites resembles the field conditions investigators encounter. When serving in that capacity, I set the stage as best I can, trying to assess quickly whether a person wants privacy or the proximity of others and whether the comfort level is greater with the door open or closed. One woman preferred to sit on the floor, surrounded by her soggy belongings, as she sought help at a shelter after the 1994 Northern California floods. This woman was agoraphobic (fearful of crowded public places) before the floods, more so afterward, and I earned her trust by bringing social workers and small-business loan specialists to her, rather than having her join the crowd in the busy service center.

To set the stage for an interview, remember that the person may be in a daze, may be numb, may be easily startled, may be hypervigilant, may be confused. But the victim usually can tell you which setting will suit him or her best. This may require a companion, an open door, and several breaks for self-composure.

Eliciting Emotion

As an interviewer, you can either elicit or avoid emotion. Do you want to see and hear a person's emotional state? Or do you want the individual to describe his or her feelings without displaying them? A person can tell you, "I was very upset, crying all the time, unable to work...". Or they can sob as they speak.

Most interviewers would prefer to have their interviewees describe rather than display strong emotions (TV talk-show hosts excepted). So would I in initial interviews with trauma survivors. My ultimate objective is to help them master their uncontrolled feelings. Therefore, I usually say that we can, if possible, defer dealing with the full impact of the event until we know each other better, until some progress has been made. I explain how, several weeks hence, we will get to the central part of the traumatic experience. But that is done when I am treating PTSD, by definition a persistent problem of at least a month's duration, with intrusive emotional recollections. At other times, for example, when de-briefing Red Cross volunteers, I want to see strong feelings, if they are present, to get them talked out before the volunteer goes home (and to show respect for the person and for his or her emotions). That is the point of the debriefing.

But police investigators are not PTSD therapists or after-incident crisis debriefers. You are interviewing a witness who is a subject of an investigative inquiry. It is not uncommon for tears to flow during the telling of an emotional event. Therapists offer tissues. I usually say, "I'm accustomed to hearing people while they are crying, so don't worry about me." I neither urge nor discourage someone from continuing to talk, but I do try to normalize the situation. Investigators should bring tissues if a tearful interview is anticipated.

When survivors cry during interviews, they are not necessarily reluctant to continue. They may have difficulty communicating, but they often want to tell their stories. Interrupting them may be experienced as patronizing and as being denied an opportunity to testify. Remember, if you terminate an interview unilaterally, because you find it upsetting, or you incorrectly assume that your subject wants to stop, you may be re-victimizing the victim.

Some people who have suffered greatly, for example, torture victims in Chile, have benefited psychologically from the opportunity to provide testimonials, and the benefits have been substantiated by research.

Members of the Michigan Victim Alliance, who serve as interviewees for the journalism students at Michigan State University, report some PTSD symptoms afterward (anxiety and intrusive recollections for one or two days), and an overall increase in self-esteem, because their stories have been heard.

Often, the facts are told with considerable depth of feeling. So the issue is not really should you, the interviewer, attempt to control your subjects' emotions, but rather, how can you best facilitate a factual report, a full report, and give your interviewee a sense of respect throughout.

Informed Consent

Should investigators offer the equivalent of a Miranda warning? "You have a right to remain silent. Anything you say can and will (especially if it is provocative or embarrassing to somebody important) be used on the front page."

That would not work. But the medical model of informed consent could be adapted for interviews with trauma victims. You might explain: "This procedure — interview and subsequent proceedings — has benefits for the community and may benefit you. Remembering, however, may be painful for you. And your name will be used. You might have some unwanted recollections after we talk and after your story appears in public. In the long run, telling your story to me should be a positive thing. Any questions before we begin?"

Stages of Response

The first set of responses after a shocking event involves the pathways of the autonomic nervous system, connecting the brain, the pituitary gland, the adrenal gland, and various organs of the body. Blood is shunted from the gut to the large muscles. The pupils dilate. The pulse accelerates and the stroke volume of the heart increases.

These physiological changes, shared by all mammals, prepare us for fight or flight. We are in a state of readiness for dealing with the threats our ancestors faced on the great plains of Africa: wild beasts, sudden storms, deadly enemies. We are not adapted for fine motor movements, nor for deep conscious thought. The surge of adrenaline and pounding heart we experience when the car skids on an icy highway does not help us maneuver that piece of machinery. Our danger biochemistry is atavistic. We have to fight these bodily changes as we respond to modern mechanical dangers, such as a high-speed skid.

There are perceptual changes as well. Our focus on a source of danger, be it a wild beast or a pistol pointed at us, is intensified. Objects in our peripheral vision begin to blur, a function not only of the organs of perception but the result of how impulses are received, recorded, and analyzed in the brain.

Detectives, doctors, and journalists all know the implications of this phenomenon: details are notoriously distorted, except for a few central features, when eyewitnesses report incidents of threat and sudden danger. Sometimes, a powerful threat is prolonged, as in a hostage incident, a kidnapping, some assaults, and rapes. Many natural disasters, a flash flood or hurricane, may place one in mortal danger for hours rather than seconds or minutes. Short, deadly traumas include gunshots, explosions, earthquakes, and fires.

When extreme stress is prolonged (days or weeks), adaptive mechanisms collapse. This is rare. But in animal experiments, mammals suffer hemorrhagic necrosis of the adrenal gland, literally a bloody death of that organ, and, soon after, death of the organism itself.

Far more frequently, humans in states of prolonged catastrophic stress enter a second stage of adaptation. Hans Selye, the physiologist whose stress studies guide the modern era, called this a stage of resistance following a stage of shock. Now the organism is in high gear, accustomed to the increased flow of adrenaline, consciously appraising what previously has been grasped automatically.

At this point, a crime victim knows that he or she is a victim, although the person may be thinking, "This can't be happening to me." At this point, details do become evident, particularly to the trained observer. And, in group hostage situations, there is often a ritual calm, when confusion and feelings of threat diminish. This is the time when negotiations may be successful.

Disaster workers recognize a heroic phase, a second stage after the initial bedlam, when all is shock and confusion. In the second stage, people help one another, lives are saved, lost children are found. Hope and exhilaration coexist with fear and grief.

Eventually, there is a return to some equilibrium in the body, the mind, and the community. This may be a time of depression and demoralization: the high-energy condition is gone. There is debris. There is loss. There is pain. Reality sinks in. This is also the time when the press leaves. A survivor who might have been annoyed by too much attention could feel abandoned and forgotten.

Several authors describe stages of impact and recovery after shocking events or disturbing news. Elisabeth Kubler-Ross defined the denial, fear, anger, and eventual acceptance after learning one has a fatal illness. A journalist may want to consider the particular sequence of stages or phases that an interviewee has experienced, where that person is now and how each stage affects the perception of events.

A discussion of stages may help the interview process, without actually leading the witness. Consider saying, "Sometimes people go through a stage when they act without thinking, when they don't even know what is happening," and you may elicit an interesting narrative. Some people need to be reminded that they acted instinctively. Then they can recall what occurred just before that phase and right afterward.

My patient who was thrown to the floor by the "cooler bandit" recalled months later that she hid her wedding ring under a shelf, as she lay in the fetal position expecting to be shot. She forgot this particular event during the time that she was experiencing fear and shame and all of the diagnostic PTSD symptoms.

For me, of special note was her instinctive protection of a valuable symbol, her refusal to yield that icon to her assailant. This woman was full of self-blame for not sounding the secret alarm, for behaving like a coward.

Therapy required a diligent search for evidence to the contrary, proof that would convince her. (I was already certain that she had done what any reasonable person would have done to survive an armed robbery.) She recalled hiding her ring as we talked about the instinctive, automatic things that some people do. And she finally agreed that her instincts were correct.

The Humanitarian Role of the Investigator

Investigators and therapists face similar challenges when they realize their subjects are at risk of further injury. Techniques may differ, but objectives are the same: to improve societal health. A therapist is not a lawyer or a security consultant, but a battered woman and an abused child need to know that shelters, restraining orders, and a network of advocates are available. Therapy includes such referrals.

The investigator is not responsible for individual referrals, but could give information about community resources when interviewing individuals who would benefit from them.

Secondary Traumatic Stress Disorder

Investigators are candidates for secondary traumatic stress disorder, an empathic response that affects us, therapists included, when our professional detachment is overwhelmed by certain life events. Images of dead children leave an indelible mark. Firefighters, who would rather not admit that they have tender feelings, find themselves vulnerable to the haunting memory of a burnt child or the sight of a tiny form in a body bag.

The sheer numbers of unexpected dead in one place will penetrate the defenses of hardened rescue workers. Plane crashes rank among the most difficult assignments for American Red Cross workers who normally handle floods, earthquakes, and fires. At an air disaster, there is a concentration of death images that few doctors, nurses, or ambulance drivers have ever seen.

Writing about journalists covering Rwanda, Roger Rosenblatt mused in *The New Republic*:

> *Most journalists react in three stages. In the first stage, when they are young, they respond to atrocities with shock and revulsion and perhaps a twinge of guilty excitement that they are seeing something others will never see: life at its dreadful extremes. In the second stage, the atrocities become familiar and repetitive, and journalists begin to sound like Spiro Agnew: if you have seen one loss of dignity and spirit, you've seen them all. Too many journalists get stuck in this stage. They get bogged down in the routineness of the suffering. Embittered, spiteful and inadequate to their work, they curse out their bosses back home for not according them respect; they hate the people on whom they report. Worst of all, they don't allow themselves to enter the third stage in which everything gets sadder and wiser, worse and strangely better.[1]*

In one or two decades, PTSD will be universally recognized, de-stigmatized, and well-treated. To be dazed at first, then haunted by horrible memories and made anxious and avoidant is to be part of the human family. When deliberate criminal cruelty is the cause of PTSD, we often neglect the victim and become captives of collective outrage, focusing attention on crime and criminality and those who are to blame. By understanding PTSD, we disarm PTSD. We do not prevent it, but we minimize its degrading, diminishing effects. We help victims become survivors. We help survivors regain dignity and respect.

Notes

1. *The New Republic*, Roger Rosenblatt, June 6, 1994.

Role of the Commander

13

Who's in Charge?

An incident commander may be the designated leader of a special unit charged with specific counterterrorist responsibilities. A commander may also be a ranking officer who finds himself or herself in charge of a situation involving terrorists. While specific responsibilities and a course of action vary from department to department and agency to agency, the topics of discussion and guidelines for action offered here cover the major options open to both types of command situations. For the leader of a special unit, the responsibilities can be divided into three general areas, determined largely by time sequence:

1. Pre-incident
2. During the incident
3. Post-incident

For the commander who might be thrust into a terrorist situation by virtue of being the duty officer at that moment in time or because of a particular assignment, the incident and post incident sections of this chapter will be most relevant.

Pre-Incident: Developing Guidelines

Preparing for a confrontation with terrorists or domestic incidents begins with the development of guidelines, including such things as who will take what role and who will perform what functions. These guidelines are the exposition of the department's policy and should be based on the belief that the preservation of human life is the most important aspect of any situation. This is not an extreme or radical statement. Perpetrators can be captured; money, property, or goods can always be recovered, but human life, once taken, never can be retrieved.

To start at the top, the incident commander should be of high enough rank to get things done vis-à-vis other units, yet low enough to still have knowledge of and familiarity with the community being served. In hostage situations, for example, some departments will have the tactical commander in charge of overseeing the hostage negotiations on the one hand as well as supervising the tactical people on the other.

In other departments, and this is our preference, the commander in such situations is the patrol commander. The rationale behind this is that patrol units are closer to the community. Special units (such as SWAT, tactical units, and hostage-negotiating teams) come in, do their jobs, and leave. The focus is narrowly on the assignment at hand; it is possible to do the job they are assigned, but still leave the patrol people with special problems after they pull out. A patrol commander then can make decisions designed to assist the special units, but which reflect a sensitivity to the impact on the community. More importantly, however, is that the incident commander is clearly in charge, and even other unit leaders who may have higher rank are subordinate to that person in terms of the situation at hand. Thus, a captain who is the incident commander may be outranked by a deputy inspector commanding the tactical unit, but the deputy inspector is "staff" to the incident commander for the duration of the incident. Whatever formula is used must be documented, thereby fixing authority as well as responsibility.

Make-Up of the Team

How a special-function unit is structured is not as important as the fact that there is some kind of structure. It is imperative that everyone know who is in charge, and that somewhere it is delineated exactly who has what authority and what responsibilities. The operational guidelines should be just that, guidelines, and not a step-by-step formula or lockstep prescription for action. It is also important to develop mutual aid agreements with other agencies in the region that provide various services, because many departments are too small or are under budgetary restrictions that prevent any one of them from having all emergency capabilities (Figure 13.1).

Some jurisdictions have established regional hostage recovery programs with two or three persons who are drawn from the various departments in the region and are assigned to the combined agency unit task force. They have regular training programs in which they become familiar with the guidelines, program, and equally important, each other. Teamwork and familiarity, particularly in life-and-death situations, build the confidence and trust necessary to accomplish the basic mission. A major recognition is that although several different departments in a county or region may be involved in an incident, the jurisdiction in whose area the incident occurs is the one whose commander takes charge; all units, regardless of jurisdiction, follow his or her orders.

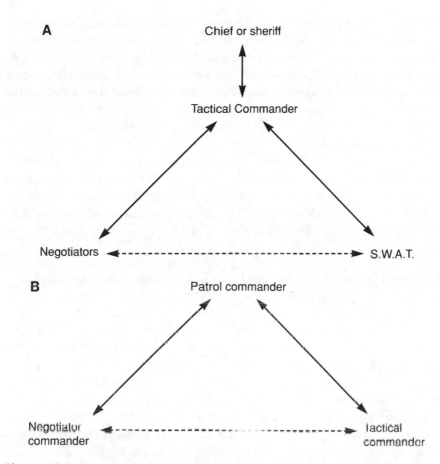

Figure 13.1 Command structure. Organization charts for two variations of command structure, depending upon the make-up of the department. The shape of the structure is not as important as the fact that a structure exists, that it is documented, and that it is understood.

Maintenance of Manpower and Equipment

It is the responsibility of the commander to constantly monitor and maintain the strength of the special units and the support equipment they need. In smaller departments, this may mean a continuous updating of mutual aid agreements with agencies in contiguous jurisdictions. Equipment concerns should include the availability of bullet-resistant garments and helmets; the proper weapons and ammunition; and radio communications equipment with mouthpieces and earpieces that provide some amount of privacy, so that perpetrators at the scene of an incident are not privy to police communications.

Not all the equipment needs to be sophisticated and expensive. Night-viewing equipment would be welcome, but so are flashlights, periscopes, mirrors, and even mundane objects like wedges and ropes to secure or maintain control of doors. Much of this equipment, if budget justifications are a concern, can be used in other police functions, but the problem here is that they must be available when an emergency situation occurs and not in the back of a car belonging to somebody who has gone fishing for two weeks.

Maintenance of equipment is extremely important, from a functional and a safety standpoint for your officers, but also from a vicarious liability standpoint because lawyers will pounce on the fact that a single piece of equipment may not have been in proper working order. Replacing batteries in equipment immediately after using it ensures its readiness when the next incident comes up unexpectedly.

Keeping Up-to-Date on New Developments and Strategies

In terms of training the operatives, if there are enough incidents for the department to deal with, then only refresher training after the initial immersion period would be needed, in addition to some periodic critiquing and evaluation. However, in departments where these special units may not be greatly utilized, say only once or twice a year, training should be required on a regular basis, at least quarterly, and preferably once a month.

Retraining, updating, in-service training (however, it is referred to) is never wasted. Weapons training for such situations results in greater control of firepower in everyday situations. Drills in hostage negotiations also can serve as aids in routine interrogation procedures. There is a spillover of specialized training into everyday assignments. This is in addition to whatever training sessions do to help defend against potential exposure to vicarious liability lawsuits.

How much training should be offered? Although this begs the question, the only real answer is as much as is necessary. All too often, hostage situations and kidnappings are covered in initial training, but nothing is offered in the way of refresher or updated courses. Such training is needed, particularly when the specialized unit does not get that many jobs during the course of a year. The training is important not only for the individual officers involved, but also for the coordination of the tactical, communications, and other units involved. The training does not have to be in the form of classroom lectures. The use of tactical people, for example, can be based on simulated reenactments of recent kidnap or hostage incidents elsewhere. Negotiators can keep their communications and sensitivity receptors fine-tuned by working suicide or other crisis telephone hotlines.

An important note to remember is that training sessions must be documented as to who did the training, what kind of training it was, how long it lasted, etc. This documentation is needed primarily in the event of lawsuits, where trial lawyers on discovery proceedings will rip into the training methods, procedures, and quality of training for police officers involved in a particular incident. More importantly, if follow-up training is not provided, then the hostage recovery team will be a special unit in name only.

Evaluate and Update

In evaluating members of the team, remember that some people may look good on paper and may even train well, but may not operate at the anticipated level of performance. Likewise, some individuals may experience burnout in a relatively short period of time, while others may function well for years, growing in the job as they gain experience. It is the responsibility of the commander to make personnel changes whenever necessary. Some departments have specified time limits for tours of duty in special units, usually two or three years, with officers transferred out automatically. The problem with this approach is that no one on the job has more than two or three years experience and, conversely, there are a lot of well-trained, experienced people out there doing other police jobs.

A unit such as a hostage-negotiating team is a voluntary assignment. Whenever an individual leaves, whether by choice or by commander's decision, the transfer should be made without prejudice. As volunteers, all team members should know they can leave, or be asked to leave, at any time without a negative evaluation landing in their personnel folders.

Liaisons with Other Agencies

The commander of a special unit should establish and maintain telephone contact, written communication, or face-to-face dialogue with agencies such as the FBI, state police, and other police departments in cities the same size or larger. Depending upon the nature of the special unit and the constituent profile of the department's jurisdiction, it also may be necessary to develop a dialogue with appropriate personnel in various state agencies, i.e., corrections departments, university systems, the Federal Aviation Administration, the Army Corps of Engineers, the Department of Energy's nuclear energy bureaus, the Department of State, various military police, Department of the Interior and some of its subunits, etc.

The reason for developing these contacts is to gain intelligence and information before a situation develops which then must be handled on an

emergency basis. The commander would know then that in an airport incident, the agency operating the terminal is in control if the incident is in a
public area of the terminal. If the incident occurs in the airport operations
area (i.e., in a location between security screening and the aircraft), the FBI
has jurisdiction. If the incident is on the aircraft itself and the doors of the
plane have not been closed, the FBI is still in charge. Once the aircraft doors
have been shut, however, it becomes the FAA's responsibility. In practical
terms, the FAA does not have much of a law enforcement arm and will usually
defer to the FBI, so the FBI remains functioning and active, but coordinates
its actions with the FAA. Even then, although the FBI is running things, many
times the local police department will be the first called to take up containment and tactical positions.

The scope of liaisons should be expanded beyond other police departments, law enforcement agencies, and enforcement arms of civilians agencies
to include local government agencies such as the fire, building, sanitation,
and traffic and highway departments. Contacts in private industry should
include security people at the electric, gas, and telephone companies, as well
as the operators (private, municipal or quasi-governmental) of airports,
docks, and harbors, and even bus and train depots, since these are favored
terrorist targets.

The information gathered should include the names and home telephone
numbers of whom to contact on a 24-hour basis. The list of potential emergency situations is virtually endless; it includes everything from cutting off
power into a building (or needing to know where underground pipelines are),
to needing building plans for a location, or having airport night lights turned
on or off with short notice. A simple thing like a telephone in a room with a
hostage-taker and his victims could play havoc with police efforts. The news
media may be able to contact the hostage-taker or, worse yet, he could initiate
calls to the media, broadcasting his demands live. Having that phone line
disconnected forces the hostage-taker to communicate with the police or
negotiator. In these days of wireless communications and cellular telephones,
knowing who can do what is a bigger challenge, but no less important.

During the Incident: Intelligence-Gathering

Another one of the primary functions of the commander during an incident
is to make sure that intelligence is being gathered. This information must be
shared with the negotiator as well as the tactical and patrol people on a need-
to-know basis. Communication is of the essence; information gathered but
not communicated to the people who need to know is worthless information.
Intelligence-gathering should begin with the number of perpetrators, num-

ber and types of weapons, number of hostages, and location of the perpetrators and hostages. Then you want to know how the incident began or was precipitated. Personal information on the perpetrators and victims should include physical descriptions, medical history, and psychological backgrounds. Finally, as much information as possible should be gleaned on the physical location where the hostages are being held: floor plans; location and type of windows; door and emergency exits; height of ceiling; the heating, ventilation, and air-conditioning (HVAC) system; what is above and below the location, etc.

A note of caution — be wary of descriptions that involve only clothing. First, people can change or be forced to change clothing. Second, color perceptions vary widely from one person to another. One person's turquoise is another person's blue and a third person's green. Clothing descriptions should be avoided particularly in target selection for sharpshooters.

At a major incident in which many innocent victims may be involved, it is inevitable that relatives and family members will begin arriving at the scene. Rather than having them mill around or wander off to restaurants or who-knows-where, it is wiser to set aside a building (or part of a building, or obtain a van or bus), and direct the relatives inside, provide them with coffee, and have detectives begin the systematic gathering of information. The last thing you want is some distraught relative being interviewed by a television or radio journalist whose broadcast could be monitored by the hostage-takers. Having them all in a bus would ease transporting them to the station house for reunions with their kin once the hostages are released.

Evaluate Alternatives

Before deciding upon a course of action, it is imperative that the commander has as much intelligence as possible. The choice, then, can be reduced to four alternatives:

1. Rescue/dynamic entry
2. Sharpshooters
3. Chemical agents
4. Contain and negotiate

Originally, when we established the courses of action, we used the term "assault." However, that term, especially when used by plaintiffs' attorneys in civil litigation was always characterized as a crime. Law enforcement people should never commit crimes. Though it may seem just a matter of semantics, it can be significant in court testimony. If there is a hostage, we use the term "rescue." If there are no hostages, just a barricade, then we call the action a "dynamic entry."

One of the most dramatic rescues in recent memory took place in Lima, Peru. The incident started in late December, 1996 at a diplomatic Christmas holiday party at the Japanese Embassy. Shortly after the function started, members of MRTA, known as the Shining Path, disguised as wait staff, produced automatic weapons and explosives. They took almost 500 guests at the party hostage. Local law enforcement officers were the first to respond to the report of gunfire and the first to become aware of what had taken place. Within the first hour, the local police and MRTA arranged for the release of almost 400 hostages, persons whom the captors deemed unimportant. The demand of the terrorists was for the release of a number of their colleagues from Peruvian prisons. Negotiations continued for almost four months, with everyone from the Red Cross to representatives of the media and church officials to family representatives of wealthy hostages getting involved. Peru's President, Alberto Fujimori, maintained a very hard line, refusing to negotiate with the hostage-takers. During the period of the ordeal, a tremendous amount of intelligence was garnered. Many listening devices were introduced into the compound in various manners. The number and description of the perpetrators and their routines were ascertained from some of the released hostages. During the protracted negotiations, the Peruvian government crafted an elaborate plan to carry out a rescue. One of the more novel aspects included digging an earthen tunnel to the inside garden area of the compound. Amazingly, the security of this information was maintained without any leaks to the media. One afternoon, while the perpetrators were playing their usual post-midday meal soccer game in the embassy ballroom, the rescue was mounted by the Peruvian army. Amidst the explosion of the flash bangs, and the gunfire, the rescue of the hostages was effected, but not without casualties. Notwithstanding the 14 perpetrators who were killed, one hostage and two soldiers also died in the rescue. In this instance, it was a military operation, and in military operations, there are acceptable casualty rates. Thus, the operation was considered a success. In police operations, however, there is no acceptable casualty rate other than zero.

Overall, the rescue/dynamic entry option is an extremely risky one. The Rand Corporation has determined that between 75 and 80% of hostages killed in hostage incidents are killed during a rescue attempt, some of which have been disastrous. On January 31, 1980, at the Spanish Embassy in Guatemala City, Guatemala, 33 terrorists disguised as peasants took over the embassy, holding 8 individuals hostage, including the Spanish ambassador. Although the Spanish government pleaded with the Guatemalan authorities not to assault, an assault was mounted. A Molotov cocktail exploded, and in the ensuing fire and police assault, 32 of the 33 terrorists and 7 of the 8 hostages died. Only one terrorist and the Spanish ambassador survived. (The terrorist was subsequently abducted from the hospital and hanged in a public square.)

There is another potential problem area involving rescue attempts. Should the perpetrators sense that an assault is near, or if capitulation is possible, there may a last-ditch effort to escape. Commotion and confusion could be created by "stampeding" the hostages, with the hostage-takers trying to escape by blending in with the crowd. One response to this tactic that has been successfully employed is for the police to herd everybody into a large bus and transport the group to a secure area, such as a station house, where the victims can be separated from their captors. Care must be taken because the terrorists may already have been singled out by their former victims, and may require police protection to save them from beatings and physical assault at the hands of the erstwhile captives.

There is one other consideration that should be made prior to going in on a rescue attempt. Make absolutely sure there is actually a hostage inside. If not, it may be a simple barricade situation, which is a major difference. If hostages are involved, the police are expected to take greater risks to protect the lives of those innocent third parties. If there are no hostages, only a perpetrator armed to the teeth, the best option is to wait him out. There is no reason to risk the safety and well-being of police officers unless the possibility of a suicide attempt exists. Police cannot just stand by if the perpetrator is bleeding to death.

One option that can be exercised in barricade situations is to have rookie negotiators use the incident for practice. If the negotiator makes a mistake in psychological procedure, no innocent person will get hurt. It would be best, however, not to call the effort "practice," particularly in the presence of media representatives who can be extremely hostile and make the police appear insensitive in their dealings with the barricaded perpetrator.

Sharpshooter

The decision to employ a sharpshooter requires highly reliable intelligence. Realistically, this is sniper fire; however, we refrain from using that terminology since the word sniper has a pejorative connotation in the public's perception. Sharpshooters should never be used to just kill the perpetrators, but rather to stop them, the fact that a perpetrator may die notwithstanding. Sharpshooters shoot to stop, not to kill. The intent is to stop the bad guys from doing whatever they are doing that is life-threatening to the officers or innocents.

Prior to giving the order to shoot, it is important to remember the rules for target identification. More than one instance has occurred in which sharpshooters selected hostages mistaken for perpetrators. Even if everything else goes right, the sharpshooter could miss or there could be a miscalculation in the number of perpetrators. If the sharpshooters have taken good cover, there should be no need to return fire and further endanger the hostages should the hostage-takers begin to exchange fire.

There are times when sharpshooters should definitely hold their fire. For example, if a person says he has a bomb, treat him as though he has a bomb. There was a case involving a bank robber in Kenora, Canada, in which the perpetrator passed a note to the teller saying he was carrying a bomb, in addition to being armed with a pistol and a long gun. The perpetrator was wired with an intricate contraption that was connected to a spring-action clothespin which he held open with his mouth to keep the contact points from closing. The note explained that if he were shot, the clothespin would close, making contact and setting off a bomb. When the robber exited the bank using an unarmed constable to carry the money, a sharpshooter who did not believe it was a bomb fired and hit the perpetrator. Unfortunately, the bomb was real and exploded. Fortunately, the constable was only inured and not killed in the explosion, sustaining leg injuries and a loss of hearing.

Another bank robber, this one in Helsinki, Finland, claiming to be armed with a bomb went mobile with three hostages. After a wild chase that ensued for nearly 100 miles, the perpetrator's car was stopped. Two hostages managed to escape and the police opened fire on the vehicle. Seconds later, the car exploded with the perpetrator and one hostage inside.

Most of the time (99.9%, in a very unscientific sampling) when a perpetrator says he has a bomb, it turns out to be a hoax or a fake explosive device. However, that .1% of the time when there is a bomb, people can and have gotten hurt and killed

Many departments or police officers are afraid of being embarrassed by letting a perpetrator with an infernal device tie up the community and half the police force for hours, only to have him laugh as he tosses his practice grenade or other harmless mock-up aside. Remember, it is easier for police to live with embarrassment, since embarrassment doesn't kill. A bomb can.

Assessments of improvised explosive devices should be made only by bomb-squad technicians. With apologies to Gertrude Stein, a bomb is a bomb, until proven otherwise.

Chemical Agents

Intelligence is also important before the decision can be made to employ chemical agents, such as tear gas. Medical background on the hostages, for example, would determine whether any of them have allergies or breathing problems. Intelligence would also indicate if infants or small children are being held. Because of children's lung capacity, the mean lethal dose of a chemical agent (i.e., the amount of agent that would preclude oxygen from the system to sustain life) is much less than that for adults. Even in situations where participants are barricaded and have all kinds of equipment including gas masks, as in Waco, Texas, with the Branch Davidians, it is not likely that there would be masks for children. A survey of chemical agent mask manufacturers in the United States revealed that none of them produced masks for children. The authors' only experience in seeing children's masks was in Israel during the Persian Gulf War in 1991 and, reportedly, in England during World War II.

Information on the location could reveal that there is volatile material or a volatile atmosphere inside which could be ignited by hot chemicals, or the agent could be rapidly dispersed by the building's ventilation system into other critical areas. There is also the possibility (more likely when it is a well-planned terrorist operation) that the perpetrators may have gas masks.

Use of a chemical agent, although intended to be nonlethal, can very nearly be the equivalent of using deadly physical force. Chemical agents come in various compounds, i.e., CS, CN, and Mace. Each has specific characteristics. For example, CS is more nauseating and disorienting than CN; however, it is more difficult to decontaminate an area where CS has been used. Compounds such as CS and CN can be delivered in a variety of ways, including projectiles of various calibers, grenades, and large area canisters to broadcast the agent more widely. The decision as to which delivery system to use will depend upon the location, distance, and type of structure, and possibly other physical characteristics. The form of agents can also vary. Mace, for example, is usually a liquid that can be squirted or streamed at the subject. CS and CN can be delivered as a vapor ignited by a burning pyrotechnic. These substances can also be micropulverized and released as a fine dust or powder. If a hot gas is involved, the fire department should be on alert and at the scene, because chemical-agent projectiles can, and have, started fires. Another chemical-agent option is oleo-capstan, or pepper spray, which can be carried on the belt of responding officers and used in the less than lethal range of the compendium of force. However, make sure that the suspension medium is not alcohol-based. One agency, after spraying an emotionally disturbed person with capstan, which at the time had an alcohol base, then used a Taser gun to stun the subject. A resulting spark ignited the alcohol and immolated the person, killing him. Ambulances should also be readily available for those affected by the chemicals.

Delivery of chemical agents should be done with care since this aspect of the operation can cause special problems. Being struck with a projectile can kill or seriously injure the subject or a hostage. There are times when a subject may be under the influence of drugs, alcohol, or just personal adrenalin. When the chemical agent is introduced, the subject may be able to withstand physically more agent than his body can handle medically. Too much agent can coat the alveoli of the lungs, inhibiting the exchange of carbon dioxide and oxygen in the bloodstream, precipitating moisture, and possibly inducing chemical pneumonia.

Food

When sending in food, don't send in ready-made meals. Rather than sending in a dozen sandwiches, for example, send in a couple of pounds of lunch meat; two loaves of bread; jars of mustard, mayonnaise, and ketchup; pickles and all the trimmings, along with some plastic utensils. The idea is to create a party atmosphere with the people inside interacting with one another. It is less likely that a hostage-taker will harm a hostage after interactive circumstances such as these.

Another thing to keep in mind when sending in food is that a great ritual should be made of getting the food into the location. (The negotiator never should deliver it personally, nor should anyone else since there is always the possibility of becoming another hostage.) Rather, the negotiator should be viewed by the hostage-taker as going to great pains and effort to get the food to the location. *Never*, repeat *never* place the food on the floor, since the hostage-taker could react extremely negatively seeing food placed before him as it would be placed before a dog.

The question of sending in food laced with sedatives or some other type of drug is a more serious one. The obvious reason this should be avoided is that it might kill somebody: an innocent hostage might eat the doped food. As long as everyone's medical history is not known and drug dosages are unpredictable in their effects on people, it would be best not to tempt fate. Even anesthesiologists working one-on-one in hospitals sometimes lose patients, and there are other side effects to drugs. In one incident in which we were involved, a 55-year-old man was holding a 5-year-old child hostage for more than 24 hours. A ranking officer, noticing that the perpetrator had requested and received some beer, but had not given any to the child, went to a nearby hospital with a six-pack of beer. He explained the situation to a doctor, who told the chief to empty about an ounce and a half of beer from each bottle. The doctor replaced it with a mixture which he assured the chief "would knock out an elephant for 20 hours" without any serious side effects. The chief returned to the scene of the incident with the six-pack, which he placed in a refrigerator for future use. The refrigerator was in a residential apartment adjacent to the command post for this incident. The chief directed an officer to watch the beer, but failed to communicate what was taking place. Half an hour later, when the chief went to retrieve the beer, three bottles were missing, apparently purloined by two tactical officers and a negotiator when the officer watching the beer went to relieve himself. When the chief indicated the beer was spiked, the three officers good-naturedly admitted they took the beer. The chief ordered all three of them to be driven home, lest the doctored beer take effect while driving themselves home. The net result of the incident was (a) the beer was not served to the perpetrator; (b) none of the officers was knocked out; and (c) two of the officers reported back on the aphrodisiac power of the adulterated beer.

When South Moluccan terrorists took over a school in The Netherlands, they held a small group of teachers and 150 children hostage. On the second or third day of the incident, all of the children got diarrhea. The Dutch authorities said overcrowding had caused the condition. One could speculate, however, that mild laxatives which affected only the children might have been introduced into food which was sent in for the group. In any event, the terrorists released the children rather than deal with that smelly situation directly.

Alcohol and Drugs

The question of whether beer, wine, or spirits should be sent in depends upon the circumstances. Intelligence here is very critical. If it is learned from family or friends that when the perpetrator drinks, he becomes belligerent or nasty, under no circumstance should alcohol be provided. If, however, intelligence indicates the subject gets mellow or sleepy when drinking, then the negotiator has the option of bargaining for hostages in exchange for the drink. There is also a chance that the perpetrator will be partying while the hostage abstains.

Should negotiators drink? Probably not, but there may be circumstances when sharing a drink or a bottle can give the negotiator an advantage or some control over the situation. When in doubt, leave it out.

If a hostage-taker asks for controlled substances such as heroin or cocaine, it is easy to turn down the request on the grounds that the police department does not deal in drugs. However, the refusal has to be stated in a way that does not to say "no" to a request. As far as pharmaceuticals are concerned, such as methadone for an addict in a rehabilitation program, this would be acceptable, but only with the approval of the perpetrator's drug counselor or physician at the scene.

Contain and Negotiate

The alternative courses of action discussed above are all violent courses of action that are irreversible. Once started, they cannot be stopped. An alternative

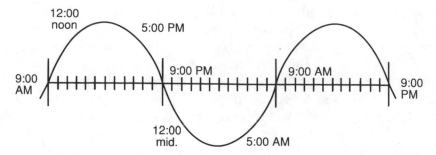

Figure 13.2 Daily biorhythm. The ups and downs of daily life are no old wives' tale. Most people have performance peaks and valleys on a 12-hour cycle, with a psychological low usually coming in the early hours of the morning between 4 and 6 a.m.

is to contain the incident, using barriers and tactical people to confine the perpetrator(s) in the smallest practical area, and then negotiate in an effort to bring about a resolution without harm to anyone. One of the prime advantages of this strategy is that it provides time. Time can be used to gather intelligence, deploy forces, and weigh options. Any of the first three alternatives is still open to the commander even after the perpetrators have been contained and negotiations have begun. Time also works on the police side in that biological functions are constantly at work (Figure 13.2). People — even well-prepared terrorists — get thirsty, become hungry, and grow tired. Toilet functions impose themselves. All the factors work in the favor of police.

Impact of the Event on the Public

The commander should be aware of the potential effect a particular incident could have on both the community at large and on the police department itself. One dramatic example of this occurred in the 1985 Philadelphia incident involving the radical group known as MOVE. Members of this group barricaded themselves inside a house and, after several months of confrontation, the decision to evict was made by authorities. After a long day of siege in which various attempts were made to remove them, including the use of fire department water towers, the decision was made to use chemical agents. In order to effectively place the chemical agent within the compound, the procedural plan called for a hole to be opened in the roof using a shaped explosive charge. The charge that was dropped proved to be too powerful. It ignited a container of gasoline that had been stored on the roof, touching off a roaring fire. Another decision was made to let the fire burn and assure that the hole in the roof would be large enough to allow the entry of the chemical agent. Unfortunately, the fire burned out of control, eventually destroying the building and approximately 60 other houses in a 2-block area.

All of the personal possessions, keepsakes, mementos, and other irre-placeable items of families in the neighborhood were destroyed. The wrath of the affected public shifted away from the MOVE radicals and was redi-rected toward the police and city government. Although this incident was precipitated by the failure of other city departments, particularly social wel-fare agencies, the situation was thrust finally into the laps of the police. The outcome had a devastating effect on both the department and the community at large. The police department lost its credibility, and the police commis-sioner resigned in the wake of the incident.

Subsequently, it was learned that an inquiry had been made of a demo-lition company about whether or not its crane and iron ball would be effective in opening a hole in the roof of the building in question. The answer was yes, it would be effective, but the cost of the effort would be $7500 to cover labor and insurance costs to the contractor. Undisclosed, Philadelphia city officials decided not to spend that much money, and the rest is history, with the result that millions of dollars had to be spent for physical rehabilitation of the area. No price has been set on the personal and psychological damage resulting from the incident.

In New York City, as a result of a liaison between the city police depart-ment and the local gas and electric utility, Consolidated Edison, at any explosion, building collapse, or other disaster, a Con Ed crane or other heavy equipment will be moved to the scene usually within the hour to provide whatever assistance is required.

Post-Incident Debriefing

Once an incident ends and the paperwork is finished, the commander should debrief as quickly as possible. Prior to the formal debriefing, however, an informal session should be held. This is simply a couple of hours with negotiators and key tactical people sitting around a restaurant or table or other informal setting, talking about the events that just transpired. At the very least, such a session helps relieve the stress created by the incident and, at best, the conversation will have a cathartic effect on the individuals involved. In the early days of the NYPD negotiating team, it was noted that if a hostage incident ended very late and each member of the team went directly home or back to regular duty, certain physical effects became man-ifest. Some officers experienced nausea, insomnia, loss of appetite, and/or sexual dysfunction. It was also reported that two officers sustained heart attacks — one while negotiating, the other shortly after returning to his home. It was further noted that under similar circumstances, members of the hostage-negotiating team would call in with related ailments.

Quite by accident, it was discovered that if all of the individuals concerned with any one incident retired to a bar or restaurant, these symptoms failed to appear or were very mild. (Alcohol was not a major factor, since some of the officers eschewed beer or a drink in favor of coffee or a soft drink.) This could be viewed as a group therapy session, and the participants should understand that it is primarily for stress management. Even if overtime pay is a concern for the officers involved, the cost to the department will still be less than having some of the officers call in sick for a day or two.

After a major incident, the negotiator will be on a high, perceiving celebrity status as a result of news interviews and television appearances. Following this high, however, there will almost inevitably be a period of mild depression as the boredom of everyday routine and reality reimposes itself. The negotiator, in fact, may be waiting for the next opportunity to star, while fellow officers may begin to exhibit resentment and jealousy. This reaction is something that negotiating team members must be told about, so they can anticipate and deal with it when it occurs. This is where a mental health professional with the operation can be most helpful in easing the pressures on everyone involved, reassuring them that these feelings are normal and represent just another challenge to be dealt with.

Formal Debriefing

Within 48 hours after the end of the incident, the commander should also oversee a more formal debriefing, which should include all the police officers who participated in the incident. Problems could arise, however, if too many persons of different ranks are involved. For example, a police officer may be reluctant to say that a deputy inspector, contrary to regulations, was in the inner perimeter without a bulletproof vest. This could present particular problems if the deputy inspector were in the room at the time. It is probably wiser to have officers of just two ranks, police officers and sergeants, lieutenants and captains, etc., participating in the same debriefing session. Later, representatives from each group can prepare the debriefing report.

During the debriefing, deficiencies should be noted, whether they are deficiencies in tactics, intelligence, equipment, or manpower. This is the essence of the debriefing: to provide information that will enable the unit to perform more effectively during the next incident. This is also why the sessions should be conducted as quickly as possible afterward. In addition, everyone involved should be aware that the debriefing will take place so that they have time to give the matter some thought and to make notes, if necessary. A concern not to be taken lightly is the question of whether or not a debriefing should be recorded. Obviously, there will be an official report, but whether or not the remarks and observations of the participants are recorded verbatim is really a policy decision for the commissioner. On the one hand, the raw material will always be available for reference and reinterpretation. On the other hand, the existence of a written transcript could encourage trial lawyers to subpoena the material in lawsuits that may grow out of the incident. Once officers become aware of the possibility of court appearances and legal ramifications, they may be reluctant to provide a free and open discussion during a debriefing session.

Evaluate New Developments and Outcomes

This is something of an amorphous responsibility but basically involves the commander's responsibility to rate new procedures and techniques which may have been used during an incident. If a new containment configuration was employed, or a different negotiating tactic tried, it is the commander's job to gauge its success and effectiveness, as well as any deficiencies, either potential or real, of the new method vis-à-vis prior procedures. It is also important to keep on top of new developmental procedures being used by other departments, and whether or not they may be appropriate for incorporation into the local department's guidelines.

The Command Post

14

The Nerve Center

Equally important as the role and responsibility of the commander are the location and administration of the command post. This is the nerve center and heart of an emergency operation. How it is set up and run could well make the difference between the successful resolution of a terrorist criminal incident and a botched assignment. It should be noted that there are regional differences in terminology in referring to command posts. They have been variously referred to as mobilization points, forward posts, and temporary headquarters, with those terms being used more or less interchangeably in some areas and having separate and distinct meaning in other jurisdictions. The preferred definitions are

1. *Forward command post.* Same as temporary headquarters; a formal location from which the operational administration of the incident is directed.
2. *Mobilization point.* A location near the site of the incident to which specialized manpower and equipment first report.
3. *Point of negotiation.* The physical location of the negotiator when in communication or direct contact with the perpetrator.

Forward Command Post

The positioning of this location is often dictated by the location of the incident. In some cases, however, pre-incident selection may be appropriate when incidents can be anticipated, such as at an airport, recreation areas, shopping center, or some other likely target location. In other instances, the site of the forward command post or temporary headquarters must be made under emergency conditions, and the selection may be a private home, an office, a store, or similar location. Among the major considerations in choosing a forward command post are the presence of telephones, adequate lighting, floor area and workspace, heat (or lack of it, depending upon the weather), toilet facilities, conveniences, and security.

A location with two or more telephones is preferred, although the increased availability of cellular telephones and other wireless communications has enhanced the flexibility in the choice of forward command posts or temporary headquarters. The use of laptop computers with wireless modems and wireless telefax capabilities enhances the effectiveness of the mobile command post. In some areas, particularly in rural areas, the use of a mobile facility may be more effective. A recreational vehicle, trailer, or even a patrol car, if appropriately equipped, could fulfill the basic needs. Vehicles seized in other actions, such as vans used in drug operations, can be outfitted even more elaborately. Remember that when placing these vehicles at the scene of an incident, safety and security are of paramount importance. Keep out of the perpetrator's line of sight as well as the line of fire.

The command post must be accessible to responding officers and backup support teams, as well as to the negotiators and supervisors at the front line. In addition, a radio frequency must be selected and communicated to the mobilization point so the newly arriving personnel can be informed.

The physical placement of the command post should be carefully screened. More than once, a post has been established in a basement or next door to an incident, only to be hastily relocated when the perpetrator began firing random gunshots at the walls, ceiling, or floor.

One of the requirements to be met, at least under ideal circumstances, is that the command post be large enough to be physically separated into distinct function areas, such as for technicians (bomb squad, negotiating team, etc.) and administrative functions, with a third area for VIP or press briefings.

Mobilization Point

The primary location to which personnel and equipment report after the initial responding officers have arrived is the mobilization point. This location is usually selected by the first supervisor to arrive at the scene, and its location is communicated via the radio dispatcher. In the event that the incident includes a report of an armed person or persons, the safest route to the mobilization point should also be indicated, as should any danger areas which may be in the line of fire. The mobilization point should be selected based on convenience, accessibility, and capacity to accommodate responding personnel. Care must be taken to insure that the location is out of the perpetrators' line of sight so they will not be able to assess the assembled resources. The idea is to increase police intelligence and information, while depriving the perpetrators of as much of the same as possible.

Point of Negotiation

In a hostage incident or a barricade situation, the point of negotiation may be closer to the location of the perpetrator than is the command post. There is no reason, however, why the point of negotiation could not be located in an area of the forward command post or temporary headquarters. However, the negotiators should have as much privacy as possible to allow them to establish rapport with the perpetrator and to insure that the perpetrator will not overhear planning, radio transmissions, or other statements made by non-negotiating officers. If the negotiating team moves up to face-to-face negotiations, the location, of course, will change. Wherever it is physically situated, however, the incident command post should be able to communicate with personnel and perhaps even monitor the actual negotiations. This can be accomplished by placing a body transmitter on the negotiator's telephone and equipping the incident commander and tactical commander with body receivers.

Staffing the Command Post

Standard operating procedure, a department's policies and procedures manual, specifies who should be the overall commander and decision-maker at an incident command post. So, too, should the staffing of the command post be spelled out well in advance. While incidents vary in nature and duration, there is a need for a chain of command. Among the positions likely to be needed are those of operations officer, logistics officer, communications officer, and intelligence officer. There should also be personnel responsible for the maintenance of a command post log and the situation map. Depending upon the incident-specific circumstances, some of these responsibilities could be combined and handled by one individual.

In hostage situations, there is also a need for a support staff. The negotiator needs a coach, ideally, another trained negotiator, who can provide advice and support, but who doesn't speak directly with the hostage-taker. In smaller departments, the coach position could be filled by a clerical officer familiar with what information the negotiator needs. Whenever possible, a mental health professional should be on hand to monitor the negotiator and, to whatever extent possible, observe the hostage-taker and his or her actions. Unless the mental health professional is actually part of the department, there should be some pre-incident affiliation or interaction to be sure everyone is on the same page.

There is also a question of how long any one person can negotiate. Perhaps 10, 12, or 18 hours is possible, although almost any negotiator will feel he can go as long as the perpetrator can. The idea is, however, to wear out the perpetrator, not the negotiator. The decision to change negotiators, or at least give one a rest, must be made by someone else, preferably the overall incident commander, upon consultation with the coach and the mental health professional. However, like a baseball manager changing pitchers, the decision is up to the person in charge.

Bomb Incident Command Post

An onsite command post is required only in the aftermath of an explosion. The immediate concern is for any persons who may have been injured in the blast, then the search for bodies, and finally, the search for physical evidence. The command post should not be located within the boundaries of the crime scene, lest evidence become contaminated or destroyed. If possible, the command post should be separated into two distinct areas: one for teams conducting the physical search, and the other for investigators and perimeter supervisory personnel. This division allows for greater safekeeping of evidence.

Recordkeeping is an important function at the command post. There should be a log recording the names of each and every person entering the crime scene area, regardless of rank or affiliation. The names, times, and dates are needed in report preparation, in developing a chain of evidence, and may be required for subpoena purposes. In addition to this log, there should be a chronological log recording the sequence of events, such as when certain pieces of evidence were recovered, when visitors arrived, when a wall collapsed, etc. These logs should be maintained by one person with sufficient authority to have all people make proper entries. The individual in charge of the log should also be able to recognize ranking officers by name, command, etc.

When major explosions occur, a command post may have to be utilized for days, even weeks, until the thorough sifting of debris is concluded. In such instances, there will inevitably be pressure to complete the job quickly in order to clear up congestion, ease traffic flow, and otherwise get the location back to normal working order. In such instances, it may be necessary to physically remove all debris from the scene to a more remote location, where the material can be picked over, sorted, and sifted.

Log and Situation Map

The command post log is a record of events and activities surrounding the particular incident. Once the basic data are recorded — when the command post was activated, its location, and the nature of the incident — information that should be recorded includes the exact location of the incident; a brief background of the incident up to the time the log was created; and the names, ranks, and affiliations of personnel assigned to the incident. Other relevant information includes the locations, names, and number of personnel deployed at the scene; which assignments are temporary and which are fixed for the duration of the incident; the number and types of vehicles and specialized equipment being employed; unit and personnel on standby or backup status; any intelligence received; any physical evidence recovered; names, and arrival and departure times of any visitors to the command post or the scene of the incident; names, time of arrest, and backgrounds of anyone arrested at the scene. The name of the authorizer should also be noted.

The situation map may be a series of maps showing the location of the incident vis-à-vis major streets, highways, and transportation routes; its location within the neighborhood; and blueprints, floor plans, and other technical drawings showing the exact location of the incident within the building. There should also be a hand-drawn sketch of the scene showing locations of the individuals involved, whether police, perpetrators, hostages, or civilians trapped by the circumstances. Other features on the hand-drawn map should include pieces of furniture, light switches, windows, and anything else that may be relevant.

Equipment and Supplies

The list of equipment required at a command post includes flip charts; markers; a blackboard (magnetic, if possible); masking tape; a large clock; a tape recorder with a telephone attachment; walkie-talkie; flashlights; Polaroid camera with extra film; one-to-one adapter; bullhorns; laptop computer with printer and connecting cable; floor plans of the building and adjacent buildings; a map of the immediate vicinity; tools and equipment for gathering physical evidence; tape measures; an AM-FM radio; a police scanner; a television monitor equipped for both over-the-air broadcasts and cable; a first-aid kit; paper or plastic cups; rope; wedges; and departmental forms and log books, for chronological recording of events and for administrative purposes such as recording overtime, etc.

Equipment at the scene should also include a field telephone or hostage phone in order to facilitate communication. A perpetrator, in the act of taking hostages, will often rip out a telephone in order to prevent anyone from notifying police, or the telephone may be torn out at some subsequent point. The field telephone will allow for easier communication than shouting back and forth or using bullhorns. A cellular telephone, on the other hand, may provide the perpetrator with greater communication. One of the disadvantages of using a telephone for negotiations, however, is that the perpetrator may not get on the phone himself, but rather will use one of the hostages to carry on the communication.

As departments get more sophisticated, they may be able to assign electronics technicians as part of the negotiation or hostage recovery team. The specialized personnel can assist in communication, intelligence, surveillance, and related areas. The equipment employed could include lock picks, mini television or video cameras, special optics, night-viewing equipment, and sophisticated listening devices. While some jurisdictions are absolutely prohibited from employing "bugs" to gather evidence, it may be possible to use such electronic eavesdropping equipment purely as a means of gathering life-saving intelligence. If there is any doubt, the local prosecutor should be consulted.

Immediately after the incident, any equipment that needs cleaning or maintenance should be attended to the same day: batteries replaced, supplies replenished, whatever. It may be days, even weeks before the equipment is needed again, but it may also be a matter of hours. On July 4, 1977, New York City had one major hostage incident followed by another in a less than four hours. The likelihood of copycat hostage situations is great enough to make agencies want to be as fully prepared as possible.

Personnel who respond to the scene should equip themselves with bullet-resistant garments and headgear and arm themselves with weapons appropriate to their assignments. Those in long-distance positions should have binoculars and scoped rifles; those closer in, shotguns and automatic weapons or both. Upon arrival at the mobilization point, arriving personnel should be given a quick briefing with as much intelligence as possible, told of the radio frequency in use at the scene, and then deployed as quickly as possible. Their first assignment should be to replace any underequipped or inadequately equipped first response officers occupying containment positions.

Communications

There are any number of aspects to a terrorist incident which can be labeled important, with no one key to the peaceful resolution of such incidents. However, lack of communication can do more than anything else to assure some degree of failure, if not total failure, in the handling of the situation (Figure 14.1).

The communications network should obviously center on the commander at the scene who, in turn, should be in direct communication with the SWAT or tactical commander and the leader of the negotiating team. The tactical and negotiating commanders also should be in direct contact, so each knows what the other is doing. In some jurisdictions, depending on the

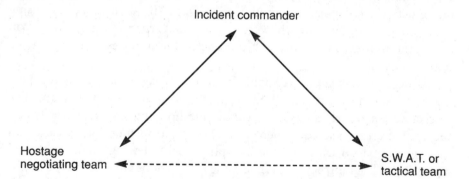

Figure 14.1 Lines of communication. In any terrorist incident, there must be two-way lines of communications between the incident commander and the hostage-negotiating team, and between the commander and the SWAT or Tactical Team. Care must be taken that communication between the negotiator and the SWAT team does not override the commander.

structure of the department, the incident commander may have to be in direct communication with the chief, the sheriff, or the police commissioner.

In addition to communicating order and relaying intelligence, efficient communications are necessary to prevent tragedies such as tactical forces taking up crossfire positions or having negotiators placed in the potential line of friendly fire. In Waco, Texas, for instance, the tactical team's command post was a considerable distance away from the point of negotiation and the official command post. Though all locations were linked by computer and there were communication and reports, the nuances of that communication seemed to have been lost on some occasions.

As mentioned above, one of the first tasks upon arriving at the scene is to establish a frequency on which communications will be carried. In jurisdictions with a large number of frequencies, a frequency predesignated for use in emergency or tactical situations may exist. In areas where there is a significant amount of interaction among different agencies, a netting frequency may be employed. There is usually at least one network, generally statewide, that employs a repeater system to permit any police agency in the state to come on to a particular frequency should it have to interact with any other police department during or in reference to an incident. If these alternatives are not available and multiple jurisdictions with differing radio frequencies are trying to work together, then a temporary radio room should be established staffed by a member of each agency whose function is to rebroadcast any information transmitted over the other frequencies.

Concealment vs. Cover

In the deployment of containment and tactical teams, an important distinction should be made between cover and concealment. Concealment will block a police officer from the view of a perpetrator, but will not stop any projectiles. Concealment blocks only the perpetrator's ability to see the target. Cover, on the other hand, will protect the officer from projectiles, the amount of protection determined by the type of weapon involved. A high-powered weapon requires better cover than does a low-caliber firearm. When adequate cover is taken, there is no need to return fire even if the perpetrator begins shooting. Police officers should not have to return fire until two things happen:

1. There is a clear necessity to shoot in order to save their own lives or someone else's life.
2. There is positive target identification and it has been determined by higher authority that deadly physical force is needed to stop or neutralize the perpetrator.

The importance of cover, or even concealment, in hostage situations is that instinctively most people will not shoot through things. They will usually wait for a good target view. Only specially trained officers, sharpshooters, and violent terrorists will shoot through objects. Randomly spraying with automatic weapons is a favorite tactic of terrorists. In such instances, mere concealment will afford little protection.

Good cover provides the police with time, time that can be used to gather as much intelligence as possible, time to identify targets, and time to get a clear target in the event the decision is made to use deadly physical force.

Handling the Media

Newspaper reporters, photographers, broadcast journalists, and sound and camera technicians should be allowed inside the outer perimeter, but kept outside the inner perimeter. It is preferable to designate a special section for media representatives, so that they can be kept away from the immediate crime-scene area where, in the case of explosion, they may destroy or disturb evidence, or in the case of a hostage situation, may incite the perpetrators to do something for the camera.

One of the most dramatic incidents of media interference with a situation occurred in Jasper, Arkansas, where members of a group called Father of Us (FOU) had taken hostages to bring attention to their message. After members of the group were interviewed by a news crew from a local television station who said they would air the tape at 6 p.m., leaders of the group said that before the night was out they were going to provoke the police into shooting them. The TV crew said that anything they did later might be too late to get on the evening news, so the hostage-takers moved up their agenda. And they did go out and get themselves shot and killed. There is no question that the media made the group members hurry to their conclusion. If the TV reporters had not pushed them along, the individuals may have lost their resolve to die for their cause.

There are numerous other incidents, particularly hostage situations, where reporters or media personalities have tied up phone lines or otherwise occupied perpetrators for on-the-air exclusives. At best, all this does is prolong a situation. At worst, it could result in the death of innocent persons.

The use of helicopters by various news agencies can have a great effect on incidents. Sometimes it seems there are so many news choppers in the air hovering above a scene that they could use their own air traffic controllers. At the 1998 Columbine High School tragedy in Colorado, the responding police and tactical teams and the scenes of escaping students were televised for all to see. Fortunately, the perpetrators did not see what was going on;

not so in Salem, Massachusetts, a year or so later. There, a bank robber led police on a multijursidictional chase for many miles. After crashing the car, the robber continued fleeing on foot. He broke into the home of a corrections officer, who was at home caring for his twin toddlers. The officer was able to negotiate with the intruder to permit the young boys to leave, although they were reluctant to go with their father still in the home. After the young boys were evacuated, the perpetrator changed the TV channel from the one the boys had been watching. On screen he found coverage of his situation, including an aerial view of the house and deployment of police around it. He also learned from one commentator that the father was a sheriffs' deputy, something the perpetrator had not previously known. This led to a demand by the perpetrator for any weapons located in the house. The incident ended successfully when the deputy wrestled with the perpetrator until the tactical team was able to immobilize him.

Media representatives have a job to do. They also serve a purpose in a constitutional democracy. By providing them with accurate, up-to-date information which will not interfere with the incident or investigation, police or corporate security personnel may be able to forestall or avert sensationalist tactics that a news blackout might precipitate.

Epilogue

"Terrorism can't happen here! Terrorism is not our responsibility! Call the people trained to handle terrorists!"

No matter what excuses politicians, managers, or law enforcement executives may try to use to get out from under, the problems of international and domestic terrorism are here and will be here for some time to come.

Whatever the social, political, or rhetorical machinations that terrorists use as justification for their actions, it will be a long time, if ever, before these real or imagined grievances can be addressed and changed to their total satisfaction.

Hostage-taking and kidnapping are mentioned in early history and in the folklore and mythology of various peoples. The only things new are the technological advances in the tools, weapons, locations, and means of communication. Instead of caves and castles, the nefarious deeds are now being carried out in huge aluminum tubes hurtling through the sky at 400, 500, or more miles per hour, 35,000 feet above ground. In the bombed-out back alleys of Beirut or the posh shopping areas of London, the actions are similar. News of the incidents travel by satellite at the speed of light into the living rooms, boardrooms, and bedrooms of the world.

It may be a hijacker with an automatic pistol, squeezing his head next to the pilot through the cockpit hatch of a commandeered jetliner; the exploding of three aircraft in a Middle Eastern desert; or the bodies of holiday travelers strewn about European airports. It may be a car laden with explosives in Lebanon or London, a dinghy loaded with explosives in Aden Harbor, or the bodies of workers sandwiched between what were once floors of an office building.

In all of these incidents, innocent people became victims.

In the 30 years since the killing of Israeli Olympic athletes in Munich by the PLO's Black September organization, much has been learned about the field of counterterrorism. Free nations have come together in a cooperative effort, albeit sometimes a limited one. Intelligence-gathering and analysis have been improved, along with communications. Selected retaliatory strikes have been carried out, disrupting terrorist-sponsoring countries' timetables. A new industry of high-technology counterterrorist equipment and consultants has flourished. Yet with all of these improvements and acquisitions, training remains the one most important factor for success of these efforts: training to be aware of the meaning of information and connections; training to ensure that someone will know how to operate the new sophisticated equipment; training to ensure that basic procedures are not pushed aside in favor of new technology; training also to ensure that as attrition from promotions or retirements trims human resources, there will be new people to fill the vacancies.

Finally, there must be a desire and dedication on the part of those involved in counterterrorist operations to pursue further the quest for knowledge. This book should be just part of your library, which ought to contain works of other related disciplines. It has been stated, "Terrorists have to be lucky only one time, we have to be lucky all of the time." But we cannot depend solely on luck. We must be prepared.

Only through dedication, equal to or surpassing that of terrorists, can the world be truly free of the fear of terrorism.

Appendix: Terrorist Organizations and Support Groups

Africa

Algeria	Arme Islamique du Salut (AIS) (Islamic Salvation Front)
Angola	Uniao Nacional para a Indendencia Total de Angola (UNITA)
Burundi	Forces pour la Defense de la Democratic (FDD)
Rwanda	Interahamwe
Somali	Somali National Alliance (SNA)
	United Somali Congress (USC)
South Africa	Afrikanner Weestand Beweeging (Boar Attack Troops)
Uganda	Lord's Resistance Movement (LRA)

Asia

Afghanistan	Jamaate e Islami
	Jumbish-i-Milli (National Islamic Movement)
Afghanistan and Pakistan	Taliban (The Seekers)
Cambodia	Khmer Rouge (Red Khmer)
Georgia and Abkhazia	Abkhazia Rebels
India	All Sikh Students Federation
	Ananda Marg (Path of Eternal Bliss)
	Bado Security Force (BSF)
	Jammu and Kashmir Liberation Front (JKLF)
	United Liberation Front of Assam (ULFA)
Japan	Aum Shinrikyo (Supreme Truth)
Laos	United Lao National Liberation Front (ULNLF)
Pakistan	Baluch People's Liberation Front (BPLF)
Philippines	New People's Army (NPA)
Sri Lanka	Liberation Tigers of Tamil Eelam (LTTE)
Tajikistan	Islamic Renaissance Party (IRP)

Europe

Corsica and France	Front de Liberation Nationale de la Corse (FLNC)
France	Group Islamique Arme (GIA)

263

Greece	Epanastikos Laikos Agonas (ELA), Revolutionary Popular Struggle
	Epanastaiki Organosi 17 Noemuri (RO-17), Revolutionary Organization November 17.
Ireland	Ulster Freedom Fighters (UFF)
	Ulster Volunteer Force (UVF)
Italy	Brigate Rosse (BR), Red Brigade
Macedonia	Unikom
Spain	Euzkadi Askatasuna (ETA), Basque Fatherland and Liberty
	Grupo de Resistencia Antifascista Primero de October GRAPO), First of October Anti-fascist Resistance Group
	Iraultza (Basque Armed Revolutionary Workers Organization)
Turkey	Armenian Liberation Army (ALA)
	Partiya Karkaren Kurdistan (PKK), Kurdistan Workers Party
	Deurimici Sol (Dev Sol), The Revolutionary Left
Yugoslavia	National Movement for the Liberation of Kosovo, Kosovo Liberation Army (KLA)

Middle East

Bahrain	Islamic Front for the Liberation of Bahrain (IFLB)
Egypt	Al-Gama'a al-Islamiyya (GAI or GI)
	Egyptian Islamic Jihad Group
Iran	Mojahein-e-Khalq (MEK)
Iraq	Kurdistan Democratic Party (KDP)
	Patriotic Union of Kurdistan (PUK)
Israel	Hammas (Islamic Resistance Movement)
	Kahane Chai (Kach Party and Revenge Underground)
	Abu Nidal Organization (ANO), Fatah Revolutionary Council, Black June
Saudi Arabia	Movement of Islamic Change
Syria	Syrian Muslim Brotherhood

The Americas

Bolivia and Colombia	Ejercito de Liberacion Nacional (ELN)
Canada	Front de Liberation du Quebec (FLQ)
	All Sikh Students Federation
Chile	Frente Patriotico Manuel Rodriquez (FPMR)
	Movimiento de la Izquierda Revolucionaria (MIR)
Colombia	Fuerzas Armadas Revolucionarias de Columbia (FARC)
	Ejercito Popular de Liberacion (EPL)

Honduras	Cinchoero Movimento Popular de Liberacion (MPL)
	Fuerzas Revolucionarias Populares Lorenzo Zelaya (FRP-LZ)
	Commandos Morazanist Popularas (FPM)
	Commandos Operatinos Especiales (COES)
Mexico	Ejercito Popular Revolucionario (EPR)
Peru	Movimento Revolucionario Tupac Amaru (MRTA)
Uruguay	Movimento de Liberacion Nacional (MLN)

Index

C

C-4, 153
Car bombs, antipersonnel, 136
Cardiopulmonary resuscitation, 162
Castro, Ernesto, 122
CBDCOM, *see* U.S. Army Chemical and
    Biological Defense Command
Central Intelligence Agency (CIA), 11, 25
Chain of command, 28
Chemical
    agents, 100, 239, 242, 243
    delays, 150
Chemical/Biological Incident Contingency
    Plan, 105
Chlorine gas, 101
Choking agents, 101
Cholera, 103
Christian extremists, 84
CIA, *see* Central Intelligence Agency
CID triad, 173
CIRG, *see* Crisis Intervention Response
    Group
Clostridium botulinum, 102
CMT, *see* Crisis Management Team
Cocaine, request for by hostage-taker, 245
Collateral damage, 202
Columbine High School tragedy, 18, 258
Command detonation, 152
Command post, 251–259
    bomb incident command post, 253–254
    communications, 256–257
    concealment vs. cover, 257–258
    equipment required at, 255
    equipment and supplies, 255–256
    handling of media, 258–259
    log and situation map, 254–255
    nerve center, 251–253
        forward command post, 251–252
        mobilization point, 252
        point of negotiation, 252–253
        staffing of command post, 253
    physical placement of, 252
    recordkeeping at, 254
    staffing of, 253
Command structure, 235
Commander, role of, 233–249
    alcohol and drugs, 245
    chemical agents, 242–244
    contain and negotiate, 245–246
    during incident, 238–239
    evaluate new developments and
        outcomes, 249
    evaluate and update, 237
    evaluation of alternatives, 239–241

    food, 244–245
    formal debriefing, 248–249
    impact of event on public, 246–247
    keeping up-to-date on new techniques
        and strategies, 236–237
    liaisons with other agencies, 237–238
    maintenance of manpower and
        equipment, 235–236
    make-up of team, 234–235
    post-incident debriefing, 247–248
    pre-incident, 233–234
    sharpshooter, 241–242
    who's in charge, 233
Communications
    officer, 253
    technology, 92
Composition B, 145
Composition C-4, 146
Concealment, cover vs., 257
Consequence management unit, 29
Containment, 160
Conventional warfare, 4
Cooler bandit, 222, 230
Counterterrorism, 3, 16
    operations, 12, 80, 262
    response capability, 10
    tactics, 16
Court testimony, 239
Cover, concealment vs., 257
CPR techniques, 177
Crime scene investigations, recording
    process in, 186
Criminal kidnappings, 114
Crisis
    intervention teams, post-incident, 165
    simulation, 29
    telephone hotlines, 236
Crisis Intervention Response Group (CIRG)
    15
Crisis Management Team (CMT), 126, 213
Cruelty, 210
Crusades, 156
Cultural icons, status of corporations as, 27
Cyberterrorism, 85
Cyclonite (RDX), 145
Cyclotol, 145

D

Daily biorhythm, 246
DCO, *see* Defense Coordinating Officer
DDNP, *see* Diazodinitrophenel
Deadline killings, 66